YALE HISTORICAL PUBLICATIONS

David Horne, Editor

Miscellany 71

Published under the direction
of the Department of History
with assistance from the income of the
Frederick John Kingsbury Memorial Fund

Frank S. and Elizabeth D. Brewer Prize Essay

of the American Society of Church History

THE

TRANSCENDENTALIST

MINISTERS

CHURCH REFORM IN THE

NEW ENGLAND RENAISSANCE

by William R. Hutchison

NEW HAVEN · YALE UNIVERSITY PRESS · 1959

TO VIRGINIA

PREFACE

THOSE WHO may remember little from a classroom introduction to the New England Transcendentalists will usually recall learning that these romantics were prone to find deep religious meanings in all created things, to discover sermons not just in stones but in bean rows at Walden Pond and mud puddles on Boston Common. Scholarly interpreters over the past century have in fact been in broad agreement that Transcendentalism was, in Perry Miller's phrase, a "religious demonstration"—a movement that strove insistently to infuse new spirituality into the common life.

The question that arises, however, is whether transcendental religion on its affirmative side was anything *more* than a tendency to appraise the universe through the spectacles of an intuitive faith. It is well known that most members of the Transcendental Club in the 1830's were Unitarian ministers and that their movement took form as a protest against the theological and social assumptions of the Boston Unitarians. But literary and general histories have nearly always conveyed an impression of the typical Transcendentalist—or at least of the typical major Transcendentalist—as a radical minister who criticized the Church, who then either left the Church or was virtually excluded from it, and who, for all his interest in religion in a general sense, took little part in theological discussion except for a passing and unproductive involvement in debate over the biblical miracles.

The need for a closer look is suggested by the fact that eleven of the seventeen clergymen in the original Transcendentalist group remained all their lives in the ministerial profession, and that all but two of the seventeen had ministerial careers lasting ten years or more.

Among these Transcendental clergymen were some who built lasting reputations as men of letters, others who did not; some who wrote extensively about their efforts as reformers of religion and others who have left us very little to go on. But in the aggregate their writings go far toward explaining what Transcendentalism meant to these ministers; how they thought the new principles could be applied within the Christian Church; and to what extent the religious applications of Transcendentalism reflected and furthered the aims of Protestant liberalism. In addition, the records of several experimental religious societies founded by Transcendentalists help to fill out this picture and make it possible to test the Transcendentalists' claim that their role in the Church was a constructive one.

The term "transcendentalist" was affixed to, or hurled at, a wide variety of persons in the period with which this study is concerned; but the focus here is on the famous group of Boston and Concord intellectuals who reluctantly accepted the designation "Transcendentalist" in the 1830's and who have always been so identified in our histories. Chronologically, the emphasis is on the period, roughly from 1830 to 1860, during which the Transcendentalist religious societies were founded and the theological controversy was acute.

The so-called Transcendentalist Controversy was one of

the important events of this period. Students of American history will be aware that the story of that dispute has been told before. They will also recognize, however, that assessments of the Controversy have been based almost entirely upon analyses supplied by the Transcendentalists themselves or by their more ardent admirers. The opinions of most of the Unitarian conservatives have been reported at second hand, if at all; and even Andrews Norton, who is generally thought to have been the representative conservative spokesman, has been quoted only in his more choleric moments. As a result, the regular Unitarians of this period have had an extremely bad press, and we have taken the word of their opponents that they deserved nothing better. Begging the question, historians have failed to examine closely a religious position that was labeled by its detractors as "pale," "corpse-cold," bigoted, and socially reactionary. Although more adequate descriptions can be found in Transcendentalist writings, hasty caricatures drawn in the heat of controversy have been taken quite seriously, and the typical Unitarian leader is usually pictured as an intolerant and hypocritical man, raging futilely against the serene Transcendental assertions.

Such portraits, often drawn with a kind of good-humored condescension, have helped to constrict our understanding of the Transcendentalist Controversy itself. Since one side, at least, is thought to have had no arguments worthy of notice, the whole dispute appears as a mere teapot tempest; and the conservative position has been variously interpreted as petty bibliolatry, a determination to suppress all difference of opinion, the expression of pompous dismay at the presumption of former pupils, or a form of collusion with the brokers and bankers of State Street.

I do not mean to caricature the caricaturists. Close students of the literary or philosophical phases of Transcendentalism have frequently suggested that the standard descriptions of both the Unitarian "reactionary" and the Transcendental "heretic" are incomplete. But such hints of a fuller interpretation have not given the writer of surveys anything very definite to work with, and the old stereotypes have retained their essential strength. Thus the main purpose of the chapters that follow is to find out what the members of the Concord group did and said as Christian ministers, and also to re-assess the traditional account of the controversy in which they became involved.

This study in an earlier form was submitted in candidacy for the degree of Doctor of Philosophy in Yale University. My first researches in mid nineteenth-century Protestantism were guided by Ralph H. Gabriel, and the thesis was directed at a later stage by David M. Potter and Sydney E. Ahlstrom. I am particularly indebted to Professor Ahlstrom, whose profound and detailed knowledge of this era in American church history has been an invaluable aid in preparation of the book.

The original dissertation was awarded the George Washington Egelston Prize for 1956 at Yale University; a revised version received the Frank S. and Elizabeth D. Brewer Prize for 1957 from the American Society of Church History. I am grateful to the members of the awarding committees for encouragement and for material assistance. The Yale University Fund for Young Scholars has also helped to make publication of the book possible. Many other persons have offered helpful criticism: H. Richard Niebuhr, John E. Smith, E. Harris Harbison, George Herbert, Mrs. Margaret Carlson, and Ralph Cooper Hutchison. Virginia Quay Hutchison has assisted in more ways than can be enumerated.

I wish also to acknowledge the special efforts of librarians and archivists at Yale University, the University of Notre

Dame, the Massachusetts Historical Society, the American Unitarian Association, and the Princeton and Harvard university libraries. The directors of the Ralph Waldo Emerson Memorial Association kindly permitted me to consult materials in the Emerson Papers.

WILLIAM R. HUTCHISON

Washington, D.C.
January 1959

CONTENTS

PREFACE   vii

SHORT TITLES   xv

1. Boston Unitarianism—the Context of Transcendentalist Reform   1
2. Transcendentalism and the Beginnings of Church Reform   22
3. Ripley, Emerson, and the Miracles Question   52
4. Theodore Parker and the Confessional Question   98
5. "The Church of the Future": Prophets and Experimenters   137
6. Transcendentalism and American Liberal Religion   190

BIBLIOGRAPHICAL ESSAY   209

INDEX   223

ILLUSTRATIONS

ANDREWS NORTON   60
   from W. C. Gannett, *Ezra Stiles Gannett, Unitarian
   Minister in Boston, 1824–1871*

GEORGE RIPLEY   60
   from Gannett, *Ezra Stiles Gannett*

EZRA STILES GANNETT   121
   from *Lamb's Biographical Dictionary of the United
   States, 3*

SAMUEL KIRKLAND LOTHROP   121
   from *National Cyclopaedia of American Biography, 12*

THE MUSIC HALL, BOSTON   181
   from John Weiss, *Life and Correspondence of Theodore
   Parker, 1*

JAMES FREEMAN CLARKE   196
   from *National Cyclopaedia of American Biography, 2*

SHORT TITLES

Allen, "Historical Sketch": Joseph H. Allen, "Historical Sketch of the Unitarian Movement since the Reformation," in J. H. Allen and Richard Eddy, *A History of the Unitarians and Universalists in the United States,* American Church History Series (New York, 1894), Vol. *10.*

Brownson, *Convert:* Orestes A. Brownson, *The Convert; or, Leaves from My Experience,* New York, 1857.

Brownson, *Orestes A. Brownson:* Henry F. Brownson, *Orestes A. Brownson's Early Life, Middle Life, Latter Life,* 3 vols. Detroit, 1898–1900.

Brownson, *Works: The Works of Orestes A. Brownson,* collected and arranged by Henry F. Brownson, 20 vols. Detroit, 1882–88.

Cabot, *Memoir:* James E. Cabot, *A Memoir of Ralph Waldo Emerson,* 2 vols. Boston, 1887.

Chadwick, *Parker:* John White Chadwick, *Theodore Parker, Preacher and Reformer,* Boston, 1900.

Commager, *Parker:* Henry Steele Commager, *Theodore Parker,* Boston, Little, Brown, 1936.

Cooke, *Dwight:* George W. Cooke, *John Sullivan Dwight: Brook-Farmer, Editor, and Critic of Music,* Boston, 1898.

Cooke, *Unitarianism:* George Willis Cooke, *Unitarianism in America: A History of Its Origin and Development,* Boston, American Unitarian Association, 1910.

Dirks, *Critical Theology:* John Edward Dirks, *The Critical Theology of Theodore Parker,* New York, Columbia University Press, 1948.

Eliot: Samuel A. Eliot, ed., *Heralds of a Liberal Faith,* 4 vols. Boston, American Unitarian Association, 1910–52.

Emerson, *Letters: The Letters of Ralph Waldo Emerson,* ed. Ralph L. Rusk, 6 vols. New York, Columbia University Press, 1939.

Emerson, *Works: The Complete Works of Ralph Waldo Emerson,* Centenary Edition, 12 vols. Boston, Houghton Mifflin, 1903–04.

Follen, *Works: The Works of Charles Follen, with a Memoir of His Life,* 5 vols. Boston, 1841–42.

Frothingham, *Channing:* Octavius B. Frothingham, *Memoir of William Henry Channing,* Boston, 1886.

Frothingham, *Parker:* Octavius B. Frothingham, *Theodore Parker: A Biography,* Boston, 1874.

Frothingham, *Ripley:* Octavius B. Frothingham, *George Ripley,* Boston, 1899.

Kern, "Transcendentalism": Alexander Kern, "The Rise of Transcendentalism," in Harry Hayden Clark, ed., *Transitions in American Literary History,* Durham, N.C., Duke University Press, 1953.

Miller, *Transcendentalists:* Perry Miller, *The Transcendentalists: An Anthology,* Cambridge, Mass., Harvard University Press, 1950.

NC: Andrews Norton Collection, Harvard University Library.

Newell, "Francis": William Newell, "Memoir of the Rev. Convers Francis, D.D.," *Proceedings of the Massachusetts Historical Society* (March 1865), pp. 233–53.

Parker, *Discourse of Religion:* Theodore Parker, *A Discourse of Matters Pertaining to Religion,* Boston, 1842.

Parker, *Sermons of Theism:* Theodore Parker, *Sermons of Theism, Atheism, and the Popular Theology,* 2d ed. Boston, 1856.

Parker, *Works:* Theodore Parker, Centenary Ed., 15 vols. (titles vary), Boston, American Unitarian Association, 1907–13.

Religious History: The Religious History of New England: King's Chapel Lectures, Cambridge, Harvard University Press, 1917.

Rusk, *Life:* Ralph L. Rusk, *The Life of Ralph Waldo Emerson,* New York, Scribner's, 1949.

Schlesinger: Arthur M. Schlesinger, Jr., *Orestes A. Brownson: A Pilgrim's Progress,* Boston, Little, Brown, 1939.

Schneider, *American Philosophy:* Herbert W. Schneider, *A History of American Philosophy,* New York, Columbia University Press, 1946.

Weiss: John Weiss, *Life and Correspondence of Theodore Parker, Minister of the Twenty-Eighth Congregational Society, Boston,* 2 vols. London, 1863.

Wells: Ronald Vale Wells, *Three Christian Transcendentalists: James Marsh, Caleb Sprague Henry, Frederic Henry Hedge,* New York, Columbia University Press, 1943.

Wilbur, *History:* Earl Morse Wilbur, *A History of Unitarianism,* 2 vols. Cambridge, Mass., Harvard University Press, 1945–52.

Williams, *Divinity School:* George H. Williams, ed., *The Harvard Divinity School: Its Place in Harvard University and in American Culture,* Boston, Beacon Press, 1954.

Chapter 1

Boston Unitarianism—the Context

of Transcendentalist Reform

SOMETHING like a law of acceleration appeared to be governing the movement of ideas in the Boston of the 1830's. Like weapons in an era of military ferment, theologies and reform programs in that period were likely to find themselves branded obsolete almost before they had been brought fully to public view.

This was the fate of Boston Unitarianism. Scarcely had the Unitarians concluded their thirty-year feud with New England Calvinism when they themselves were set upon by new reformers with new ideas: the Transcendentalists.

The older reform movement, at the time of this attack, was in the parlous position of having spent much of its early dynamism without having achieved either doctrinal explicitness or solid denominational form. There was, in fact, a deep aversion among the Unitarians, and especially among those who had participated actively in the anti-

Calvinist campaign, to any idea that a new denomination had been formed. The name "Unitarian" had been accepted by most members of the party as early as 1819, but many in the 1830's still preferred to be known simply as "liberals." Such persons argued that the more explicitly theological term failed to express the full meaning of their protest, but the decisive factor was their distaste for any sectarian designation whatever. Some were still persisting in the notion, long before proved unrealistic, that the Liberal Movement was merely a reforming party within Congregationalism.

One serious result of these attitudes was that they created a popular impression, which Calvinists enthusiastically encouraged, that Unitarianism was a purely negative system. Individual Unitarian preachers might be, and were, practically unanimous in their acceptance of such positive doctrines as the supernatural origin of Christianity and the essential infallibility of Scripture; they might preach these affirmative doctrines regularly to their congregations, who after all had little need by the 1830's to be reminded of the fallacies of Calvinism; but still the fact would remain that their most conspicuous assertions as a party had been negative ones.

Here was a situation which could be corrected only by greater assertiveness on the part of the Unitarians themselves; but this course, too, could have unfortunate consequences. The Transcendentalists in 1835 were joining the Calvinists in branding Unitarianism as a mere tissue of "pale negations," but it was not difficult to foresee that the declaration of a positive Unitarian creed would be treated as a reversion to Orthodox methods.

Unitarians did eventually make a concerted declaration of their beliefs, and out of the reaction to that later statement came the now time-honored estimate of nineteenth-century Unitarianism as a faith which managed to be both too negative and too positive.[1] But the Transcendental protest cannot be understood unless it is seen that the younger radicals were contending from the start against a system whose vital assumptions were far from negative, and whose very denials were built upon the biblical faith of earlier Puritanism.

The "orthodox" standard of belief in the American Congregational churches from the mid-seventeenth century onward was Genevan Calvinism as interpreted by English churchmen of the Cromwellian period. This was the system to some points of which the Unitarians took exception. It affirmed first and most decisively the absolute sovereignty of God, and went on to describe the methods by which this omnipotent God reveals himself, and the mode of his dealing with men. It asserted that the one God reveals himself in three persons, that Holy Scripture is the final authority for human faith and action, that men are elected to salvation or condemned to perdition by a divine decree promulgated before the creation of the world, and that those who are chosen for salvation can neither refuse the gift of grace nor act in such a way as to cause it to be withdrawn. Jesus Christ, who was recognized as an equal member of the Godhead and as both God and man, had obtained the salvation of the Elect by accepting the just punishment due to all men because of the essential depravity of their nature since Adam's fall.[2]

1. See the writings of O. B. Frothingham, below, p. 217, and his *Boston Unitarianism 1820–1850: A Study of the Life and Work of Nathaniel Langdon Frothingham*, New York, 1890. Also Wilbur, *History*, pp. 435–36, 456–61; Miller, *Transcendentalists*, pp. 3–15 passim; Kern, "Transcendentalism," pp. 285–86. But cf. Williams, *Divinity School*; and Conrad Wright, *The Beginnings of Unitarianism in America*, Boston, Starr King Press, 1955.

2. Williston Walker, *The Creeds and Platforms of Congregationalism* (New York, 1893), pp. 367–402, 438–39.

It is desirable to make clear at this point that the nominal center of Unitarian dissent from this system and the practical source of dissent were not precisely the same, although they complemented each other. The nominal point of contention was of course the doctrine of the Trinity; Unitarians denied that Jesus Christ was God or a "person" of the Godhead. But the practical disagreement was over the nature of man and his ability to contribute to his own salvation. This divergence was the "practical" one in the sense that it was the primary motivation of those who dissented from Calvinism; it is safe to say that relatively few of the liberals would have bothered to argue the profoundly difficult question of the Trinity had it not involved for them an estimate of human nature which they felt was wrong. With this in mind, we may attempt a further amplification of the Unitarian position as it existed at the time of the Transcendentalist outbreak in the 1830's.[3]

Unitarians believed, first of all, in the *personality* of God, which means that they did not regard God simply as an idea in the human mind or a semantic device used to express the totality of universal laws. They asserted, along with the Calvinists, that this personal God reveals himself in numerous ways, most importantly through his Son and the workings of the Holy Spirit; but for the Unitarian these distinct forms of revelation did not warrant the conclusion that there are three Gods or even three "persons." Christ was therefore an intermediate divine being, a messenger supernaturally and uniquely endowed and sent as a special, indispensable revelation to man.

3. The following summary of Unitarian theology is most heavily indebted to Sydney E. Ahlstrom's work in progress, "The Christian Unitarian Mind: An Anthology of Early American Unitarian Writings." See also William W. Fenn, "The Unitarians," in *Religious History;* and Ahlstrom, "The Middle Period," in Williams, *Divinity School*, pp. 116–30; and idem, "The Scottish Philosophers and American Theology," *Church History, 24* (1955), 257–72.

Along with the personality and oneness of God Unitarians were convinced of his *moral perfection*. It was because of the latter attribute that God could not be conceived as acting in the arbitrary fashion outlined in Calvinist theology. "Moral perfection" is something that men can judge only according to their own notions of right and wrong, but Unitarians tried to avoid the charge of arrogant presumption by pointing out that man's reasoning capacity, and hence his moral ideas, are themselves God-given. They were sure, too, that the New Testament, God's best revelation, corroborates the conclusions of human reason.

As heir to the long tradition of Protestant dissent, Unitarianism was a consciously and vociferously biblical faith. John Pierce, liberal pastor in Brookline, justified a persistent ignoring of the trinitarian issue by counting all of the trinitarian and unitarian texts in Holy Writ and determining that they were exactly equal in number.[4] Not all were such literalists as this, but Unitarian rejections of Calvinism, and even their most extravagant claims for human rationality, were conscientiously buttressed at all points by appeals to Scripture as the infallible authority and final rule of faith.

The focal point of the Unitarian creed was, as has been suggested, its doctrine of human nature rather than its doctrine of God. Without denying man's proneness to do evil, Unitarians stressed his almost infinite capacity for good, and categorically rejected the Calvinist notion that there is a class of sinners whose strivings toward a good life must forever be fruitless. They did believe that a process of personal regeneration is necessary, and also that Christ by his example and sacrifice has made such regeneration possible, but they refused to regard Christ's death on the Cross as part of a legal settlement or bargain with God; it was rather a necessary episode in God's fullest revelation, which he

4. Eliot, *1*, 236.

completed, in the Resurrection, by a demonstration of the
Divine purpose of defeating sin and death.

Optimism about human nature formed the substructure
for a ramifying set of beliefs about individual and social
progress. Since men are endowed by God with reason and
with innate capacities for good, and have been enabled
through the revelation in Christ to know the way of salvation, they can defeat the evil that is within and around
them by leading blameless lives and by prevailing upon
others to do the same. Here was the rationale of the common
Unitarian assertion that "character is more important than
creed," and perhaps also for the reluctance of some Unitarians to engage in schemes of social, as distinct from personal, regeneration.[5]

All of the foregoing beliefs affected Unitarian attitudes
toward the Church and its functions. The Church they regarded as a divine institution especially set apart to do God's
work. It was not, however, the earthly communion of an
Elect; and they thought it should include all who confess
Christ to be the Son of God. Holy Communion, which they
tended to interpret as a commemoration, was open to all
who might wish its aid in their personal effort of regeneration, and was not restricted to the already saved. Baptism
signified a dedication to the Church and membership in it,
but had lost its Orthodox character as a sacramental purging
of sin. In the polity of the Unitarian churches, the Puritan
tradition of congregational autonomy was strictly observed.
And worship was conducted essentially in the old Puritan
manner.

The distinguishing beliefs and practices of Unitarianism
had diverse sources in Christian history. Anti-Trinitarianism
was rooted in the earliest experience of the faith, specifically in the protests of Arius and his followers against the
creed formalized by the Council of Nicea in A.D. 325. As a

5. See Schlesinger, chap. 2.

Protestant heresy, denial of the Trinity had become widespread in Poland and Transylvania during the sixteenth century, and in the writings of Faustus Socinus (1539–1604) it had taken a turn more radical than mere Arianism. While Arius had regarded Christ as a kind of intermediate or archangelic being, Socinus asserted the complete humanity of Jesus. The eastern European congregations which called themselves "Unitarian" from about 1638 onward, and the English Unitarian movement dating from the 1770's, were essentially Socinian.

Since Unitarians in Europe were known to believe in the strict humanity of Jesus, it was easy for opponents of the American Unitarians to accuse the latter of adherence, secret or otherwise, to the same view. In fact, however, the American movement drew its inspiration not from Socinus but from rationalistic and Arian writers such as Locke, Chillingworth, Milton, and Clarke, who represented the liberal element in the English churches during the seventeenth and eighteenth centuries. English and Dutch Unitarians of the Socinian school had made some scattered conquests in America by the early nineteenth century, but their influence upon the New England liberals appears to have been negligible.[6]

Arian opinions, coupled with protests against points of Calvinist doctrine, had been preached in Massachusetts pulpits during the eighteenth century by numerous ministers, of whom the most influential were Ebenezer Gay, Charles Chauncy, Jonathan Mayhew, and James Freeman. These forerunners of the Unitarian Movement quite properly considered their views no more heretical than some which were widespread in the English churches. Despite their Arianism, they believed Christ to have been sinless, infallible, and a complete incarnation of the love and power

6. Wilbur, *History*, *1*, 271–343, 379–80; Wright, *The Beginnings of Unitarianism*, pp. 210–17.

of God. They accepted biblical authority and insisted upon faith in Christ as the prime requisite for salvation.

The eighteenth-century New England liberals stirred more controversy by their attacks upon distinctive Calvinist doctrines than by their questioning of the Trinity. Most disquieting to conservatives was their partial concurrence in the opinions of the Dutch theologian Arminius (1560–1609), who had asserted that men can contribute to their own salvation. New England ministers in some cases were dismissed by their congregations or subjected to a more general ostracism by their colleagues for urging this doctrine, but neither Arminian nor Arian preaching caused widespread disruption of the Puritan churches until the last years of the eighteenth century. By then, the unresolved differences had brought about conscious alignments within many congregations, and intraparish factional disputes flared up, typically at the time when a new pastor was to be elected. The earliest such incident, and the first separation of a parish on doctrinal grounds in New England history, came about in 1784. A minority faction in the church at Worcester at that date supported the candidacy of the liberal Aaron Bancroft (father of the historian George Bancroft) and withdrew when he was not elected.[7]

It is at this point that one sees a third tradition coming into play along with those of anti-Trinitarianism and anti-Calvinism. This was the tradition of congregational church order, which strongly affected the spread of Unitarianism, and later of Transcendentalism, through New England parishes.

The relative smoothness of liberal advances owed much to the freedom of individual churches, under the Congregational system, to alter doctrine without either changing the original church covenant or gaining the assent of a superior

7. Wright, passim; Cooke, *Unitarianism*, pp. 48–49; Wilbur, *History*, 1, 401.

denominational authority. The covenant was the organic law drawn up by each congregation as the foundation for the religious life of their community. Under its most typical form, the subscribers simply bound themselves "in the presence of God, to walk together in all his ways, according as he is pleased to reveal himself unto us in his blessed word of truth." [8] Doctrinal regularity was expected, and could be enforced by many external means, but was not defined for all time in the church's constituting document.

Although interchurch cooperation was an honored custom and was capable of extension into some form of denominational control, Massachusetts Puritans guarded their congregational autonomy with the greatest diligence. They wanted no part of a "consociation" system such as had been adopted in Connecticut. Individual societies did develop statements of belief to which candidates for membership had to assent, but general denominational statements such as that embodied in the Cambridge Platform of 1648 were considered authoritative only after ratification by the several churches.[9]

Another feature of Congregationalism which aided the free movement of opinion was its conception of the pastoral office. The minister's authority was delegated to him by the people of his own church, not by an ecclesiastical or synodical body. Local ministerial associations "licensed" candidates who wished to engage in missionary work or general supply preaching, but election and ordination to a regular pastorate were kept in the hands of the individual churches. When other clergy participated in the service of ordination, they did so at the request of the candidate's own congregation. Theoretically, a clergyman who for any

8. Walker, *Creeds and Platforms*, p. 116; John W. Platner, "The Congregationalists," in *Religious History*, pp. 8–11.

9. Platner, in *Religious History*, pp. 19, 35–36; Walker, *Creeds and Platforms*, pp. 106–7, 186–88, 422.

reason ceased to hold a pastoral charge was for the time being deprived of his ministerial standing.[10]

A further characteristic of New England church organization, one which came to have vital significance during the Unitarian-Calvinist controversy, was the distinction between Church and Parish. The Church was made up of those who had offered evidence of conversion and had been accepted as communicants. The Parish consisted of all citizens of the community, of whom attendance at services was expected and financial support was, to varying degrees, required. Although requirements for Church membership had gradually been relaxed in many communities through the use of the so-called "Half-Way Covenant" and other devices, the number of communicants in most instances continued to be much smaller than the total constituency of the Parish.[11] Since, after the first century of New England history, political privileges were not restricted to communicants of the Church, noncommunicants could make their influence felt in any ecclesiastical matter which could be said to affect the entire community.

As the Arminian and Arian disputes evolved into a major controversy causing seemingly irreconcilable divisions, the Congregational customs which have been discussed were fully exploited by the more liberal party. The tradition of congregational autonomy aided them because it meant that an individual church could adhere to the new opinions, or

10. Platner, in *Religious History*, pp. 7–9. This rule of forfeiture was widely ignored in practice, and was formally disallowed in 1865. G. G. Atkins and F. L. Fagley, *History of American Congregationalism* (Boston, Pilgrim Press, 1942), pp. 361–65.

11. After the disestablishment which occurred in Massachusetts in 1833, The Parish or "Corporation" consisted of those who provided the church revenues by owning or renting pews. Cooke, *Unitarianism*, pp. 120–23; Henry M. Dexter, *Congregationalism: What It Is; Whence It Is; How It Works* . . . (Boston, 1865), pp. 208–13.

choose a liberal·minister, whether neighboring churches were doing so or not. The political strength of the Parish assisted the liberals because Parish majorities were generally more favorable to the new opinions than Church majorities.

The growing power of the Parish was demonstrated, and at the same time made more formidable, when the Massachusetts legislature in 1799 provided that Church members must secure the assent of the Parish to their choice of a minister. And twenty-one years later, when the revolt against Calvinism was at its height, the state Supreme Court ruled that ownership of buildings and properties rested with the Parish and not with the Church. As a consequence of these pronouncements, conservative Church members who were forced by Parish vote to call a minister unacceptable to them could secede from the Parish only by accepting a crippling material loss. The tempo of liberal growth was markedly increased by these arrangements, and by 1825 ninety-six formerly Orthodox churches, most of them in Eastern Massachusetts, had been captured by the Unitarians.[12]

The liberal victory in Harvard College was no less striking. The Hollis professorship of divinity went to the Arian Henry Ware in 1805 after a closely fought contest, and the election shortly afterward of a Unitarian president and four liberal faculty members showed that the Orthodox stood little chance of regaining control. The latter, there-

12. William W. Fenn, "The Revolt against the Standing Order," in *Religious History*, pp. 106–9. Of a total of 125 Unitarian churches existing in 1825, 100 were in Massachusetts, only 20 in the rest of New England, and only five west of the Hudson: Cooke, *Unitarianism*, p. 118. Unitarians were a minority in Massachusetts, but by the 1830's held more than half the Congregational churches in Boston, including all of the original eleven except Old South: Wilbur, *History*, p. 433; Cooke, *Unitarianism*, p. 118; Atkins and Fagley, p. 132; *Boston Almanac*, 1837.

fore, in 1808 founded a rival institution, Andover Seminary, for the training of ministers. Liberal Harvard in turn recognized the need for a more systematized training in divinity, and President Kirkland in 1816 initiated a Society for the Promotion of Theological Education, which organized a Faculty of Theology, built Divinity Hall, and in 1830 put the new institution, as "Harvard Divinity School," under direct university control.[13]

This period of intense theological dispute, roughly from 1805 to 1833, has always been known as the age of the "Unitarian Controversy," and it was in these years that the liberals gained that reputation for negative polemics which they later found so hard to live down. Nearly all of the most famous Unitarian documents and statements, however, show the profound conservatism which accompanied the advocacy of dissent and free inquiry. It is notable that the first major statement of the Unitarian position was a pamphlet intended primarily to clarify what the liberals believed, not what they were attacking. William Ellery Channing, the saintly leader and chief inspiration of this generation of Unitarians, in 1815 wrote and published an open letter in which he denied that he or other liberals were preaching Socinian views, as an Orthodox writer had contended they were. The liberals, he said, believed firmly that Christ was more than human, denying only that he was an equal member or "person" of the Godhead.[14] Four years later, speaking at the ordination of Jared Sparks to the liberal church of Baltimore, Channing gave the Unitarianism of his own day its most nearly definitive expression, and here again he attempted to state the positive as well as the critical features of

13. Wilbur, *History*, pp. 406, 422–23. Cf. Conrad Wright, "The Early Period," in Williams, *Divinity School*, pp. 21–36.

14. *Letter to the Reverend Samuel C. Thacher, on the Aspersions Contained in a Late Number of the Panoplist, on the Ministers of Boston and the Vicinity*, Boston, 1815.

the new faith. The Unitarian party, he said, stood for the use of reason in the interpretation of the Bible, and believed that such a rational reading of Scripture confirmed the oneness and "moral perfection" of God, the divinity (but not deity) of Christ, and the primary importance of good character, as distinguished from mere acceptance of a creed.[15] Throughout his subsequent career, Channing's chief emphasis was upon the immanence of God in human nature,[16] a positive doctrine which was the focal point of the Unitarian creed and which underlay all of their activities as a party of protest.

Andrews Norton and Henry Ware, who shared with Channing the leadership of this reformist phase of Unitarianism, were the most active controversialists in the new school. Norton, Dexter Professor of Biblical Literature at Harvard, edited the aggressive *General Repository and Review* during the earliest stages of the struggle, and in 1819 published a *Statement of Reasons for Not Believing the Doctrines of Trinitarians*.[17] Ware, Hollis Professor of Divinity in Harvard College and later Professor of Systematic Theology in the Divinity School, engaged in a three-year pamphlet warfare in the course of which he defined Unitarian objections to the entire system of Calvinist doctrines.[18]

15. "Unitarian Christianity: Discourse at the Ordination of the Reverend Jared Sparks, Baltimore, 1819," in *The Works of William E. Channing, D.D.* (Boston, 1877), pp. 367–84.

16. See Robert L. Patterson, *The Philosophy of William Ellery Channing* (New York, Bookman Associates, 1952), pp. 61–148.

17. *A Statement of Reasons for Not Believing The Doctrines of Trinitarians Concerning the Nature of God and the Person of Christ*, Boston, 1819. Nine further editions, progressively enlarged, appeared between 1833 and 1877. For memoirs of Norton see, in addition to the sources listed in the Bibliography, below, William Newell in *Christian Examiner*, 55 (1853), 425–52.

18. Ware stated his basic position in *Letters to Trinitarians and Calvinists, Occasioned by Dr. Woods' Letters to Unitarians*, Cam-

But the necessity of speaking out in a negative way with respect to Calvinism made these men the more ready to emphasize their respect for Scripture as the ultimate authority. Although rational analysis seemed to them to show that the Bible gives no clear sanction to Calvinist and Trinitarian views, nevertheless those elements of the faith which are clearly and unambiguously stated were not to be questioned —as Norton attempted to prove in his major work on the *Genuineness of the Gospels*.[19] Norton, together with his co-worker John G. Palfrey, was an American pioneer in the movement of "higher criticism," which sought to clarify Scripture through an analysis of the language and culture of biblical authors; but he refused, as did the Unitarian party generally, to go further and question the authenticity of Scripture or its divine inspiration.[20]

bridge, Mass., 1820. For a recent discussion of the major point in dispute see H. Shelton Smith, *Changing Conceptions of Original Sin: A Study in American Theology since 1750* (New York, Scribner's, 1955), chap. 4.

19. Three vols. Boston, 1837–44.

20. George Rappall Noyes, who in 1839 succeeded Palfrey as Dexter Professor of Biblical Literature at the Divinity School, came to somewhat more radical conclusions about the authorship of Scripture but confined his doubts of authenticity to certain of the Old Testament prophecies: Williams, *Divinity School*, pp. 52, 107–8, 132. Others of note in the generation of Channing and Norton were Joseph S. Buckminster (1784–1812), a brilliant early exponent of the German methods in biblical criticism; Noah Worcester (1758–1837), who published *Bible News of the Father, Son, and Holy Ghost* (1810), an early tract in the Liberal campaign; John T. Kirkland (1770–1840), whose election as Harvard president in 1810 was a confirmation of the Unitarian success in that institution; Joseph Tuckerman (1778–1840), minister-at-large in Boston, who helped implement Channing's theories on the improvement and self-culture of the poorer classes; Edward Everett (1794–1865), in this early period the successor of Buckminster at the Brattle Street Church and later holder of the Eliot chair of Greek Literature in Harvard University; Francis Parkman (1788–1852), pastor of the

A marked characteristic of these early leaders in the Unitarian Movement was their reluctance to see the party organize itself into a new "sect." In the 1820's, however, younger men saw that some form of denominational unity was required if Unitarianism was to evolve from a reformist faction into an independent and effective Church.

The prime embodiment of this new organizing spirit was Channing's assistant and eventual successor in the pastorate of the Boston Federal Street Church, Ezra Stiles Gannett. Intense, methodical, and almost painfully sensitive to the need of balancing the liberal and the confessional traditions of Unitarianism, Gannett was the moving force behind the founding of the American Unitarian Association in 1825. A later historian, lamenting the failure of the early Unitarians to organize more effectively, remarked of Gannett that "ten such men would have carried Unitarianism like a prairie fire from border to border of our country." [21] Whether or not this is so, it is literally true that there were not ten such. Organizational advances were most meager and disappointing in the years between Gannett's founding of the Unitarian Association and Henry W. Bellows' organization of the National Conference in 1865.

The Unitarian Association itself had only very limited authority, since ministers and laymen joined as individuals and not, ordinarily, as representatives of their congregations. But even this mild approach to unity was distrusted by many Unitarians, particularly by those in the Boston area; the first

---

New North Church and father of the historian; Bernard Whitman (1796–1834), editor, and leader of the liberal faction in a bitter interchurch controversy in Waltham; and Alvan Lamson (1792–1864), whose settlement over the parish at Dedham was the occasion of the famous Supreme Court decision of 1820. Eliot, Vols. *1, 2.*

21. Joseph Henry Allen, *Our Liberal Movement in Theology, Chiefly as Shown in Recollections of the History of Unitarianism in New England* (Boston, 1882), p. 28.

roster of the Association included only sixty-five Bostonians in a total membership of 891, and during the first twenty-five years (1825–50) a mere one-third to one-half of the Boston churches offered financial assistance.[22]

Outside of the American Unitarian Association, the chief agencies of the denomination were the Boston Association of Congregational Ministers, the Evangelical Missionary Society, and the "Berry Street Conference." The Boston Association had become predominantly Unitarian in the early nineteenth century, and exclusively so after the Orthodox formed their own ministerial group in 1811.[23] As in the case of the national organization, the functions of the Boston Association were severely limited; it could only "advise, resolve, and suggest," and its utmost reach of authority was the certifying of candidates for general preaching duties. The Berry Street Conference, founded by Channing in 1820, was likewise an advisory body, but served all of the Unitarian ministers of Massachusetts. The Missionary Society, also a statewide organization, devoted itself to the sponsoring of religious societies in rural areas.[24]

To most Unitarians the written word was a more acceptable vehicle for spreading the liberal faith than were denominational organizations. Indeed the prodigious amount and high literary quality of Unitarian writings provides perhaps the major explanation of the wide nineteenth-century influence of this small and struggling religious body. In addition to the 300 tracts published by the Unitarian Association, which discussed ably many of the primary questions of religious liberalism, nearly a dozen newspapers and periodicals were founded during the first fifty years of

22. Wilbur, *History*, p. 441.

23. William B. Sprague, *The Life of Jedidiah Morse, D.D.* (New York, 1874), p. 89.

24. Frothingham (n. 1, above), pp. 213–27; Atkins and Fagley (n. 10, above), p. 102; Cooke, *Unitarianism*, pp. 104–7.

the movement. Of the latter, the *Monthly Anthology* and the *North American Review* have been justly celebrated for their contributions to literary and scientific studies; the quarterly *Christian Examiner* (1824–69) has been ranked among the ablest of American theological journals; and the *Christian Register* was a weekly newspaper of high merit which has been continued in various forms to the present day.[25] The roster of contributors to these publications would provide a fairly complete index to the literary and religious "flowering" of nineteenth-century New England; and even a listing of editors includes the names of Edward Everett, William Emerson, George Ticknor, Jared Sparks, R. H. Dana, Henry Adams, James Russell Lowell, and Edward Everett Hale.[26]

Combined literary and organizational efforts were not, however, sufficient to make Unitarian religion the pervasive and powerful force which its originators expected it would be. Compared with the respectable figure of 125 Unitarian churches founded before 1825 over a limited area, the 105 additional ones begun throughout the country between 1825 and 1850 were not much to boast about.[27] The instinct of Gannett, who favored active proselytizing in the 1820's, was more correct than he could know; for changes in the

25. Frank L. Mott, *A History of American Magazines* (Cambridge, Harvard University Press, 1938–57) 2, 219–61; Cooke, *Unitarianism*, pp. 95–96; Van Wyck Brooks, *The Flowering of New England, 1815–1865* (New York, Dutton, 1936), pp. 17–20, 111–34; and Mott, *American Magazines*, 1, 284–92.

26. Other Unitarian periodicals appearing in the early nineteenth century were the *Christian Monitor* (1806–11); Norton's *General Repository* (1812–13); the *Christian Disciple* (1813–24); Gannett's *Monthly Miscellany* (1839–43); the *Monthly Religious Magazine* (1844–74); and the *Quarterly* (later the *Monthly*) *Journal of the American Unitarian Association* (1853–69). See Cooke, *Unitarianism*, pp. 95–101, 107, 162, 448.

27. Wilbur, *History*, p. 455.

American religious scene in the next decades were to rob Unitarian liberalism of much of its appeal. Revivalism and perfectionism on the frontier and in urban centers and "progressive orthodoxy" in the Calvinist churches would make it possible for many a Christian to have his humanistic religion without apparently committing himself to a denial of Christ's deity.[28]

By the same token, of course, one can argue that Unitarianism could not have taken hold of the popular imagination, even with ten or twenty Gannetts to organize and guide it. Certainly the creed of the young denomination contained ambiguities which, until they were resolved, marred its effectiveness both in evangelization and in facing such attacks as that of the Transcendentalists.

Unitarians could justly be charged with inconsistency, not primarily because of the doctrinal positions taken, but more because of the groundwork of authority which was presupposed for those positions. It was this question of the source of religious authority which was imperfectly resolved in the Unitarian system; and it was no mere accident that Transcendentalist criticism took form in that area, nor was it simply bad fortune that the conservatives at first showed lack of concert in their answers.

The difficulty was that despite an implicit confidence on the part of Unitarians that reason and revelation, both given by the Ruler of a rational universe, would always be found to be in harmony, the question of priority cried out for an answer, and leading Unitarians did not always respond to it in the same way. Henry Ware, Jr., told his Divinity School classes that where reason appears to conflict with the plain meaning of Scripture, the latter must prevail; but Channing,

28. For the relation between Unitarianism and midcentury revivalism see Timothy L. Smith. *Revivalism and Social Reform in Mid-Nineteenth-Century America* (New York, Abingdon Press, 1957), chaps. 5, 6.

whose utterances on this point often contradicted each other, seemed to lean toward the opposite view. He once said, for example, that "nothing but the approving sentence of reason binds us to receive and obey revelation." [29]

Another sticking-point was the relationship between nature and the supernatural. Unitarians sought support for their theological doctrines in the natural world, as well as in the "approving sentence of reason," and critics could and did ask why the Unitarians supposed that God, if he has revealed himself so fully in an orderly universe, had found it necessary to disturb this natural harmony simply in order to make a further revelation. Conversely, it could be asked why, if the Unitarians were certain about the supernatural proofs of Christianity, they should be as avid as they were in seeking natural evidences.

The whole position was made more vulnerable by the dependence of the Unitarian scheme of evidences upon a theory of knowledge which was coming increasingly under attack in both Europe and America. That theory, as formulated by Locke and modified by the Scottish realist philosophers, placed a heavy emphasis on sense experience as the source of religious ideas. Unitarians therefore defended the miracles and other supernatural evidences by arguing that God had no mode of conveying specific religious truths to the human mind except by manifestations which men could see or hear. Some of them conceded that general ideas of right and wrong were perhaps, as the Scottish philosophers thought, given in the very structure of the human mind, but the more specific truths of religion, they said, are not so given, and can only be known through a direct confrontation of the senses. Here again the Unitarians could be accused of inconsistency, of having exalted the God-given rationality

29. Fenn, in *Religious History*, p. 126; John W. Chadwick, *William Ellery Channing, Minister of Religion* (Boston, Houghton Mifflin, 1903) p. 221.

of the human mind when denouncing Calvinist doctrines which they thought absurd, only to denigrate these same human powers as soon as their own presuppositions were subjected to rational tests.

In practical argument during the Transcendentalist period over the definition and limits of the Unitarian faith, these technical difficulties on the subject of authority tended to become subsumed in the broader question of the limits of free inquiry and free expression, and here again there was no complete agreement among denominational spokesmen. Early Unitarians had repeatedly denounced their Orthodox opponents for setting arbitrary limits to the free search for truth.[30] When the Calvinists had protested that in their opinion the Unitarian "search for truth" had passed the limits of Christianity, liberals had taken this as a sign of the narrowness and bigotry of the more conservative system. But it became evident during the Transcendentalist Controversy that Unitarians were not willing to see free inquiry carried beyond the boundaries of what they themselves considered to be essential Christianity. "Surely," Dr. Nathaniel Frothingham argued in 1845, "there is a liberty of enclosure, as well as of spread." [31] Free inquiry, they began to say, must remain within the boundaries of confessional Christianity. Once the special authority of Jesus or the Bible is denied, the inquirer can no longer ask to be called a Christian.

But the principle of free expression, to which Unitarians had appealed when their movement was in its reformist period, had attained an unwonted dominance in the Unitarian mind and also in the public conception of their movement. Ironically, in the Transcendentalist period it inhibited the "free expression" of some Unitarians who would have liked to denounce what they believed was harmful.

30. Clarence Faust, "The Background of the Unitarian Opposition to Transcendentalism," *Modern Philology*, 35 (1938), 307–13.
31. Quoted in Frothingham, *Boston Unitarianism*, p. 40.

The heavily worked stereotype of early Unitarianism, despite all its contradictory taunts about pale negation and flushed assertiveness, is not utterly without foundation. As the institutionalized form of a once dynamic critical movement, the Unitarian Church was subject to all the dangers which frequently accompany the success of such movements. Signs of intellectual stagnation and social complacency were not lacking; and the special fact in this case, that success had come overwhelmingly in Boston and very uncertainly elsewhere, gave an added coloring of parochialism to a system that had aspired confidently to universal appeal.

Still, the Transcendentalist characterization of conservative Unitarianism was too facile, as its very contradictions would suggest. The creed which the conservatives finally got around to stating in the controversy of the 1840's and 1850's was not something newly wrought for an urgent occasion, nor was it a reversion to the system they had denounced. Their temper in answering their Transcendentalist critics may or may not have been "angry" and "dogmatic." Any Unitarian assertions, however, would have seemed dogmatic in contrast with the restrained silence which their opponents ridiculed but nonetheless expected them to maintain.

Chapter 2

Transcendentalism and the Beginnings of

Church Reform

THE late eminent historian James G. Randall once remarked that "there are times when the avoidance of a readable formula of broad interpretation requires downright force of character." Everyone likes brief definitions which are not only readable but recallable, and most writers feel under a certain obligation to provide them if possible. But many significant historical movements defy reduction to rough-and-ready formulae; and the Transcendental Movement clearly is one of that class. Almost any concise definition of the methods and aims of this group will either be theoretically broad enough to include all philosophical idealists from Plato through Bradley or else so narrowly technical as to exclude persons who were consciously and actively a part of what is called American Transcendentalism.

The very name "Transcendentalism," unfortunately, suggests a more extensive agreement in technical philosophy than actually existed in the group; and its members, fully aware of this, did all they could to avoid having that name attached to their movement. If there had to be a party designation, this, they thought, was an improper one, and they tried to bring other names into currency. "Disciples of the Newness" or simply the "New School" were favorite and sufficiently vague terms; "The Symposium" was Alcott's preferred name for their Club; Orestes Brownson tried for years to popularize the term "Eclecticism"; and the designation "Hedge's Club" did make some headway with the public. When they finally began answering to the name "Transcendentalists," it was not because they had come to terms with a set of philosophical principles that all could accept but because the public, delighted with the term, had refused to accept any other.

The name was deplored not as an entire misrepresentation of the spirit and aims of the group, for that it certainly was not, but rather as an ambiguous term which had several popular and several technical definitions, no one of which was suitable for what the American group had in common.

Popularly, the adjective "transcendental" was affixed to any philosophy thought to be "enthusiastic, mystical, extravagant, impractical, ethereal, supernatural, vague, abstruse, [or] lacking in common sense." [1] Sir William Schwenck Gilbert's parody, in *Patience*, of transcendental aestheticism reflected both the common man's disdain for such nonsense and his tendency to confuse Transcendentalism with such distantly related groups as the medievalist Pre-Raphaelite Brotherhood:

If you're anxious for to shine in the high aesthetic line, as a
    man of culture rare,

1. *The Dictionary of Philosophy*, ed. Dagobert D. Runes, New York, Philosophical Library, 1942.

You must get up all the germs of the Transcendental terms,
    and plant them everywhere.
You must lie among the daisies and discourse in novel phrases
    of your complicated state of mind
(The meaning doesn't matter if it's only idle chatter of a
    transcendental kind) . . .
Though the Philistines may jostle, you will rank as an apostle
    in the high aesthetic band,
If you walk down Piccadilly with a poppy or a lily in your
    medieval hand . . .

The technical definitions were usually, though not invariably, more rigorous than the popular ones. Perhaps the
most specific meaning the term was ever to enjoy was given
to it by Immanuel Kant, who first coined the term for the
kind of application it was to have in nineteenth-century
usage. The "transcendental philosophy" which Kant proposed, and for which he provided the "architectonic plan"
in his *Critique of Pure Reason,* was to be a systematic exposition of the nature and conditions of a priori knowledge. This
philosophy would concern itself, he said, "not so much with
objects as with the mode of our knowledge of objects in so
far as this mode of knowledge is to be possible *a priori.*" [2]
According to Kant, the contribution of Pure Reason is
its provision of the "forms" of sensibility and the "categories" of understanding which are imposed upon sensory
material by the perceiving mind. Concepts such as space,
time, and causality belong to the nature of the human mind,
and thus are logically prior to experience, even though in a
chronological sense "all our knowledge begins with experience." The mind is furnished with pure concepts and forms
of intuition which it could not obtain through induction but

2. *Critique of Pure Reason,* trans. Norman Kemp Smith (London, Macmillan, 1929), pp. 59–61.

which are necessary conditions for a reliable knowledge of the world of phenomena.[3]

Kant set definite limits to the area within which Pure Reason can function. He made a distinction between the "transcendental" concepts which relate to the substructure of experience and those "transcendent" concepts which have to do with a sphere of reality that is beyond experience. Such objects of thought as God, freedom, and immortality, he argued, are "transcendent" (rather than transcendental) and are known by Practical Reason, not by Pure Reason. These two spheres of knowledge, he explained, must not be confused, for the objects in each are not equally knowable. Practical Reason does make possible a knowledge of "transcendent" things which is sufficient to guide moral action, but it cannot provide the scientifically accurate account which is gained in the experiential realm by the interworkings of Pure Reason and the faculties of sense perception.[4]

The post-Kantian idealists of Europe accepted the spirit and many of the hints of Kant's system without always observing this distinction between the two types of Reason and the proper functions of each. German idealists, for example, far from agreeing with Kant that the conclusions of the Practical Reason could not be the basis for reliable scientific knowledge, sought to "unify" his system by removing or blurring the distinction between Pure and Practical Reason, and by making a single "self-determining spiritual principle"—a unified "Reason"—the common basis for their variously articulated systems of knowledge. The most im-

3. Ibid., pp. 41–42, 65–119. Sterling P. Lamprecht, *Our Philosophical Traditions: A Brief History of Philosophy in Western Civilization* (New York, Appleton Century Crofts, 1955), pp. 363–70.

4. *Pure Reason*, pp. 299, 380–81, 483–84; *Critique of Practical Reason*, trans. Lewis W. Beck (Chicago, University of Chicago Press, 1949), pp. 118–20.

portant of these revisers of Kant were Fichte, Schelling, and Hegel, but such lesser figures as Jacobi, Schiller, Richter, Novalis, Schlegel, and Baader each contributed in his own way to the same development.[5]

Still another turn was given to the definition of the transcendental method by the French Eclectic School dominated by Victor Cousin and Theodore Jouffroy. The name given this school suggests accurately what they thought the true philosophy would be, namely an extraction and recombining of the best from all other systems; but an epistemological method of determining what is "best" in any philosophy had also to be selected, and their insistence upon "psychological introspection" as "the supreme criterion of philosophical truth" is the primary justification for linking them to the German post-Kantian idealists, and particularly to Schelling. What differentiates them, however, from the Germans is their insistence upon objective validation, through both psychological and historical analysis, for the truths given in intuition.[6]

Coleridge and Carlyle, whose transmission of German idealism was especially important in the early stages of the American Transcendental Movement, provided no systematic redefinition of transcendentalism, but in the manner of the Eclectics brought some of its elements into bold relief. Coleridge, drawing most heavily on Schelling's philosophy, stressed the introspective method, the distinction between Reason and Understanding, and an evolutionary theory of natural-spiritual "correspondences" derived from Schelling's

5. Frank Thilly, *A History of Philosophy*, rev. Ledger Wood (New York, Holt, 1951), pp. 451–53; Harald Høffding, *A History of Modern Philosophy . . . from the Close of the Renaissance to Our Own Day*, trans. B. E. Meyer (London, Macmillan, 1900), *2*, 110–92.

6. William Turner, *History of Philosophy* (Boston, Ginn, 1903), pp. 606–8; "Cousin," in Runes, *Dictionary of Philosophy*.

Naturphilosophie. Carlyle made pronounced use of Fichte's assertive "transcendental ego." [7]

The American school of idealists, who followed Coleridge in a vast oversimplification of the relations between Reason and Understanding, sometimes invoked the name of Kant in their pursuit of speculations which Kant would have regarded as unsound, and attached the term "transcendental" to concepts which he had labeled "transcendent." As Francis Bowen of Harvard wrote in 1877:

> Kant's influence was but indirect, and his opinions were imperfectly known. . . . Hence it was, that, misled by the term Transcendentalism, applied to his philosophy as a whole, and by his doctrine of the subjective character of space and time, the opinion became general, that his system was rather Platonic than Aristotelian, placing the essence of things and the characteristics of true knowledge in the realm of pure ideas and supersensual intuitions of the truth,—the very region, according to his philosophy, of necessary illusions and abortive attempts of the intellect to overstep its natural boundaries. [8]

Thus any claim on the part of the Concord group to be thoroughgoing disciples of Kant would have been unjustified. But in fact their misapprehensions of the Kantian system did not result in any such claim. They acknowledged varying degrees of indebtedness to the critics and reinterpreters of Kant. And they knew the extent to which they

7. Kern, "Transcendentalism," pp. 274–75.

8. *Modern Philosophy from Descartes to Schopenhauer and Hartmann* (New York, 1877), p. 160. For a recent appraisal of the interpretation and frequent misapprehension of Kantian ideas by New England writers see Henry A. Pochmann, *German Culture in America, Philosophical and Literary Influences 1600–1900* (Madison, University of Wisconsin Press, 1957), pp. 119, and 79–242 passim.

had drawn upon Plato, Neoplatonism, Swedenborg, and Oriental religions, together with the concepts of universal order in Newton and Paley, the mystical elements in American Puritanism, and the moral theories of the Scottish philosophy.[9] They resisted the "Transcendentalist" tag, then, not only because its popular connotations were insulting and its technical meaning uncertain, but also because they knew the name would mislead others into expecting from them a concerted adherence to one or another of the systems going by that name.

The Transcendentalists' fears in this respect were only too well borne out in later assessments of their movement. Although most writers have recognized that their essential agreements were not in technical philosophy, a few have devised "readable formulas" which exclude one or more of the most active participants. Orestes Brownson, Theodore Parker, Bronson Alcott, and even Ralph Waldo Emerson have all been told by one writer or another that they do not deserve to be called Transcendentalists.[10]

9. Stanley M. Vogel, *German Literary Influences on the American Transcendentalists*, New Haven, Yale University Press, 1955; René Wellek, "Emerson and German Philosophy," *New England Quarterly*, 16 (1943), 41–62; "The Minor Transcendentalists and German Philosophy," ibid., 15 (1942), 652–80; Goddard, chap. 2; Kern, "Transcendentalism," pp. 270–75.

10. Parker is read out of the movement by Dirks in *Critical Theology*, p. 136; Parker and Brownson by Herbert W. Schneider in *American Philosophy*, pp. 262–68; and Alcott by Caroline H. Dall in *Transcendentalism in New England: A Lecture . . .* (Boston, 1897), pp. 22–23. O. B. Frothingham, who does not at all deny Emerson's central place in the American movement, nonetheless illustrates the confusion of definitions. "A Transcendentalist," Frothingham writes, "in the technical sense of the term, it cannot be clearly affirmed that he was. Certainly he cannot be reckoned a disciple of Kant, or Jacobi, or Fichte, or Schelling." Frothingham, *Transcendentalism in New England: A History* (New York, 1876), p. 226.

The wide-eyed sense of discovery which has sometimes been manifested by such revisionists would no doubt have caused innocent merriment at the meetings of Hedge's Club, for the Transcendentalists were fully aware of their disagreements and were rather prone to take pride in them. James Freeman Clarke once remarked that their group was called "the Club of the Like-Minded," and added that he supposed this was "because no two of us thought alike." All were agreed, as Emerson said, on the value of the "spiritual principle," but they did not always concur on the question of how it should be articulated and applied to contemporary problems. In epistemology, Parker, Brownson, and several others modified their faith in intuition by a Cousinian emphasis upon historical and scientific verifications. Despite general agreement on a symbolic theory of the universe, Thoreau's writings (his later ones in particular) showed an intense interest in recording natural facts for their own sake; and the tendencies toward Pantheism in the writings of Emerson were scrupulously avoided in the work of most of the others. In their attitudes toward religious institutions, most Transcendentalists dissented from the extreme iconoclasm of Parker and Emerson. In social theory, despite a common aim of protesting against commercial materialism, the spectrum of divergence extended from Thoreau's intense individualism, through the Utopian collectivism of George Ripley and W. H. Channing, to the radical reformism of Brownson. Only in the field of aesthetic theory—that is, in their advocacy of organic expression of the intuitions instead of classical regularity—does the group appear to have been free from significant internal disagreement.[11]

Their similarities of basic philosophy, of background, and of temperament, however, were more marked than these differences, and produced a unity of purpose which was as apparent to their amused contemporaries as it was to the

11. Kern, "Transcendentalism," pp. 252–309 passim.

Transcendentalists themselves. Most conspicuous among the unifying factors were their common tendency toward an intuitive philosophical method, their generally romantic approach to the universe, their almost invariable optimism about human nature, and their common feeling of participation in a movement of awakening and protest. Solutions differed, and so did the philosophical rationales for those solutions, but they agreed in placing "intuition" above all traditions and conformities, all sacred books and special revelations. They were fundamentally united in condemning formalism in religion and literature, Lockean "sensationalism" in philosophy, and all that was inhuman or materialistic in the popular social morality. Between such ways of thinking and the accepted attitudes of their time and place there was a gulf much wider than any of the divergences within Transcendentalist ranks.[12]

On September 19, 1836, Bronson Alcott recorded in his diary that the "Symposeum" (as he preferred to spell it) had had its first meeting that evening at George Ripley's home.[13]

12. Kern has compiled a list of 20 specific matters in which there was significant agreement among the Transcendentalists. "Transcendentalism," pp. 250–51.

13. For accounts of the early meetings, see *The Journals of Bronson Alcott*, ed. Odell Shepard (Boston, Little, Brown, 1938), pp. 78–79; *The Journals of Ralph Waldo Emerson*, ed. E. W. Emerson and W. E. Forbes (10 vols. Boston, Houghton Mifflin, 1909–14), *4*, 85–87. The number of years during which the Club was in existence is hard to determine. Estimates have ranged from "three to four years"—Alcott, quoted in George W. Cooke, *An Historical and Biographical Introduction to Accompany the Dial* (2 vols. Cleveland, the Rowfant Club, 1902), *1*, 51—to "a dozen years" (Cooke in ibid., p. 55). The longer estimate undoubtedly includes later informal meetings, such as the "conversations" at Miss Peabody's bookshop in the 1840's, which were attended by some of the same persons. As for frequency of the meetings, Alcott later remembered it as "probably" four or five times a year. Ibid., p. 51.

In attendance, besides Alcott and Ripley, had been Emerson, Brownson, Clarke, Convers Francis, and Frederic Henry Hedge. The main topic of conversation had been the organization and membership of the group, and though a high degree of informality had been agreed upon, it had been decided that membership should be by invitation. Hedge, who had made the original proposal of a Club in a letter to Emerson during the preceding summer, had suggested it be limited to ministers, but Emerson had demurred, insisting that Alcott, "a God-made priest," must not be excluded. The rule decided upon at the first meeting was "that no man should be admitted whose presence excluded any one topic," and with this criterion in mind the charter members agreed to invite four of the elder statesmen of Unitarianism —James Walker, Nathaniel Frothingham, Dr. Channing, and the free-thinking layman Jonathan Phillips. They also voted to include three young ministers—John Dwight, Cyrus Bartol, and W. H. Channing.[14]

Of the twenty-six persons who became closely associated with the Club and its activities, seventeen were Unitarian ministers—all but four, that is, of the male members. The story of Transcendental church reform centers around seven of them: Emerson and Ripley, who first announced and argued the program of reform; Parker, who carried forward and expanded that program in its later stages; Hedge, who above all others saw the reform of Unitarianism within the context of universal Christianity; and finally Clarke, Brownson, and W. H. Channing, founders, along with Parker, of experimental religious societies in which the Transcendentalist principles were applied. In addition, Convers Francis and William H. Furness were of importance in the earliest phase of the movement, while Bartol, Charles Brooks, Chris-

14. None of the older men became a regular member. Convers Francis, 41 years of age in 1836, remained the senior member of the Club throughout its existence.

topher Cranch, John Dwight, Sylvester Judd, Samuel Osgood, Caleb Stetson, and Jones Very made less tangible contributions during ministerial careers of varying length.[15]

To a remarkable degree the program of the Transcendentalists, and especially its application to formal religion, was set forth within a few months of the year 1836. Hedge understated the case when he recalled later that there had been, in that summer, "a promise in the air of a new era of intellectual life." [16] Among the Transcendentalist writings published in 1836 were Alcott's *Conversations on the Gospels*; Brownson's *New Views of Christianity, Society, and the Church*; Emerson's *Nature*; a highly controversial review by George Ripley of James Martineau's *Rationale of Religious Inquiry*; Furness' *Remarks on the Four Gospels*; a tract, *Christianity as a Purely Internal Principle*, from the pen of Francis; and a semitranscendental work by Charles Follen, *Religion and the Church*.[17] "The spiritualists," as

15. The roster of the Club is completed with the names of Bronson Alcott, Ellery Channing, Margaret Fuller, Ellen Hooper, Elizabeth Peabody, Sophia Ripley, Caroline Sturgis Tappan, Henry Thoreau, and Charles Wheeler. Dr. Channing, James Marsh, and Sampson Reed are frequently and justly mentioned as precursors of the movement. Moncure Conway, O. B. Frothingham, Thomas Wentworth Higginson, Samuel Johnson, Samuel Longfellow, Charles Newcomb, Franklin B. Sanborn, David Wasson, and John Weiss were later converts to Transcendentalism. George Bancroft and Caleb Sprague Henry were significant as philosophical adherents to transcendentalism but were not closely associated with the Concord group. See Kern, "Transcendentalism," p. 249.

16. Quoted in Cabot, *Memoir, 1*, 245.

17. A. Bronson Alcott, *Conversations with Children on the Gospels*, 2 vols. Boston, 1836–37; Brownson, *Works, 4*, 1–56; Emerson, *Works, 1*, 3–77; William H. Furness, *Remarks on the Four Gospels*, Philadelphia, 1836; Convers Francis, *Christianity as a Purely Internal Principle*, American Unitarian Association Tract Series, 105, Boston, 1836; *The Works of Charles Follen, with a Memoir by His Wife* (5 vols. Boston, 1841–42), *5*, 254–313; George

Francis remarked at the time, appeared suddenly to be "taking the field in force." [18]

Alcott's *Conversations on the Gospels*, though not directly concerned with church reform, had an important part in the general excitement. This extraordinary man, who was largely self-educated and who for several years had been a peddler in Virginia, had already attracted notice as an educational innovator. During short-lived experiments in Boston, Philadelphia, and several Connecticut towns over the previous decade, he had pleased many by his ability and warmth, and frightened others with his strange methods and heterodox religious philosophy. In the Temple School, which he had established in Boston in 1834, the children were taught not by the usual devices of exposition and recitation but by the "conversational" method, which presupposed in the young an intuitive knowledge of religion and morality, and assumed that true teaching consists in "drawing them out" on these and other subjects.[19]

Bronson Alcott drew the children out on some subjects—childbirth, for example—which Bostonians thought unfit for childish lips, however plainly the underlying truths might be written on their hearts. When the Transcendentalists began their meetings in the fall of 1836, the storm of public criticism was still several months in the future but Alcott's record of the pedagogical conversations was about to be published, and Elizabeth Peabody, his collaborator, had already informed Alcott that she could not share responsibility for publishing those passages which, as she correctly

---

Ripley, "Martineau's *Rationale of Religious Inquiry*," *Examiner*, 21 (1836), 225–54.

18. Quoted in Clarence L. F. Gohdes, *The Periodicals of American Transcendentalism* (Durham, N.C., Duke University Press, 1931), p. 40.

19. Odell Shepard, *Pedlar's Progress: The Life of Bronson Alcott* (Boston, Little, Brown, 1937), pp. 112–84.

foresaw, the public would consider indecent.[20] Until March of 1837, however, when the bitter attacks upon Alcott began, the Temple School was to the other Transcendentalists an inspiring example of successful reform activity.

Emerson's *Nature*, the most significant expression of Transcendentalist philosophical ideas to appear in this early period and one of the several great manifestoes of the movement, had been published in early September 1836 and was already being discussed among the *illuminati* when they first met on the nineteenth. Within a month, moreover, five hundred copies had been sold, and the first Unitarian reaction, in the *Register*, had been highly favorable, if somewhat puzzled.[21]

For the Transcendentalists the importance of *Nature* was its teaching of the correspondences between natural facts and spiritual truths, and its insistence upon the primacy of "spirit," whose laws nature both obeys and teaches. For Emerson himself, the book, and the warmth of its reception in some quarters, also had an importance in deciding the course of his career.

Thirty-three years of age in 1836, Emerson had spent the preceding decade in search of his vocation; and the story of that search reveals much about his relation to the Transcendentalist efforts of reform. After graduation from Harvard College in 1825 he had entered the Divinity School, where all efforts to apply himself steadily had been vitiated by the necessity of teaching, by bouts with rheumatism, and by an

20. Alcott, typically, exercised the best intentions and the worst practical judgment by segregating the offensive passages in appendices, where the guardians of public morals could and did peruse them out of context. Shepard, *Alcott*, pp. 187–91.

21. Rusk, *Life*, pp. 242–43. For other reactions see Alcott, *Journals*, p. 78; Emerson, *Letters*, 2, 36.

eye ailment which prevented him from writing or taking part in recitations. None of this was conducive to a very thorough theological indoctrination. But Emerson even in normal circumstances would not have been one to indulge in doctrinal certainties. His religious and vocational ideas were constantly in flux. Like his brother William, who had doubted himself out of the ministerial profession, Waldo was accustomed to harboring unorthodox ideas; and his preoccupation with the art of eloquent self-expression made him especially impatient with theological systems and parish details.

Settlement as a regular minister in 1829, while quieting some of his vocational doubts, had raised new ones. In March of that year he had been elected colleague of Henry Ware, Jr., at the Hanover Street Church, and he had assumed full charge of the pastorate shortly afterward. He had immediately discovered that he disliked leading public prayers, and his earlier doubts about institutional Christianity had been intensified when he was obliged to administer rites in which he did not wholly believe. Since he cared still less for visiting and similar parish duties, there had been little but preaching to make the young Emerson glad in his calling.[22]

The accumulation of doubts expressed itself in his sermons, in which he began to complain about what he called "historical Christianity." Too many pious people, he told his parishioners, "see God in Judea and in Egypt, in Moses and in Jesus, but not around them."[23] In February of 1832 he addressed a letter to the church members in which he suggested revisions in the service of Holy Communion. He wished, he said, to give that rite a more exclusively com-

22. Rusk, *Life*, pp. 76–81, 110–19, 139.
23. Arthur C. McGiffert, Jr., ed., *Young Emerson Speaks: Unpublished Discourses on Many Subjects by Ralph Waldo Emerson* (Boston, Houghton Mifflin, 1938), p. xxxv.

memorative character and to diminish the role of the pastor in administering it.

Emerson, though he may have been aware from the beginning that separation from his pastorate could follow if he persevered in this protest, was undoubtedly sincere in thinking that his parishioners might agree to his proposals. "I had hoped," he said later, "to carry them with me." He had chosen the Communion as target of his protest not only because it seemed to him an especially noxious example of religious formalism, but also because the New England churches had had a long history of changing ideas on the subject. If the innovator sought an entering wedge, this was not an illogical one.[24]

The extent to which Emerson was acting as a "reformer" in this episode must nonetheless be stated cautiously. After a summer of negotiations, during which his proposals were rejected first by a special committee and then by the church membership, the young pastor concluded that he could not "go habitually to an institution which they esteem holiest [i.e. Communion] with indifference and dislike," [25] and he accordingly submitted his resignation, which was accepted by the church in October. Charles Emerson thought that his brother's actions bore the stamp of the true reformer, and predicted that Waldo would found a new society conforming to his own ideals. But their aunt, the astute Mary Moody Emerson, scouted any such expectation. "You talk of his being a *reformer*," she protested to Charles:

> A reformer! and beginn at the wrong end? annuling a simple rite w'h has bound the followers of Jesus together for ages & announced his resurrection! A reformer—who on earth with his genius is less able to cope with opposition? Who with his good sense less

24. Rusk, *Life*, pp. 160–64.
25. Emerson, *Journals*, 2, 497.

force of mind—and while it invents new universes is lost in the surrounding halo . . . No, he never loved his holy offices—and it is well he has left them.[26]

What Mary Emerson saw more clearly than others was that while Waldo might speak out in favor of sweeping changes, he would never make himself responsible for carrying them through. He had placed himself accurately among reformers when he said, in the sermon announcing his final refusal to administer the traditional Communion: "That is the end of my opposition, that I am not interested in it." He was content, as he told his parishioners in perfect sincerity, that the rite should "stand to the end of the world." [27]

From the point of view of the intensely spiritual individualist, seeking to give vent to all positive intuitions of his own mind, lack of interest was indeed a decisive objection against any human activity. But the thoroughgoing reformer is likely to make lack of interest the beginning rather than the end of his protest. From the latter perspective Emerson's position could be thought a supine and even an irresponsible one.

During a nine-months' tour of Europe in 1833, Emerson apparently did entertain thoughts of gathering "a parish of his own" on his return to the United States; but subsequently he made no definite moves in this direction. His nearest approach to the role of reformer in the next few years was a suggestion to the church in New Bedford that he might become their pastor if they would relieve him of the duties of administering Communion and leading prayers. Members of the New Bedford pastoral committee were so shocked that they suppressed the letter in which these proposals were made, and negotiations appear not to have been resumed.[28]

26. Emerson, *Letters, 1,* 355; Rusk, *Life,* pp. 165–67.
27. Quoted in Frothingham, *Transcendentalism,* p. 380.
28. Rusk, *Life,* pp. 186, 199–200.

If Emerson shrank from assuming the place of an active reformer, however, he did not cease to be a Unitarian preacher. His break with the ministerial profession had not been so complete as has sometimes been imagined.[29] From 1834 through 1837 he occupied an average of forty-one Sundays each year with ministerial duties, acting as regular supply preacher for several extended periods at New Bedford and East Lexington. At East Lexington his commitment ran from mid-1835 until February 1838—nearly as long a period as he had served in the Second Church. He did not preach for the last time until January 20, 1839.[30]

It does seem clear, however, that Emerson continued to preach in this period mainly because his income was as yet only partially sustained by lecturing and writing. His attachment to the ministry declined as those other ventures succeeded. The ending of negotiations with the New Bedford church occurred shortly after his first season (winter 1833–34) as a public lecturer, and though he made a three-year arrangement at East Lexington in 1835, he was doing his best to get out of that responsibility by late 1837, after the public had responded favorably to *Nature* and to his "American Scholar" address of the summer of 1837.[31] The fact that he wrote his last new sermon in July of 1836,

29. Frothingham called the events of 1832 "his resignation of the Christian ministry." *Transcendentalism*, p. 120.

30. "Preaching Record," Emerson Papers, Harvard University Library. The agreement with the East Lexington church called for Emerson to preach until May 1838, but he arranged for John Dwight to take most of the services in the last few months. Cooke, *Dwight*, pp. 17–18; McGiffert, *Young Emerson Speaks*, p. xxxvii. A pulpit appearance at Nantucket in 1847, sometimes cited as Emerson's last sermon, was differently interpreted by the speaker himself: Cabot, *Memoir*, 2, 498.

31. For public response to the "American Scholar" see Rusk, *Life*, p. 266.

and that the frequency of his preaching declined from fifty Sundays in 1836 to thirty-four in 1837 [32] would in fact give grounds to argue that the publication of *Nature* was at least as much a turning point in Emerson's career as was the resignation of 1832.

Another of the Transcendentalist group who eventually left the ministry was George Ripley.[33] In the fall of 1836 his resignation was four years in the future, and Ripley at this time was an active and highly respected member of the Boston clergy. Though still in his early thirties, he was, as O. B. Frothingham later recalled, "formal, punctilious, a trifle forbidding" in manner. Gold-rimmed spectacles betokened the scholar, but the intense black eyes behind them betrayed the reformer. He had been graduated at the head of his Harvard class in 1823 and then had taught mathematics in Harvard College while attending the Divinity School. His pastorate at Purchase Street Church, in Boston, had begun in 1826 under the most favorable auspices, the church having been organized expressly for him in what was then a fashionable quarter of the city.[34]

Ripley's high expectations for the success of this society were, however, not realized. The church did not become large or prosperous; and though this was partly because of a sudden movement of wealth and respectability from the Purchase Street area, the young preacher tended to be-

32. "Preaching Record."

33. Of the seventeen Transcendentalist ministers, eleven remained permanently in that calling, and ten of the latter continued as Unitarians. Samuel Osgood became an Episcopalian minister. Emerson, Ripley, Brownson, Cranch, Dwight, and Very left the profession altogether.

34. Frothingham, *Ripley*, pp. 36–37, 45. The church building stood at the corner of Purchase and Pearl streets (near present-day South Station). Ibid., p. 36.

rate himself and to doubt his qualifications as a parish minister.[35]

Another development which influenced Ripley's eventual decision to quit the ministry was the increasing liberalism of his theology as he became better acquainted with German speculations. His fondness for the new "transcendental" themes was evidenced throughout the 1830's in articles written for the *Christian Examiner;* [36] and his preaching began to show the effects of these investigations.

Ripley's sermon entitled "Jesus Christ, the Same Yesterday, Today, and Forever," first preached in 1834, anticipated not only his own later heresies but also Theodore Parker's celebrated discourse of 1841, *The Transient and Permanent in Christianity.* Ripley's sermon contained little of Parker's severe denunciation of the "transient" elements in the popular faith, but there was a similar conception of what constitutes permanence. "Religion," he said, drawing upon the theology of Schleiermacher, "has always existed, and in its essential elements is always the same. Its ideas are inseparable from man." When it is said that Christ is "the same yesterday, today, and forever," he explained, the true meaning is not the eternal existence of the person of Christ, but "the Immutability of the religious truths which he taught." Thus, departing from the

35. Ibid., p. 61.
36. For Ripley's articles of the 1830's see William Cushing, *Index to the Christian Examiner*, Boston, 1879. Ripley also had been acting editor of the *Christian Register* for a brief period in 1833 (Frothingham, *Ripley*, p. 94) and had established his own newspaper, *The Boston Observer and Religious Intelligencer*, in January 1835. The *Observer* was merged with the *Register* in June of the same year. For an excellent study of Ripley's relation to foreign thought see Arthur R. Schultz and Henry A. Pochmann, "George Ripley: Unitarian, Transcendentalist, or Infidel?" *American Literature 14* (1942), 1–8, 18–19.

standard Unitarian belief, Ripley portrayed Jesus as merely the enunciator, albeit the clearest and best enunciator, of principles which the human race has always known. The implication was that all religious systems, Christianity included, are based upon "natural" human sentiments and ideas, rather than upon supernatural occurrences.[37]

This interpretation was not likely to cause widespread alarm so long as it was merely preached to a congregation unschooled in theological niceties, and so long as Ripley and the other Transcendentalists did not attack specific doctrines of supernaturalism. An *Examiner* article by Ripley in November 1836, however, did adopt this more negative tack, arguing that Christian truths can be made plain to the human mind without the aid of miraculous confirmation. Since this article was "the opening gun in a long battle" between Transcendentalists and conservative Unitarians, fuller discussion of it is reserved for the chapters dealing with that controversy. Here it is enough to say that Ripley's turning of long-pondered "spiritualistic" ideas to an attack on Unitarian doctrines was one symptom of the increasing self-assurance of the younger intellectuals in the period when they first came together.

A volume somewhat ambitiously titled *New Views of Christianity, Society, and the Church* was published in December 1836 by Ripley's close friend, Orestes Brownson. It brought to public notice an emphasis in Transcendentalist thought which differed from either Emerson's or Ripley's. Though broadly critical of both Catholic and Protestant theology, the book's radicalism was far more social than doctrinal. It was the work of a man whose chief interest was to make Christianity a more suitable vehicle for social amelioration, and who after much searching be-

37. George Ripley, "Jesus Christ, the Same Yesterday, Today and Forever," in Miller, *Transcendentalists*, pp. 284–93.

lieved he had found, in Unitarianism, the most promising starting-point for this endeavor.

Orestes Augustus Brownson was easily the most colorful of the Transcendentalists—as a speaker, writer, and disputant as well as in appearance. Well over six feet in height and powerfully built, he accented the strange complexities of his nature by wearing a black swallow-tail coat that fluttered behind him, a kerchief tied at the neck, books on each arm, a quid of tobacco in the mouth. In the pulpit he was a fiery and convincing orator, on the printed page a relentless logician.

Brownson had had the most turbulent personal religious history of all the Transcendentalists. As a Vermont farm lad he had been exposed to a variety of sectarian influences, most notably to the mild Congregationalism of an elderly couple who had become his foster parents. At the age of nineteen, when living at Ballston Spa in upstate New York, he had joined the Presbyterian church; but shortly thereafter, finding himself unable to accept Calvinist doctrine, he had gone over to the Universalists. In his twenty-third year, prepared by wide reading which served in the place of formal education, he had been ordained as a Universalist minister. While serving as a preacher and newspaper editor for that sect, he had found himself gradually losing confidence in the internal consistency of Universalist doctrine, and colleagues had begun to complain of his wavering in the faith. By 1830, at age 27, he had entered upon a brief agnostic period, during which he had aided in the formation of the abortive Workingmen's party in New York City and had become an editor of their newspaper, the *Free Inquirer*.

In 1832 Brownson had exercised his acute analytic powers on the premises of skepticism and discovered that that system, too, was wanting in consistency. Strongly influenced by the theological and social writings of W. E.

Channing, he had rejected both the agnostic position and the Owenites' environmental approach to social reform. He had come to believe, with Channing, that social salvation would be achieved not by the uprooting of institutions, but through individual regeneration, and that the Christian religion provided the only hope for such regeneration. He had resumed his ministerial career by accepting the Unitarian pastorate in Walpole, New Hampshire, where he remained until 1834.

It was during this stay in Walpole that Brownson had begun to attract the attention of the Boston Unitarians. In 1834 he had contributed a series of "Letters to an Unbeliever" to the *Christian Register*, and these had been widely praised as a convincing refutation of the rationalistic skepticism with which one Abner Kneeland was then making a successful appeal to the working class. Brownson, with his argumentative skill and his first-hand knowledge of the byways of infidelity, had seemed especially fitted to lead a Christian counteroffensive against Kneeland. George Ripley and Channing had encouraged him to come to Boston, and Bernard Whitman, editor of the *Unitarian*, had assured Brownson that his newspaper writings on infidelity had gained wide reading and hearty acceptance among the liberal clergy.

Brownson's first response to these solicitations had been to take a church nearer to Boston, in Canton, Massachusetts. Then, in the spring of 1836, he had moved into the metropolis to initiate the work which was to give him a major place as a religious reformer. On May 29 he formally inaugurated an experimental church, called the "Society for Christian Union and Progress," and in July obtained a literary vehicle by securing appointment as editor of the weekly *Boston Reformer*. *New Views*, his volume of December 1836, was the manifesto of this experimental ministry to the working class, laying out its theological rationale and expressing the reformer's confidence that a transcendentalized Unitarianism would bring the Kingdom of God in the not-too-distant future.[38]

It is an additional commentary on the unusual potency of the transcendentalizing atmosphere of 1836 that the least outspoken of the Club members published, in the summer of that year, his first and only defense of the new religious ideas. Convers Francis, the mildest and at age 41 the most venerable of the transcendental group, produced a brief tract called *Christianity as a Purely Internal Principle*. In this he argued that the Christian religion is unique precisely because of its entire independence of "forms." Insofar as the churches set credal standards or demand adherence to particular rituals, Francis said, they revert to pagan practices which Christ himself abhorred. True Christianity judges men by their personal virtue and not by their stated beliefs.

In thus exalting morality over creed, Francis was no doubt following a well-beaten Unitarian path, but the sharp distinction which he made between the internal and external in religion showed his participation in the Transcendentalist movement of thought.

Despite his general lack of assertiveness, Francis had given other earnests of his sympathy with the new school, most notably in his championing of German philosophy. During the early years of his long pastorate at Watertown, Massachusetts (1819–42), he had begun to acquaint himself with scholarly works of every description. One year's authors included Henry More, Cicero, Plato, Tacitus, Sophocles, Coleridge, Herder, DeWette, Eckermann, Lardner, Baur, and Constant.[39] Owner of a considerable library, and of an infinitely receptive if not acutely discriminating

38. Schlesinger, pp. 8–27, 64; Brownson, *Orestes A. Brownson, 1*, 85–110, 140.
39. Newell, "Francis," p. 241.

mind, he gained a reputation for "all-sidedness" which was to be confirmed all too well for his Transcendentalist friends when he appeared in the 1840's to be suppressing his liberal principles for the sake of his Harvard professorship. In the early years, however, Francis was the revered elder statesman of the Club and the moderator—probably in more than one sense—of their discussions.

William Henry Furness, a close friend and former schoolmate of Emerson, was pastor of the Unitarian society which Joseph Priestley had founded in Philadelphia in 1796. Although he was rarely in Boston to meet with the Transcendental Club, he was considered a leading spirit of their movement.

Furness' *Remarks on the Four Gospels*, published in late 1836, showed the marked coincidence of his biblical views with those which Ripley and others were putting forward. Like the others, Furness had no intention of denying that the miracles recorded in Scripture had actually occurred. On the contrary, he argued that the substantial agreement and uniform ingenuousness of the Gospel writers makes it impossible to suppose that their accounts are unreliable. But turning to a refutation of common attitudes about the miracles, he took the position, similar to Ripley's, that the miracles were not performed for the purpose of convincing men of the truths of Christianity. It is true, he acknowledged, that Christ's resurrection and wonderful acts provide added confirmation of Christian teachings; but the human mind, which has direct intuitions of religious truths, needs no such confirmations, and would have received the Gospel with equal assurance had the miracles never been recorded.[40]

Furness' special contribution to the Transcendentalist

40. Furness, *Four Gospels*, pp. ix–x, 252–53, 310–12. His lengthy argument for the accuracy of the Gospel narratives is contained in chaps. 2–7.

discussion of miracles, besides his intense insistence upon their validity, was a naturalistic theory which links him to David Friederich Strauss and the Tübingen School on the one hand, and the theology of the American Horace Bushnell on the other. Rejecting the standard Unitarian and Orthodox interpretation of the miraculous as constituting an "interruption" of the natural order, he held that such manifestations belong to a "spiritual" realm which indeed is beyond the sphere of ordinary human activities, but still is a part of the natural world. To deny that the miraculous can occur within the natural realm, he said, is to make the presumptuous assertion that we know all there is to know about our universe.

The place of Jesus in this scheme was that of a man uniquely endowed and enabled to draw upon the resources of the "spiritual" stratum of nature, and to make real the power that would otherwise have remained merely potential in this higher realm. Such a singular endowment, Furness thought, makes Jesus "divine" in a sense that other men are not, and constitutes his special claim to veneration.[41]

By the time Furness had finished insisting upon the moral grandeur of Jesus and the authenticity of the Gospel narratives, his rejection of the word "supernatural" rested on little more than semantic hair-splitting, and the book caused a minimum of discomfort in conservative circles. What allied him most clearly with the Transcendentalists was his assertion of the dispensability of miracles as Christian proofs, together with his championing of a naturalism which could easily be carried to conclusions more startling than his own.

Frederic Henry Hedge, although he contributed nothing of first importance to the spate of New School writ-

41. Ibid., pp. 145–88, 217–18.

ings in 1836, had played a major part throughout the 1830's in bringing transcendental doctrines to the fore. Hedge at age thirty had already acquired a wide reputation for scholarship, and particularly for erudition in the field of German metaphysics. Since 1832 he had contributed major articles to the *Examiner* on Coleridge, Swedenborg, and Schiller, and on phrenology. Although he had been outspoken for transcendental philosophy in these writings, such criticisms as he had made of prevailing Unitarian ideas had as yet caused no serious reaction, and in fact had been praised highly by so conservative a Unitarian as Henry Ware, Jr.[42]

Hedge was the only member of the immediate Transcendentalist circle who had been educated in Germany. His father, professor of logic at Harvard, had sent him abroad in the company of George Bancroft in 1819, and young Hedge had spent three years there before entering Harvard College. By 1829 he had completed his theological studies and had been ordained in the church at West Cambridge. Six years later he had accepted a call to the Unitarian society in Bangor, Maine. Although he was a regular attendant at meetings of the Club—which acquired one of its names because it met when he came to Boston—this timely removal from the hotbed of religious radicalism may have helped to determine his eventual position in the more conservative wing of the Transcendentalist Movement.[43]

42. Hedge's article on Coleridge, despite its air of profundity and a few supercilious remarks about the mental qualities requisite to an understanding of transcendental philosophy, apparently did not "infuriate the opponents," as Perry Miller suggests (*Transcendentalists*, p. 67). Ware thanked Hedge for "the pleasure I have received and which I hear expressed in every quarter": Wells, p. 97. For Hedge's articles of the 1830's see Cushing, *Index to the Christian Examiner.*

43. Eliot, 3, 162.

The optimism of the Transcendentalists as they took the field in force during 1836 was increased by their belief that some older Unitarians would come to their aid. Channing, James Walker, and Charles Follen were the leaders upon whom they placed most reliance. All of these men, and Channing in particular, had given constant emphasis to the free search for truth, and to the need for expanding and developing Unitarian doctrine.[44]

Walker, as editor of the *Examiner,* had seemed to show a friendly disposition toward the younger intellectuals by welcoming their writings for that periodical in the early 1830's.[45] What seemed even more conclusive, however, were his frequent protests against the Lockean philosophy. Walker's lecture of 1834 called "The Foundations of Faith" had stated the good transcendental principle that the "rightly constituted" soul receives the truths of religion "with a degree of intuitive clearness, and certainty, equal at least to that of the objects of sense." He had called for "a better philosophy than the degrading sensualism out of which most forms of modern infidelity have grown." [46]

Walker's "better philosophy" was Scottish, not German, and he wished less extreme innovations in theology and the Church than those which the Transcendentalists were adumbrating. But the younger group expected tolerance if not active support from Walker, and in this, at least, they were not to be disappointed.

44. See, for example, his letters to Sismondi and Martineau, in Charles T. Brooks, *William Ellery Channing: A Centennial Memory* (Boston, 1880), pp. 155, 159; and in W. H. Channing, *The Life of William Ellery Channing, D.D.* (Boston, 1880), p. 435. Henry A. Pochmann has assailed "the common impression that Unitarians consistently and implacably opposed German ideas" in his *German Culture in America* (above, n. 8), pp. 148–51.

45. But cf., for Walker's warnings against excessive radicalism, Brownson, *Orestes A. Brownson, 1,* 120–21.

46. *Examiner, 17* (1834), 13, 14.

Charles Follen, a theological and political liberal who had escaped from Germany to the United States in 1824, had expressed sympathy for transcendental reform ideas in a work entitled *Religion and the Church*, which he brought out during the summer of 1836.[47] In this treatise he had drawn heavily upon the work of Friederich Schleiermacher and Benjamin Constant, making particular use of Constant's belief that religious institutions must undergo constant modification as society itself advances.[48] In the volume which appeared in 1836, Follen had made the human "religious sentiment" the starting-point of the theological system he intended to elaborate. The intuitions of the mind, he said, rather than "those records, which, by different portions of mankind, are considered as of divine origin," must form the basis for reforms in religion; and the new theology, when completed, must contain not simply the best insights of the Christian religion, but an historical synthesis of the true elements in all earlier faiths.[49]

Follen has generally been excluded from listings of the Transcendentalists, or at most has been considered a transitional figure. He was preaching in New York and the West during the early years of the Transcendental Club, and he died when returning to Boston in 1840; so it is difficult to say precisely what his position would have been in the controversy of the 1840's. It is plain, however, that in certain respects—notably in his emphasis on the intuitional basis of religion and in the syncretism of his theological

47. This was intended as the first installment in a major study of religious institutions, but Follen's death by shipwreck in 1840 prevented completion of the work. One additional chapter was published posthumously in Follen, *Works*, 5, 293–313.

48. Constant's theory of religious institutions had its fullest expression in his *De la Religion, considerée dans sa source, ses formes, et ses developpements*, 5 vols. Paris, 1824–31.

49. *Works*, 5, 256–57, 287–90.

method—he contributed to the structure of Transcendentalist reforming thought.[50]

In view of the prodigious output of the younger intellectuals in the latter part of 1836, it is easy to see why that year has been called the *annus mirabilis* of their movement. In the field of religious reform alone, nearly all the characteristic Transcendentalist themes had been introduced, with Alcott and Emerson advocating reliance on the intuitions and moral awareness of the individual, Ripley and Furness initiating a critique of accepted canons of authority, and Brownson, Francis, and Follen interpreting the Christian Church as a mutable expression of man's evolving religious conceptions.

The strong note of reforming optimism which pervades these writings makes the terms "ferment" and "enthusiasm," so often used to describe Transcendentalism, seem especially applicable to this early period. The Transcendentalists were never so united as in the fall of 1836, when they had just begun to find each other out, and had not yet elaborated the varied schemes of action and revolt which were later to cause divergence among them. It was this "enthusiasm"—a common resolution that society could be changed for the better if reliance were placed upon human intuitions—which provided the center and integrating force for their movement.

The probability of disagreement was inherent in the very form of this common enthusiasm. Clarke's witticism meets the case almost exactly; they were perhaps most like-minded in their unabashed eclecticism, in a determination that beyond a certain point no two of them should think alike. This is why technical philosophical definitions of

50. Eliot, *2*, 286–88. For Follen's influence upon Brownson see Brownson, *Works*, *4*, 2; for his connection with Dwight see Cooke, *Dwight*, pp. 39–40.

American Transcendentalism are so unsatisfactory, and always tend to exclude persons who considered themselves part of the movement. Such "readable formulae" trace circles which cut across the area in question but are not concentric with it. The reach and variety of this group's accomplishments stemmed not from a philosophy, or even a set of related philosophies, but from a complex interaction of ideas, of the men who held them, and of the times in which they lived.

Chapter 3

Ripley, Emerson, and the Miracles Question

CORNELIUS FELTON, Eliot Professor of Greek at Harvard, admitted to his friend Andrews Norton in 1840 that he had a somewhat personal reason for disliking Transcendentalist ideas. "German metaphysics and philosophical religion," he said, "make me feel like a mouse under an air pump." [1] Norton himself, who led the Unitarian opposition to Transcendentalism in the 1830's, had no similar feelings of helplessness; or if he had, he was not the kind to acknowledge them. As James Walker was later to say, Norton was a man who not only disliked groping in the dark, but who also made it a policy to keep his own counsel about such uncertainties as did beset him. When he announced scholarly findings and doctrinal interpretations, he invariably spoke with the self-assurance of one who has found the only possible answer. As a teacher in the Divinity School, he gained a reputation that was the exact reverse of the one Convers Francis was later to acquire. While Francis' students were annoyed by his insistence on considering all

1. Felton to Norton, December, 1840, NC.

sides of all questions, Norton's complained of their teacher's impatient refusal to sympathize with their doubtings. Norton, as Walker recalled, "never put himself to much trouble to comprehend the ignorance or the errors of other people." If students appeared unconvinced by a conclusion which to him was clear and unarguable, he simply gave them up.[2]

In the Transcendentalist controversy which first broke out in November 1836, Norton applied these lecture-hall methods in the larger arena of public dispute, where they aroused enough indignation to make his name a lasting symbol of dogmatism and utter illiberality. Indeed, historians have sometimes given the impression that Norton's name stood for little else in the public mind of his own day. But contemporaries found Norton personally admirable, as well as formidable in the field of scholarship. In ordinary intercourse, if not always in the classroom, he was known to be amiable and generous, "modest even to diffidence." "Few men have ever lived," Walker said, "who had less of ill-will or unkindness."[3] And George Ripley, Norton's foremost opponent among the Transcendentalists, in later years paid tribute to the man's "thorough scholarship . . . refined and exquisite taste . . . hatred of pretension [and] devotion to truth."[4] Norton's excellence as a scholar was well known to his contemporaries, and so was his early record as a champion of liberality in opposition to Calvinist dogmas. The public estimate rested as much upon his *Genuineness of the Gospels* and his *Statement of Reasons* as upon the *Discourse on the Latest Form of Infidelity*, which is now commonly treated as his chief claim to attention. Norton exercised a degree of influence which

2. Eliot, 2, 197–98.
3. Ibid., pp. 195, 197.
4. In Justin Winsor, ed., *The Memorial History of Boston . . .* (Boston, 1880–81), 4, 299.

would not have been possible to such an unreasoning pedant as the usual caricature presents.

His attitude toward the European philosophies and biblical studies of his time was, however, an illustration of the positiveness for which Norton has been remembered most widely. If he ever experienced Felton's sense of being tossed about intellectually by those powerful Germanic currents, he had no intention of admitting it. He was perfectly confident that he knew which of the foreign speculations had validity and which had not.

As a biblical scholar, Norton stood firmly in the tradition of literary and historical analysis in which the names of Simon, Bentley, John Mill, Wettstein, and Griesbach were most prominent. The general tendency of these critics, whose work spanned the period from the end of the seventeenth to the end of the eighteenth century, had been toward a rejection of the theory of verbal inspiration. Their researches, which led at first to a recognition of the internal contradictions of Scripture, by the beginning of the nineteenth century had influenced such scholars as Norton to take historical circumstances, peculiarities of idiom, and the prepossessions of writer and audience into account when interpreting a scriptural passage or inquiring into its authorship.[5]

Among the types of speculation which Norton opposed were, first of all, those which presupposed a suprasensory mode of receiving religious truth, and which therefore tended to minimize the importance of such manifestations as the biblical miracles. Locke and the Scottish realist phi-

5. George A. Buttrick, et al., eds., *The Interpreter's Bible* (New York, Abingdon-Cokesbury, 1952–57), *1*, 128–32; Wright, in Williams, *Divinity School*, pp. 46–49. For Norton's acknowledgments to this group of biblical critics, see his *The Evidences of the Genuineness of the Gospels* (abridged ed. Boston, 1867), pp. 202, 417–25, 450–53.

losophy formed the basis for his thought, and for his opposition to romantic intuitionism. He criticized Schleiermacher, along with Spinoza before him and such later theologians as DeWette, Paulus, and Strauss, for their alleged
reduction of Divine Personality to a pantheistic omni-
presence in the soul and in Nature.[6] He also rejected the
conclusions reached by German biblical scholars in the
"quest for the historical Jesus" which Schleiermacher's
Reden über die Religion (1799) had initiated. Belief in
both the personality of God and the divinity of Christ was
being undermined, Norton believed, by the interpretations
of Eichhorn, who doubted the traditional authorship of
the Gospels; of DeWette, who advanced a theory of "com-
plements and interpolations" to account for the inconsistencies of Scripture; of Baur and the "Tübingen School,"
advocates of an Hegelian explanation of the emergence of
early Christian doctrine; and of Strauss, whose *Leben Jesu*
(1835) denied scriptural authority and treated the New
Testament narratives as chiefly mythical. Norton's work
on the *Genuineness of the Gospels* was a defense of the
Bible's claim to divine inspiration against the incursions
made by these critics.[7]

In the fall of 1836 George Ripley in Boston and William
Furness in Philadelphia both became open advocates of
theories of biblical interpretation which Norton had rejected. Both of them made the argument, among others,
that the miracles of Jesus, though perfectly authentic, were
not performed for the purpose of confirming the truth of
Christ's teachings. Norton reacted violently to Ripley's

6. Andrews Norton, *A Discourse on the Latest Form of Infidelity
. . . 19th of July, 1839* (Cambridge, Mass., 1839) pp. 41–47; *Remarks
on a Pamphlet Entitled " 'The Latest Form of Infidelity' Examined"*
(Cambridge, Mass., 1839), pp. 11–70.

7. Buttrick, *Interpreter's Bible, 1*, 132–34; Norton, *Genuineness
of the Gospels*, pp. 24–27, 45–47, 180–82, and passim.

article, in a letter to the *Boston Daily Advertiser*, but oddly enough offered no public objection to the speculations of Furness.

Furness, to be sure, had given a more conservative appearance to his thought by expatiating on the beauty of Christ's character and the absolute reliability of the Gospel accounts; but the differences between Furness' ideas and Ripley's were not sufficient to explain the variance between Norton's reactions to the two writings. The real reason for that variance grew out of the respective circumstances of publication.

All of Norton's protests in this and later stages of the "miracles" controversy showed a marked concern not only about dangerous opinions but also about the auspices under which the opinions were expressed. His usual justification for entering a dispute of this nature was that he believed the Unitarian reputation (and indirectly his own) was at stake. In the dispute of 1836, Norton was protesting against Ripley's ideas, but almost equally against the bad judgment of the editor of the *Examiner* in allowing such heresies to appear in an official Unitarian organ.

This interpretation is confirmed in the correspondence which took place between Furness and Norton before and after publication of the *Four Gospels*. Furness, too cautious a man to plunge boldly into controversy, had shown his manuscript to several friends in Philadelphia during the summer of 1836; and when some of these persons were doubtful whether he ought to publish it, he had written asking Norton to read the work and give his opinion. Norton apparently sent a polite refusal, explaining that although he could not agree with the thesis which Furness had outlined to him, he did not believe an authoritative stamp of approval was necessary for a manuscript published on the author's own responsibility. Furness accordingly sent the work to the press in mid-August, and it was on sale in Boston by November 12.[8] By December, Norton had read the *Four Gospels,* and he told Furness that his views were mistaken but not especially dangerous. Since, by that time, Norton's denunciation of Ripley had already appeared in the Boston papers, Furness was understandably gratified that his book had escaped censure.[9]

The importance of the question of "auspices" is further underlined by the fact that the opinions to which Norton took such violent exception in Ripley's article not only were similar to those of Furness' book but were announced in a much less formidable way. They appeared somewhat incidentally in the last seven pages of a thirty-page review.

The work reviewed, James Martineau's *Rationale of Religious Inquiry,* was an attempt to find the "seat of certainty" in Christianity by critical analysis of both Catholic and Protestant doctrines, and by application of the inductive method to religious practices. Ripley applauded this attempt to promote a scientific approach to the study of theology. Where he took exception to Martineau's ideas, he did so, ironically enough, more from a conservative than from a radical point of view: his complaint was that Martineau seemed to deny the divine inspiration of the writers of Scripture. He thought that this denial marked a peculiar inconsistency in an author who appeared to rest almost the entire case for Christianity on the authenticity of the miracles of Jesus.[10]

It was in his remarks on the second half of this alleged inconsistency that Ripley ventured into dangerous territory. Although miracles are important and are entirely credible, he argued, acceptance of them had never in the past been demanded of all who call themselves Christian, and ought not to be now. He admitted that Jesus may

8. *Register,* November 12, 1836.
9. Furness to Norton, July 15, August 14, December 12, 1836, NC.
10. *Examiner, 21* (1836), 225–45.

sometimes have used miraculous displays to help in confirming the source of his authority, but thought that neither
divine authority nor moral teachings could have been
authenticated by miracles alone, since in the time of Jesus
miracle-workers were everywhere. If Christ's doctrines had
not been true and convincing in themselves, no one would
have believed that he came from God, nor would they
have obeyed his teachings.[11] Ripley thus brought into public discussion, through the medium of a representative Unitarian publication, the view he had been preaching since
1834 that Christ was simply the enunciator of religious
truths which would have been equally valid had he never
come.

The young theologian was not unmindful of the opposition which his doctrine of miracles would arouse among
orthodox Unitarians. Despite the apparently casual manner in which he had broached the subject, the move had
been a deliberate one. He had discussed his intention with
Theodore Parker, who had warned him that "the first one
who lifted a hand in this work would have to suffer," and
had advised him to "push some old veteran German to the
forefront of the battle, who would not care for a few
blows." [12]

The vehemence of Andrews Norton's reaction justified
such apprehensions as those of Parker. Norton's first im-
pulse on reading the article expressed itself in a letter which
he drafted, but evidently did not send, to James Walker,
editor of the *Examiner*. He asked Walker to announce in
the next issue that Andrews Norton had severed his connection with the journal.[13] He regretted, he said, that the
managing editors had not seen fit to consult him "before

11. Ibid., pp. 249–53.
12. Frothingham, *Parker*, pp. 78–79.
13. Norton since 1835 had been one of the "sponsors" of the
magazine. Mott, *American Magazines, 1,* 287.

anyone was allowed to take such grounds" in the *Examiner*. Since the mischief was now irremediable, he said, he had no course but to disassociate himself from the magazine. "Every individual has some influence," he added modestly; and he was unwilling that his own should be perverted to "the publication of such doctrines in a work of popular instruction." [14]

Whether or not this letter was ever dispatched, Norton shortly decided upon a somewhat different course. Instead of announcing withdrawal of his support from the *Examiner*, he contented himself with a public letter expressing his disapproval of Ripley's position. Sidney Willard, editor of the weekly *Christian Register*, declined "from personal considerations" to print this missive,[15] and it appeared instead in the *Daily Advertiser* of November 5.

Norton's letter began by expressing the "surprise and sorrow" which he felt on reading the concluding passages of Ripley's review. The theory outlined there was not only wrong, he said, but also capable of doing infinite damage, since it tended to destroy faith in "the only evidence on which the truth of Christianity *as a revelation* must ultimately rest." He had no wish, he said, to interfere with "the rights of free discussion," but it seemed to him that those rights were too often misunderstood. Certain limits must be fixed for the good of the community.

Norton then suggested, in what was by far the most objectionable part of his communication, that two rules

14. Norton to Walker, November 1, 1836, NC.

15. It was characteristic of Willard to avoid controversy, but his motive in this case may have been a feeling of deference toward his predecessor Ripley. Willard was a former Hancock Professor of Hebrew and Oriental Languages in Harvard College. After 1830 he devoted his time to editing various periodicals, and to public office. He died in 1856. See his *Memories of Youth and Manhood*, Cambridge, Mass., 1855.

should in future be followed by writers attempting to controvert doctrines which those "who have thought most concerning them" consider true and important. The first rule was that such innovators must be perfectly certain that they have "ability to discuss the subject." The second was that they should withhold their views from publication pending approval by "those who are capable of judging of their correctness." [16]

To Ripley, whose reputation for careful scholarship was not greatly inferior to that of his former teacher, and who had been a preacher and editor long enough to know something about his responsibilities to the public, it was

Andrews Norton

George Ripley

not pleasant to receive a knuckle-rapping for neglecting to have his composition approved. His reply appeared in the *Advertiser* on November 9, and under the circumstances it showed admirable restraint. "I would have to forget the benefits I have received from the severity of your taste and the minuteness of your learning," he told Norton, ". . . before I can persuade myself to discuss any subject

16. *Advertiser*, November 5, 1836.

with you in a manner incompatible with your superiority in years and attainments to myself." He felt, however, that Norton's charge of "heresy" could only be called absurd; and he added, in a phrase that must have struck home for non-Unitarian readers, that "we are both too deeply laden with offences of that kind to make the spectacle of our flinging stones at each other anything but ludicrous." The public would be especially amused, he thought, to find Norton showing such outraged concern about a signed article in a periodical of which he was not the editor. They would be asking whether the writer were not "of age to assume his own responsibilities."

Aside from all this, he said, the charges of heresy had been put forward in an unfair manner. Norton, "with singular indefiniteness," and without deigning to discuss the issues, had pronounced Ripley's article injurious to the public good. Was it not rather late in the day, Ripley asked, for this kind of demagogic appeal "to the fears of the uninstructed?"

The younger man proposed to lay the whole case before the reading public, "to whose verdict, on such points, I attach more importance, than you think it deserves." To show that his understanding of the miracles had ample precedent, he cited the Scriptures, the Fathers of the early Church, the Protestant reformers, and several modern theologians. He trusted that these citations would at least indicate "that I did not utter my opinion without thought." [17]

The editor of the *Register*, despite his earlier refusal to publish Norton's letter, now, at Ripley's request, printed the whole exchange, though he was circumspect enough to ask his readers to observe that "we make no comments." [18] Few further contributions to the argument ap-

17. Ibid., November 9, 1836.
18. *Register*, November 12. After a month of the controversy,

peared in the *Register* for a month; but on the tenth of December an unsigned letter appeared which deserves to rank far above Norton's as a statement of conservative objections to Ripley's views.

Ripley's very justifiable complaint that Norton had tried to suppress his arguments instead of discussing them was fully recognized by this later correspondent. The writer decried Norton's alarmism and expressed his own appreciation of the desirable spiritual emphasis which the Transcendentalists were bringing into Unitarianism. Then, after making every concession to the spatial limitations under which Ripley's remarks had been set down, he proceeded to give a detailed reply from the conservative point of view.

The true issue, this correspondent said, was whether or not Christianity is merely a set of moral and ethical teachings. If it is nothing more than this, he argued, then the miracles are at most a kind of seal of approval used to inspire confidence in the authority of the teacher; but if, as Christians have always believed, the primary importance of Jesus was his announcement of a divine interposition in human affairs, then miracles confirm this special divine action. While it may be true, he said, that the mere ethical teachings of Christianity could have been conveyed by a natural process, God's sending of his Son to redeem the world constituted a supernatural intervention which could be confirmed only by supernatural occurrences.[19]

Although this balanced criticism represented the reaction of a considerable body of Unitarians, and in fact

---

Willard still found it impossible to disagree with either participant; see his editorial of December 10. Cf. letters from correspondents, *Register*, November 19, December 10.

19. *Register*, December 10. The tone and logical preciseness of this composition suggest Gannett as the author.

reflected the position of the *Register* itself,[20] Norton's stronger aspersions also found support. Professor George Noyes of Harvard Divinity School and Charles W. Upham, pastor of the First Church in Salem,[21] both wrote to Norton to express support of his stand. Upham stated that, while he regretted that his friend Ripley had been exposed to censure, he was relieved that someone of influence had spoken out against Transcendentalism, which he considered "absolutely and not remotely, of infidel tendency and import." [22]

Another Salem minister, eager to discipline the *Examiner* though singularly vague about its offenses, reported to Norton that, while he had not read Ripley's article, he could judge from Norton's letter in the *Advertiser* "what its import is," and he suggested, somewhat cabalistically, "a meeting of a few persons, at some convenient place," to take concerted measures for bringing the *Examiner's* editorial policy into line. He had recently written the *Examiner*, he said, to complain about certain articles on the Resurrection and "on Swedenborg (I believe it was)," but had received very unsatisfactory replies from the editor. He had also been disturbed by "some papers published by Mr. Brownson" in praise of Thomas Carlyle. He found it impossible, he said, to understand what Mr. Carlyle's opinions really were, but he did know "that his admirers belong to the class of persons" who were endangering the morals of the community.[23]

20. Ibid.

21. An able Unitarian controversialist, Upham later attracted notice as a Whig politician, and gained literary immortality as the supposed prototype of Hawthorne's Judge Pyncheon. *DAB*.

22. Noyes to Norton, July 25, 1837; Upham to Norton, November 5, 1836, NC.

23. John Brazer to Norton, November 7, 1836, NC. Brazer had been Professor of Latin in Harvard College 1817 to 1820; Merle

William Henry Furness, whose good fortune and ob-
servance of protocol had helped him to escape Norton's
censure, was not entirely spared by other critics of Transcendentalism. An *Examiner* review of *Remarks on the
Four Gospels* expressed "unqualified dissent" from Furness'
naturalistic theory of miracles, and linked that heresy to
Ripley's. "There is a class of writers among us," said this
reviewer, "who are, consciously or unconsciously, *philosophizing* away the peculiarities of the Gospel, and reducing
it to a level with mere naturalism." Although Furness
might not consider himself one of this class, the reviewer
added, it was undeniable that his theories tended in a harmful direction. "The arrow has been discharged from the
bow; where it may fall, or whom it may wound, is not for
him to determine." On the whole, despite a personal veneration for the ideal of free expression, the writer was
"disposed to regret" the publication of the work.[24]

James Walker, as editor of the *Examiner*, apparently felt
little concern about Furness' "dangerous tendencies"; for
the latter was allowed to answer his critic in the next issue.
In this article Furness re-affirmed his "naturalistic" explanation of the miracles, though he side-stepped the question
of indispensability which had so aroused Norton against
Ripley.[25]

This first stage of controversy had run its course by mid-
1837, but the attack upon conventional religion which the
Examiner had seen as merely a "tendency" was made ex-

E. Curti, in the *DAB*, interprets Brazer's leanings toward natural
religion as anticipations of Emersonian thought, but it appears that
Brazer himself would have been scandalized by this suggestion.

24. *Examiner*, 22 (1837), 104. The reviewer was M. L. Hurlbut,
a teacher and Unitarian clergyman of Philadelphia. See H. H. Hurlbut, *The Hurlbut Genealogy* . . . Albany, 1888.

25. "The Miracles of Jesus," *Examiner*, 22 (1837), 283–321.

plicit in Emerson's Divinity School Address of 1838, and the reaction this time was not so short-lived. Again, as in the disturbance of two years earlier, the question of sponsorship was prominent, for the speaker to this official gathering had been invited by vote of the graduating seniors.

Under such circumstances, even a vague statement of transcendental commonplaces might have caused something of a stir. It is not surprising, therefore that Emerson's premeditated and for him systematic attack upon the popular theology provoked a major controversy. The ideas in the Divinity School Address were not new.[26] The pronouncement achieved its status as epoch-making because it was the first Transcendentalist attack upon Unitarianism which left no avenue of escape from open conflict. If the reformers followed Emerson's prescription as given in this famous sermon, they would not attempt "to project and establish a Cultus with new rites and forms," but would concentrate instead upon breathing "the breath of new life . . . through the forms already existing." [27] Reforming energies were not to be siphoned off harmlessly into a new and eccentric religious sect, but were to be applied to the radical remaking of Unitarianism.

Emerson began his address by setting forth the philosophical basis for the reforms which he proposed. Reiterating the thesis of *Nature,* he pointed out the correspondence between the consummate beauties of the Earth "in this refulgent summer" and the perfection of those spiritual laws which "traverse the universe and make things what they are." He then carried the discussion immediately into the realm of morality by explaining a further correspondence: that between the "spiritual laws" of the universe and the

26. See Clarence L. F. Gohdes, "Some Remarks on Emerson's 'Divinity School Address,' " *American Literature, 1* (1929), pp. 27–31.

27. Emerson, *Works, 1,* 149–50.

moral law within the human mind. "The sentiment of virtue," he said, is nothing but the response of the receptive heart to "certain divine laws" which are perceived by introspection and are immediately recognized to be the laws of the universe as well as of the mind. The spiritual laws cannot be made into formulae, he explained, but their operations can be described: these laws oversee all moral activities, and with a "rapid intrinsic energy" execute rewards and punishments for each human deed at the very moment it is being carried out. The operations of the spiritual laws have always "suggested to man the sublime creed" that the world is the product "of one will, of one mind"; and it is this conviction, he said, which originally creates and shapes religious institutions.

The speaker's complaint against conventional Christianity was that this intuitive basis of religious institutions and creeds has been forgotten. In Christianity, as in some other religions, he said, men have lost their belief in direct inspiration. Having, nonetheless, a sort of nostalgia for their lost faith, they pretend that one man or a few men in all of history have been capable of receiving direct intuitions of truth, and they accordingly attribute to these favored individuals the "divinity" which rightly belongs to all men.

Jesus, Emerson explained, proclaimed not his own divinity, but that of the human soul. Though Christ spoke of miracles, he meant only that all of life is a miracle. And when the writers of Scripture claimed to be inspired of God, their meaning was simply that all men are inspired. It is, he claimed, only the later interpreters—the formulators of "historical Christianity"—who have imagined otherwise.

The Christian Church, Emerson thought, has not only fostered false and redundant doctrines, but also, conversely, has neglected to preach Christ's real message, namely man's direct access to the spiritual laws. Popular preaching, he said, is ineffectual because ministers of the Gospel are unaware even of the possibility of direct inspiration, and therefore have not attempted to attain that experience or lead others to it.

Emerson's basic prescription for remedying the ills of the Church was the replacing of "second-hand" formulae with spiritual insights gained at first hand. Opponents afterward liked to quote his declaration that "the remedy . . . is first, soul, and second, soul, and evermore, soul"; but he also stated the solution in more precise terms. He told the young graduates to "go alone," to eschew conformity, and to have higher than common standards of morality. Instead of attempting revolutionary departures from the existing institutional forms, they were to make use of the instruments which Christianity provides, especially those of preaching and the Sabbath. Above all, they were to communicate "a faith like Christ's in the infinitude of man." [28]

The phrasing of this last admonition suggests the most fundamental of the disagreements between Emerson and standard Unitarianism. The doctrine he advocated was "faith in man," a faith not "in Christ" but "like Christ's." This implicit rejection of the usual Christian Confession was made more galling to conservatives by Emerson's searing allusions to formalism and coldness in the pulpit, and by his sometimes deprecatory phrasing. His remark, for example, that "Miracle, as pronounced by Christian churches, is Monster," was regarded as irreverent. His call for "a new Teacher" seemed clearly to be a denial that the religion of Jesus is God's final or even his most complete revelation.[29]

28. Ibid., p. 144.
29. Ibid., pp. 136–42, 129, 151.

The first manifestation of the bitter controversy stirred by this discourse was not an argument about Emerson's opinions but rather a confused attempt to fix responsibility. Emerson himself clearly had no wish to be looked on as a spokesman for anyone else,[30] but he was, after all, a prominent alumnus of the College and Divinity School, and one who had been preaching with some regularity in Unitarian pulpits for over a decade. Cambridge theologians, therefore, asked indignantly whether the Senior Class was willing to sponsor Emerson's heresies; Unitarian clergymen asked the same about the faculty of the Divinity School; and non-Unitarians queried and happily affirmed, by turns, the responsibility of the whole denomination.[31]

The young seniors were in the least enviable position in this crossfire. They wrote Emerson to say that although some of them disagreed with the ideas he had expressed, all thanked him for speaking at their graduation. They were uncertain, they said, whether under the circumstances the address should be published or merely printed and circulated privately.[32]

Publication eventually was decided upon. After August 25, when the *Address* was placed in the hands of the public,

30. Letter to Henry Ware, Jr., October 8, 1838, Emerson, *Letters*, 2, 166–67.

31. Theodore Parker penned an amusing account of this exchange of recriminations in a letter to George Ellis (August 7, 1838), in Franklin B. Sanborn and William T. Harris, *A. Bronson Alcott, His Life and Philosophy* (2 vols. Boston, 1893), *1*, 279–81.

32. Emerson, *Letters*, 2, 147. The seven members of the Class of 1838 were Benjamin Fiske Barrett, Harrison Gray Otis Blake, Theodore H. Dorr, Crawford Nightingale, George F. Simmons, Frederick A. Whitney, and William D. Wilson. *Harvard University Quinquennial Catalogue* (Cambridge, Mass., 1930), p. 1114. Robert C. Waterston, who studied at Cambridge "under the personal charge" of Drs. Ware and Palfrey, was co-signer of some of the group's communications with Emerson. Eliot, 2; Emerson, *Letters*, 2, 147.

there was no longer any reason for Unitarian conservatives to hold their fire, and within two days Norton had expressed his reaction in the pages of the *Advertiser*. The vitriol in this outburst made the attack upon Ripley two years earlier seem relatively mild. Norton began by ridiculing the entire New School in the most abusive terms. Their aberrations had arisen, he said, because of a "restless craving for notoriety and excitement," which had recently been intensified by the praise which "that foolish woman" Harriet Martineau had accorded the Transcendentalists in her work *Society in America*.[33] Transcendentalist ideas, he said, were the outgrowth of "ill-understood notions, obtained by blundering through the crabbed and disgusting obscurity of some of the worst German speculatists." Most of the American Transcendentalists, Norton thought, had not even bothered to read the Germans at first hand but had relied upon the interpretations of Carlyle and Cousin—both of whom received suitably derogatory epithets from Norton's angry pen. And he added a denunciation of "the atheist Shelley," whose sole relevance to this discussion was that the Transcendentalist *Western Messenger* had printed something favorable about his poetry.

Norton then elaborated upon some of the less technical characteristics of the New School, its "extraordinary assumption . . . great ignorance . . . incapacity for reasoning . . . contempt for good taste . . ." and "buffoonery and affectation of manner." Ordinarily, he said, such absurd persons as the Transcendentalists would not merit notice of any kind; but Emerson's recent discourse had attacked principles basic to the good of society, and apparently some "silly" people were being persuaded to abandon Christianity for Transcendentalism. The situation therefore had become "disastrous and alarming."

33. (3 vols. London, 1837), *3*, 284–85, 342–59.

As in his reprimand of Ripley, the author again disdained to examine the arguments he was condemning. "It is not necessary," he explained, "to remark particularly on this [Emerson's] composition. It will be sufficient to state generally, that the author professes to reject all belief in Christianity as a revelation," and "makes a general attack upon the Clergy, on the ground that they preach what he calls 'Historical Christianity.'" Emerson, so far as Norton could discern, did not believe in God in any "proper" sense of the term.

Having stated his adversary's views to his own satisfaction, Norton remarked that "what *his* opinions may be" was a matter of minor concern. Emerson might believe whatever he liked; and it could hardly be expected "that his vanity would suffer him long to keep his philosophy wholly to himself." A more serious question was how such a dangerous man had been permitted to speak before the Divinity School on an official occasion. The Senior Class, by inviting Emerson, had made themselves accessories, and Norton thought they owed an explanation to the public for their part in this "great offense." [34]

This denunciatory retort from Norton is the one that has been remembered by historians of the Transcendentalist Movement, but it was nonetheless unrepresentative of the general Unitarian reaction. Some members of the Boston Association raised the question whether Emerson should be called a Christian,[35] but most of the earliest conservative commentaries on the Divinity School Address show as much embarrassment and annoyance about Norton as disagreement with Emerson.

Theophilus Parsons, a prominent lawyer who later became a Professor in the Harvard Law School, wrote to the *Advertiser* on August 30 attempting to set the conserva-

34. *Daily Advertiser*, August 27, 1838.
35. Frothingham, *Parker*, pp. 107–8.

tive argument on sound footing.[36] He first reprimanded Norton for his "outbreak of indignant contempt." While he agreed that Emerson and the new philosophy were dangerous, he could not believe that error would be defeated by "anger, derision, intolerance, and blind and fierce denunciation." The effect of Norton's arguments, he thought, had been to show that their author was afraid of new ideas merely because of their newness; certainly no more plausible objection to Emerson's philosophy had been stated. As for the letter's charges of "assumption," "ignorance," and "incapacity of reasoning," Parsons could only inquire incredulously: "Where sits the judge who passes such a sentence?" [37]

Even more critical of Norton's stand was another correspondent, writing to the Boston *Morning Post*.[38] Like Parsons, this conservative thought Emerson's opinions were wrong. The attitude of "the Cambridge Professors," however, seemed to him to verify the maxim "whom the gods will destroy they first deprive of reason." If it was true, he suggested, that young people were being led astray by Emerson, it might be that these young people had looked to the Cambridge professors for support in free inquiry, and had not received it. The followers of Emer-

36. Authorship of this letter is noted by Norton on his own clipping; NC.

37. Norton, answering the Parsons letter several days later, wrote that there had been no need to use reasoned arguments in answering Emerson, since the latter had himself used no arguments but had confined himself to "professions of infidelity and irreligion." *Advertiser*, September 1, 1838. A rebuttal by Parsons appeared on September 3.

38. The writer, according to Norton's notation, was "G. T. Davis." Probably the reference is to George Thomas Davis, lawyer and editor of Greenfield who was then serving in the Massachusetts House of Representatives; he later became a Whig Congressman. NC; *Lamb's Biographical Dictionary*.

son, as this writer remarked in words that remind one of a similar appraisal by Matthew Arnold, undoubtedly valued him less for his opinions than for his insistence upon spiritual freedom. "It is as the advocate of the rights of the mind, as the defender of personal independence in the spiritual world, not as the Idealist, the Pantheist, or the Atheist, that he is run after." [39]

Norton's tirade, far from placing the Unitarian conservatives in a less vulnerable position, had aggravated an already delicate problem in disentanglement. Some who would have joined immediately in a tactfully engineered disavowal of Emerson's ideas were now unwilling to associate their names with Norton's in such an effort. Of those who found themselves in this situation, none was more painfully tried than the Rev. Chandler Robbins, a young man twenty-eight years of age who a year earlier had been chosen editor of the *Register*.

Robbins, though staunchly orthodox, was Emerson's personal friend and his successor at the Second Church. For this reason, and also, perhaps, because the *Register* had always tried to remain neutral in intra-Unitarian disputes, the paper took no stand on the current controversy until it had raged a full month. Direct challenges from non-Unitarians, however, finally provoked Robbins into entering the fight.

Early in October the Rev. M. A. DeWolfe Howe,[40] an editor of the Episcopal *Christian Witness*, jabbed at the entire Unitarian party by telling his readers that in the absence of any official pronouncements to the contrary, it must be assumed that Transcendentalism had infected at least one entire wing of Unitarians. "Let it not be supposed . . . that the young saplings alone have

39. Boston *Morning Post*, August 31, 1838.

40. Howe (1808–95) became a bishop of the Episcopal Church, and was the father of the noted writer of the same name.

bowed before this 'wind of doctrine:' No—some of the sturdiest cedars in their Lebanon have felt its influence." [41] When another outsider, two weeks later, addressed a letter directly to Robbins, asking him whether the *Register*, "as the organ of the Unitarian body," regarded Emerson as a "fair representative" of that Church, the detached attitude could no longer be maintained.

Robbins' answer to the challenge was that neither the Unitarian Church nor any of its members made themselves responsible for opinions expressed by one of their number. Speaking for himself, he said that he dissented from Emerson's ideas but had a high regard for their expositor as a person, and disliked the "popular roar" which had arisen against him. "That liberal Christians are called upon to father and answer for all his peculiarities of opinion," Robbins said in summary, "this we stoutly deny . . . but, that he is a highly gifted, accomplished and holy man, and at heart and in life a Christian, we shall not cease to believe and to declare, until we see the best of reasons . . ." [42]

Norton, who had just finished explaining to the public that Emerson was not a Christian, of course found it unsettling to have the *Register* declare that he was. With characteristic impulsiveness he immediately drafted a public letter criticizing editor Robbins. Instead of sending this one immediately to the papers, however, he took the precaution of showing it first to his brother-in-law, Samuel A. Eliot, [43] who suggested some dozen changes "which, without altering the meaning or the force of the article, will qualify the manner." Eliot advised his relative to add "we conceive," or "it seems to us that . . ." to some of

41. Quoted in the *Register*, October 13, 1838.
42. Ibid., September 29, 1838.
43. Eliot, who was mayor of Boston at this time, had married one of Norton's sisters; President Charles Eliot of Harvard was their son. *DAB*.

the stronger assertions. He also suggested that Norton's description of the Transcendentalists as "puffed up with mystical, irreligious speculations" would impress some readers as "slightly contemptuous." [44]

Norton did accept these modifications, and the letter in its final form somewhat restored his reputation as a polite controversialist. Transcendentalism was still branded as Atheism, but the arguments against it were now more reasoned and the angry epithets were missing. Norton argued that the *Register's* disclaimer of responsibility for Emerson's opinions was nugatory, since it could "be made equally of any individual," however damaging his heresies. The plain fact was, he said, that un-Christian doctrines were being preached by professedly Christian and Unitarian ministers. Robbins' assertion that Emerson was not an infidel amounted only to the use of words "in a new, arbitrary, false sense." As far as opinions (as distinguished from morals) were concerned, he could think of "no infidel who is not entitled to the name of Christian, if it be due to Mr. Emerson." The total effect, he thought, of Robbins' editorial had been to place a major Unitarian newspaper squarely behind infidelity. [45]

Robbins' hurt reply three days later accused Norton of having "ranked me with a class of men to which I do not belong," and thus of jeopardizing his standing with the public and his congregation. Norton, he complained, had chosen to overlook all of his distinct disavowals of Emersonian opinions. If he was to be censured for commending Emerson, he ought also to be commended for censuring him. [46]

In a *Register* editorial that same week, Robbins reiterated his personal distaste for the "popular roar" against Emer-

44. Eliot to Norton, October 10, 1838, NC.
45. *Advertiser*, October 15, 1838.
46. Ibid., October 18, 1838.

son, and with some bitterness asked his readers' forgiveness "for not always chiming with the prevailing tone of censure." Unfortunately, he said, he found himself "constitutionally prone to sympathize" with good men whose real and supposed faults have become "the fashionable quarry" among critics who "should hold their peace, and do penance in secret before God for their own unworthiness." He realized, he added sarcastically, that a penchant for noticing the good qualities of an unpopular figure "is almost an *intolerable* fault in the editor of a paper devoted to Christian Liberality." For this and other reasons, he declared, he would soon cease to impose himself upon the readers of the *Register*.[47]

At this juncture, Eliot interposed his good offices to end the increasingly personal dispute between his relative and Robbins. When Norton showed him another letter, a tedious defense of his dealings with the young editor, Eliot instead of suggesting revisions proposed a settlement out of the journalistic court. In a frank appeal to Norton's paternal instincts, Eliot assured him that Robbins was actually a lad of sound heart and good intentions, lacking only "a little force of character" to make him a man of thoroughly proper opinions.[48] Norton, who for all his assertiveness seems to have valued the advice of his peers, agreed to send the letter directly to Robbins instead of to the papers, and Robbins replied to this magnanimity in a deferential if not thoroughly chastened manner.[49]

In the sequel to this small drama, the *Register* continued its advocacy of fair treatment for Emerson; and when Robbins eventually carried out his earlier threat of resignation, he was able to state triumphantly that many readers had written supporting his position. The paper had gained

47. *Register*, October 20, 1838.
48. Eliot to Norton, October 21, 1838, NC.
49. Norton to Robbins, October 23; Robbins to Norton, n.d., NC.

more subscribers than it had lost. Robbins had discovered, in other words, that "the popular roar" was not so universal as it had appeared to be at first. His Parthian shot as he took leave of his critics was that he "would not now erase one sentiment to which they have objected" in his editorials.[50] Robbins had marshaled enough "force of character" to effect a successful holding action, if not an outright victory, for the party of tolerance.

If Emerson's successor at the Second Church was torn between personal loyalties and public responsibilities, the situation of his former colleague in that church was equally painful. Henry Ware, Jr., owed a heavy debt of gratitude to the young man who, in the earlier years of Ware's ill health, had assumed the heaviest burdens of the Second Church pastorate; and to Emerson, Ware had always been *le bon Henri*. Writers on Transcendentalism, nonetheless, have usually pictured Ware as hastening rather angrily to rebuke Emerson for the Divinity School Address, and of attempting to goad him into a public debate.[51] The facts of the episode do not entirely support this interpretation.

On the evening of July 15, 1838, Emerson and his wife, though declining Ware's invitation to stay the night at his home, remained long enough to discuss the discourse which Emerson had just delivered at the Divinity School. In the course of their conversation, Emerson made some qualifying remarks which caused Ware to say that he might be able to assent to the ideas in the Address if such qualifications were added to them. On the following day, however, feeling that he had conceded too much, Ware wrote Emerson to say that the discourse had contained some statements which he could not accept even with

50. *Register*, January 26, February 2, March 30, 1839.
51. Miller, *Transcendentalists*, p. 196; Commager, *Parker*, p. 67; Rusk, *Life*, p. 271.

modifications. Some of Waldo's ideas, he had decided, were "more than doubtful," and would "tend to overthrow the authority and influence of Christianity" if widely accepted. He added that he rejoiced in Emerson's "lofty ideas and beautiful images of spiritual life," and that he would never have mentioned the reservations which he felt if "a proper frankness" had not required it.[52]

Emerson, in reply, acknowledged that while he could not have withheld any part of his thought, he had been aware that his words would offend "dear friends and benefactors of mine." He promised Ware that the manuscript would be carefully revised before it was sent to the printer. "I heartily thank you," Emerson added, "for this renewed expression of your tried toleration and love." [53]

In September 1838 Ware put some of his objections to Transcendentalist ideas in a sermon called *The Personality of the Deity*. Christianity, he declared, asserts that God is a Person who wills and acts, who loves and exacts obedience. Attempts to reduce God to an abstract set of laws or moral relations are, therefore, essentially vicious. Some men, he acknowledged, may hold erroneous beliefs about God and yet live blameless lives, for "to the pure, all things are pure." But in general, a doctrine of Divine Impersonality robs morality of its sanctions and makes true piety impossible.[54]

Although Ware did not mention Emerson in this discourse, or specifically identify the theories he was opposing

52. Ware to Emerson, July 16, 1838, in Cabot, *Memoir*, 2, 689–90.

53. Emerson to Ware, July 28, in Cabot, *Memoir*, 2, 690–91. Emerson subsequently decided against making any revisions, believing that to do so would be to take unfair advantage of his critics. Elizabeth P. Peabody, *Reminiscences of Rev. Wm. Ellery Channing, D.D.* (Boston, 1880), p. 373.

54. Henry Ware, Jr., *The Personality of the Diety* . . . (Boston, 1838), p. 22 and passim.

as "transcendental," it was clear that Emersonian ideas had been prominently in his mind as he wrote. Using some of the very words and phrases of Emerson's Divinity School Address, Ware denied that the laws of God are comparable to the law of gravitation, that reverence for the ordinances of Nature is what produces all forms of worship, or that laws which "execute themselves" can be the laws of God. He seemed clearly to be answering Emerson when he denied that a man's ultimate responsibility is to his own conscience. And his assertion that Christ cannot be ranked with "Plato or Mahomet . . . Luther or Confucius . . . Fénélon or Swedenborg," even reflected the cataloguing device which was a trademark of Emerson's prose style.[55]

These apparently obvious though inexplicit allusions to the controversial Address caused Ware's colleagues to seize upon his sermon as an authoritative and direct rebuke to Emerson. At their request he had the discourse published, and immediately felt under obligation to send a copy to Emerson with an explanatory word. He told Emerson that he had meant to controvert current errors of doctrine, including some which he believed were present in the Divinity School Address. The sermon, however, had been one of a series on the doctrine of God, and had been planned before Emerson's Address was given. "If I assail positions, or reply to arguments, which are none of yours," Ware wrote, "I am solicitous that nobody should persuade you that I suppose them to be yours." He was, he said, "particularly unhappy to be thus brought into a sort of public opposition to you." [56] Ware was perhaps less than candid in trying to minimize the degree to which his sermon had been directed against Emerson, but it would

55. Ibid., pp. 8, 13–14, 17, 20–21.
56. Ware to Emerson, October 3, 1838, in Cabot, *Memoir, 2,* 691–92.

seem that he had little intention of drawing his former colleague into open debate.[57]

If Ware was unwilling to say precisely whom the shoe was supposed to fit, other conservatives were not so cautious. The *Christian Examiner*, by reviewing Emerson's discourse and Ware's sermon together, succeeded in confirming the impression which Ware himself—somewhat belatedly—had sought to avoid. Some of the "intolerant" suggestions in this brief and anonymous notice [58] were destined to be associated with Ware's name long after his own painstaking fairness had been forgotten. The reviewer began by assuring readers that he was taking note of Emerson's "strange notions" solely because the community desired to know whether or not Unitarians approved them. The answer, he said, was that most Unitarians considered Emerson's theories "so far as they are intelligible . . . to be neither good divinity nor good sense."

The reviewer was not equally certain about the reactions to Emerson among students in the Divinity School. He assumed that they had not been taken in; but he thought that in the future, measures should be taken to prevent

57. Ware issued no "challenge" to Emerson. He wrote as follows: "I am anxious to have it understood that, as I am not perfectly aware of the precise nature of your opinions . . . I do not therefore pretend especially to enter the lists with them . . . I do not know by what arguments the doctrine that 'the soul knows no persons' is justified to your mind." Emerson's reply, so often quoted without this context, was: "I could not give account of myself, if challenged. I could not possibly give you one of the 'arguments' you cruelly hint at, on which any doctrine of mine stands. For I do not know what arguments mean in reference to any expression of a thought." Cabot, *Memoir*, 2, 691–93.

58. Presumably the writer was one of the new editors—F. W. P. Greenwood and William Ware—who had taken over from James Walker in 1838; but Cushing apparently was uncertain about the authorship. *Index to the Examiner*, p. 38.

student exposure to such doctrines: "The instructors of
the School should hereafter guard themselves, by a right
of veto . . . against the probability of hearing sentiments,
on a public and most interesting occasion, and within their
own walls, altogether repugnant to their feelings, and
opposed to the whole tenor of their own teachings." [59]

This suggestion, both in content and in phrasing, was too
reminiscent of classic illiberalism to be appreciably softened
by anything else the reviewer might say. He did, however,
attempt to reconcile it with the Unitarian pretensions to
open-mindedness. "We beg to be understood," he said, "as
not questioning the right of the author of this address to
utter his own thoughts in his own way." The reviewer had
no wish "to fetter the human mind by the bonds of prescription and antiquity"; but surely it was not persecution
when Emerson had exercised his own right to speak "freely
and boldly," for others to dissent with equal boldness.[60]

For the defenders of Emerson, this gesture in the direction of free inquiry hardly met the case. Denouncing
heterodox opinions, they said, was one thing, but banning
them from expression at Harvard was quite another. The
Transcendentalist *Western Messenger* asked why there
should be such solicitude for the "feelings" of certain professors. "Was the Cambridge Divinity School built up for
the benefit of its instructors? Were its professorships endowed for the purpose of giving certain gentlemen the
opportunity of disseminating *their* opinions?" [61] As for

59. *Examiner*, 25 (1838), 266.
60. Ibid., pp. 266–67.
61. *Western Messenger*, 6 (1838), 118–21. The *Messenger* was a
monthly theological and literary magazine published at Cincinnati
from June 1835 to April 1841. The principal contributors were the
Transcendentalists James Freeman Clarke, Christopher Cranch,
Samuel Osgood, and W. H. Channing. See Gohdes, *Periodicals of
Transcendentalism*, chap. 2.

Norton's apparent desire for an official condemnation of
Emerson, the *Messenger* reminded Unitarians that their
church, having no synods or formal creeds, could have no
use for the weapon of excommunication. The editors suggested that "if Mr. Emerson has taught anything very
wrong," it would be found out, and he and other Unitarians
would quietly part company.

Readers were also cautioned against Norton's ill-con-
sidered attempt to link the opinions of the New School to
those of a miscellaneous list of foreign writers. The Transcendentalists, said the *Messenger*, had their unity not in
common attachment to any set of foreign writers whatever, but simply in their desire for "more of LIFE, soul,
energy, originality" in religion and letters.[62]

Orestes Brownson also came to the aid of his fellow
Transcendentalists. Before Norton's intervention had raised
the issue of free inquiry, Brownson had expressed serious
reservations about the Divinity School Address. He had
criticized Emerson's idea of "obedience to self" as tending
toward "pure egotism." It amounted, he thought, to "deifi-
cation of the soul with a vengeance." Such a position could
hardly escape atheism, since "the soul's conception of God
is not God, and if there be no God out of the soul, out of
the *me*, to answer to the soul's conception, then is there no
God." Brownson also had thought Emerson's thrusts against
"historical Christianity" too extreme. The Church, he
acknowledged, plainly has erred "by giving us only the
historical Christ, but let us not now err, by preaching only
a psychological Christ." In spite of all these reservations,
Brownson brought the heavy ordnance of his argumentative powers to the support of Emerson once Norton's ill-
tempered attack had given a new turn to the controversy.

62. *Messenger*, 6, 37–47. See also the answers of Clarke and Osgood to Norton's taunts about "the atheist Shelley." *Advertiser*,
September 28, October 5, 16, 1838.

Norton's heresy-hunting, Brownson said, was inexcusable. "The brand of heresy is and long has been as deep on him as it can be on anyone else . . ." And Brownson suggested that the charge of skepticism was more clearly applicable to those who could believe nothing without the miracles than to others who could believe everything without them.[63]

Emerson himself had not spoken a controversial word since the Divinity School Address, and he was to be even less a participant in the next phase of the dispute. Oliver Wendell Holmes aptly likened Emerson's position at this time to that of Patroclus when the Greeks and Trojans fought over his body.[64] By late 1839 George Ripley had stepped into the role which Emerson declined to fill—that of chief polemicist and champion of Transcendentalism against the conservative attack.

Ripley's former altercation with Norton, over the Martineau review of 1836, had had little apparent effect upon his high standing among Unitarians. His markedly transcendental *Discourses on the Philosophy of Religion*, published in Boston in late 1836, and the first volumes of *Specimens of Foreign Standard Literature*, issued under his editorship in 1838, had been praised by the Unitarian periodicals.[65]

Late in 1839 Ripley was drawn back into active controversy to answer Norton's *Discourse on the Latest Form*

63. *Boston Quarterly Review*, 1 (1838), 504–12; 2 (1839), 87, 112.

64. Holmes, *Ralph Waldo Emerson* (Boston, Houghton Mifflin, 1885), p. 116.

65. The *Specimens* (14 vols. Boston, 1838–42) contained translations of works by Cousin, Jouffroy, Constant, Goethe, Schiller, De-Wette, and others. For reviews of the *Discourses* see the *Register*, December 3, 1836; *Messenger*, 3 (1837), 576–83; *Examiner*, 21 (1837), 402–3.

of Infidelity. Norton had delivered this in July at the behest
of the newly formed "Association of the Alumni" of the
Divinity School. Arguing clearly and without the denunciatory language of his newspaper appearances, the conservative champion had pointed out the difficulty of explaining the words and actions of Jesus if the place of
miracles is depreciated. Christ, Norton said, indicated
clearly that his miracles attested his mission. If we do not
believe that they had this function, then we must believe
Jesus either a fiend or a madman for having spoken as he
did. What is more, said Norton, the absence of miracles
would leave Christianity without any authentication whatever; for the transcendental "religious sentiment," despite
all claims made for it, is ultimately less dependable than
the testimony of the senses. Those who belittle sense experience because it is contingent and uncertain, Norton
argued, are asking for a degree of metaphysical certainty
which simply is not attainable. In religion, as in all other
areas of human knowledge, we must be content to rest our
belief upon the strongest probabilities, as these are determined by the wisest teachers.[66]

The Transcendentalists' objections to this argument were
intensified by Norton's addition, in the published version,
of appendices in which he analyzed the "infidel" speculations of Hume, Spinoza, Schleiermacher, Hegel, Strauss,
and DeWette—and clearly implied that the New School
in America were guilty of the same errors. This implication
was bitterly resented, as was Norton's pompous assumption
that ordinary persons must rely for their interpretation of
Christian truth upon the findings of such learned persons as
himself. Another major objection was that Norton, having
placed the foregoing philosophers and their supposed
American adherents under a common antimiracle rubric,

66. Norton, *Latest Form of Infidelity,* pp. 21–35.

denied the right of the Transcendentalists to appear before a credulous public as "Christian" teachers.[67]

George Ripley's rejoinder, published anonymously as *"The Latest Form of Infidelity" Examined*, recorded the Transcendentalists' demurrer to all of the foregoing assertions,[68] and, leaving the defensive, reproached Norton for pretending that his own peculiar views were universally accepted Christian doctrines. The "personal dogma" of which Ripley particularly complained was Norton's alleged insistence that miracles are the only possible proof of Christianity,[69] and he attempted to show, by lengthy citations of Christian writers of all periods, that this was a doctrine almost unique with Norton, and not even espoused by that theologian himself at an earlier time.[70]

Norton's reply to this charge was that Ripley had gone to great pains to prove something which had not in the least been denied. What he had meant, Norton said, was that miracles are the only means of authenticating a revelation and proving that it is actually from God, not that men are convinced of the truth of Christianity by no other evidence than the miraculous.[71] The distinction here would seem to be a small one, since Norton still held that miracles are the decisive form of evidence; that is, that without them no other proof of Christian doctrine would be convincing. But a certain amount of accommodation had been achieved between the two schools of opinion. Norton had implicitly made the concession, significant to the Transcendentalists,

67. Ibid., pp. 8–13, 37–39, 50–64.

68. *"The Latest Form of Infidelity" Examined: A Letter to Mr. Andrews Norton, Occasioned by His "Discourse before the Alumni of the Cambridge Theological School,"* by "An Alumnus of That School" (Boston, 1839), pp. 16–23, 154–60.

69. Ibid., p. 31.

70. Ibid., pp. 23–29, 43–95.

71. Andrews Norton, *Remarks on . . . "'The Latest Form of Infidelity' Examined"* (n. 6, above), pp. 4–8.

that men are sometimes persuaded of the truth of Christianity by other evidences than the purely empirical.

Except for his clarification on this point, Norton's second pamphlet was merely an attempt to vindicate the author's former aspersions against Spinoza, DeWette, and Schleiermacher, all of whom he had accused of denying the personality of the Deity.[72] And Ripley, the somewhat over-conscientious scholar, unfortunately allowed himself to be lured into this irrelevant textual analysis. This was an especially grave tactical blunder, since it seemed to confirm what Norton had assumed from the beginning, that the Transcendentalists were committed to defend these writers. Ripley's last two pamphlets in the series [73] gave 218 pages in all to this scholarly analysis and only nine pages, at the end of the second pamphlet, to a treatment of the real issue.

In those final passages Ripley gave an able summary which might have attracted some notice if published separately. Norton's form of supernaturalism, he said, was a logical deduction from the Lockean philosophy, but both the doctrines and the philosophy are rejected by "the universal consciousness of man." "Does the body see, and is the spirit blind?" Ripley asked. If the spirit were "blind," then Norton would be right, and religious truths would be "a mere balance of probability, decided by intellectual researches." The certainty of faith would then have to proceed from "reliance on others; not from a spiritual witness in ourselves." But most men, he said, will never believe that this is so.[74]

Young Theodore Parker entered the controversy at this

72. Ibid., pp. 11–70.
73. *Defence of "'The Latest Form of Infidelity' Examined," A Second Letter to Mr. Andrews Norton* . . . Boston, 1840; *A Third Letter to Mr. Andrews Norton* . . . Boston, 1840.
74. Ripley, *Third Letter*, pp. 148–53.

point, under the pseudonym of "Levi Blodgett." Parker's pamphlet served the purpose of publishing the Transcendentalist case in a form which the public would read. "Blodgett" declared that to unlearned persons like himself it certainly seemed that faith in Christ precedes and does not depend upon faith in miracles. The miracles, whose validity he cordially affirmed, are only added confirmations for an essentially intuitive belief.[75]

If Ripley allowed another person to give the final word on the Transcendentalist side, his adversary also stepped aside at this point, and the current stage of the Transcendentalist controversy was brought to a close with Norton's republication of *Two Articles from the "Princeton Review."* These articles constituted a systematic and hard-hitting criticism of the "impious temerity" of German philosophizing, and of its "hideous and godless" results. Though sympathetic to the need for a more spiritual philosophy in American religion, the authors deplored the fact that foreign imports, rather than native intelligence, had been appealed to for a corrective.[76]

75. Theodore Parker, *The Previous Question between Mr. Andrews Norton and His Alumni, Moved and Handled in a Letter to All Those Gentlemen,* Boston, 1840.

76. *Two Articles from the "Princeton Review,"* Concerning the *Transcendental Philosophy of the Germans and of Cousin, and Its Influence on Opinion in this Country,* Cambridge, Mass., 1840. The authors of the articles, one of which was a cooperative effort, were Charles Hodge, A. B. Dod, and J. W. Alexander, all of Princeton Theological Seminary. Norton's sponsorship of this reprinting has been taken as indicating "to what straits" he had been reduced (Miller, *Transcendentalists,* p. 232). It should be noted, however, that the articles in question expressed sympathy with the Unitarians of New England not only in their defense against German speculations but also in their dispute of longer standing with the New England Theology, which the Princetonians believed had become overly rigid in the post-Edwardean period (*Two Articles,* pp. 7–10). Norton's action, in other words, was not so desperate as it might at

It has been usual in accounts of the Transcendentalist controversy to accept a somewhat overcaricatured Andrews Norton as typical of the Unitarian conservatives. The truth is that Norton gave way to more even-tempered men after the first four years of a controversy which continued for seventeen years. It is also highly probable that one reason for Norton's complete abstention from debate after 1840 was the the stubborn refusal of the denomination in the 1830's to support his program of exclusion. Whether from timidity or some better reason, the men most in agreement with Norton doggedly refused to come out publicly for his measures. Thus the almost reverential attitude which Norton's colleagues expressed toward his leadership has overtones of polite appeasement, and the bold champion of conservatism may well have felt that he was being humored. It is clear that he felt and deeply resented his isolation.

Typical of the encomiums heaped upon Norton through private correspondence was that contained in a letter from the Rev. Charles Upham. "We look to you alone in this exigency," Upham wrote.

> Dr. Channing favors the new views. . . . Dr. Walker has never lifted a finger against them. In point of fact he has favored them, and his appointment to Cambridge was hailed as the first step towards bringing the college and Unitarianism to Transcendentalism. My only hope is in you. May your life be spared to

---

first appear. Hodge's letters to Norton at this time indicate that both men felt their agreements—their common supernaturalist emphasis, their reliance upon Locke and the Scottish philosophers, and their partial concurrence on the faults of New England Calvinism—were stronger than their disagreements, making an alliance natural at this particular juncture. They agreed to delete some mild criticisms of Norton from the Boston reprinting of the *Two Articles*. Hodge to Norton, February 27 and March 12, 1840, NC.

deliver us from a state of things which . . . could only issue in the destruction of the faith . . .[77]

A Philadelphia Unitarian wrote that he had been shocked to hear two of his fellow citizens, shortly after the Divinity School Address, discussing the "open and formal declaration of unbelief in Christianity" which had been made by Emerson on behalf of Harvard University. The writer had "speedily communicated this fact," he said, to Harvard authorities, but no official disclaimers had been forthcoming.[78]

Henry Ware, Jr., praised Norton for his "noble and astonishing forbearance," and another writer contrasted the "calmness and elevation of spirit" in Norton's pamphlets with Ripley's "bitterness and unkind feeling." This correspondent said he had been confident from the beginning that the Cambridge leader would answer "*triumphantly*," and had found his arguments "perfectly satisfactory and convincing." Ezra Gannett thanked Norton for having put his mind at rest about German philosophy, which he said he had previously opposed without fully understanding.[79]

The profound deference felt for Norton is further evidenced in letters from two Unitarians whose support Ripley might have hoped to gain in this dispute. George R. Noyes, the biblical scholar who because of suspicions raised in 1834 about his orthodoxy has sometimes been cast as a sort of forerunner of Transcendentalism,[80] told Nor-

77. Upham to Norton, September 4 and December 21, 1839, NC.
78. James Taylor to Norton, September 10, 1839, NC.
79. Ware to Norton, December 7, Samuel K. Lothrop to Norton, December 16, Gannett to Norton, August 27, 1839, NC. Similar letters came from Harm Jan Huidekoper, John Ware, George F. Simmons, and Alexander Young, NC.
80. Henry S. Commager, "Tempest in a Boston Tea Cup," *New England Quarterly*, 6 (1933), 651–52.

ton that while he had not read Ripley's pamphlets, he had known in advance "what his views are, and what his mode of defending them, viz. by the use of language which means one thing to the initiated, and another to common people." And the Transcendentalist William H. Furness again notified Norton that his own orthodoxy was intact despite his unusual theory of the miracles. "However peculiar my own views," Furness wrote, "I cannot endure that these important facts should be rejected, or thrown into the shade." [81]

The *Christian Register*, even under the new and "safer" editor who had replaced Chandler Robbins, tried to maintain a neutral position. "If this subject must be discussed," the Rev. Rufus Johnson pleaded, "let us do it in perfectly good humor." But the *Register* later devoted four long editorials to a good-humored defense of Norton. Waxing ecstatic and almost lyrical, Johnson assured readers that "he ever moves in light. Mists disperse as he advances . . . It is really refreshing in the midst of those flitting phantoms, shadows and clouds which are lowering on the regions of theology, to hear a certain, decided, penetrating, calmly confident voice." [82]

But this kind of support, even in the public prints, was no substitute for a real participation in Norton's campaign by such men as the Wares, Channing, Walker, Gannett, Palfrey, and Noyes. What was worse, the two men who shared pre-eminence with Norton in Unitarian leadership, Walker and Channing, had flatly and openly rejected his view of the Transcendentalist danger. Walker in 1840, addressing the same group of Divinity School alumni who had heard *The Latest Form of Infidelity* the previous year, had the effrontery to call for a more balanced understand-

81. Noyes to Norton, February 21, 1840; Furness to Norton, September 13, 1839, NC.
82. *Register*, July 27, October 26, November 2, 23, December 14, 1839; January 4, 1840.

ing of the foreign philosophies and less unreasoning alarm about them. After pointing out the valuable contributions of Schleiermacher, DeWette, Kant, Cousin, and others, Walker declared that though "men may put down Transcendentalism if they can . . . they must first deign to comprehend its principles." [83] And Dr. Channing, who in 1838 had said he doubted whether Emerson meant to deny a personal Deity, greeted Walker's conciliatory speech of 1840 by saying he was "glad to learn that Dr. Walker understands the spirit of our alarmists." Opponents of Transcendentalism, he said, were showing "a want of faith in religion . . . more alarming than the infidelity which they condemn." [84]

As if this show of high-echelon complacency were not bad enough, it suddenly appeared that Norton's three-year campaign to control the Unitarian publications had been a labor of Sisyphus. The *Examiner* published an article by Andrew Peabody, the Unitarian minister in Portsmouth, New Hampshire, which agreed with the Transcendentalists that "a belief in miracles constitutes no part of a sanctifying faith in Christ." Peabody, aiming at conciliation, asserted that Norton's charge of "infidelity" had been leveled only against the German philosophers; and he innocently represented Norton as valuing miracles mainly because they bolster the faith of the unlearned masses. "The vast majority of the ignorant, the unspiritual, and the sinning," Peabody explained, must rely upon supernatural evidences; and the chief error of the Transcendentalists was that "in the retirement of their studies" they had simply forgotten "that all men were not as spiritual as themselves." [85]

83. Quoted in O. B. Frothingham, *Transcendentalism in New England: A History* (New York, 1876), p. 122. See also *Register*, July 25, 1840.

84. Peabody, *Reminiscences*, pp. 379–81, 416.

85. *Examiner*, 27 (1839), 223, 224, 226.

Truly dismayed by this new evidence of the *Examiner's* waywardness, Norton wrote an angry private letter to the editor, William Ware.[86] With his usual tact he told Ware that "it is clear from the manner in which the *Christian Examiner* has been conducted that you have not thought and felt on this subject as I do, probably because you have known less about it." The *Examiner's* delinquency, he said, was symptomatic of a general attitude on the part of conservative leaders, whose course "with some honorable exceptions" has been "equally ruinous and discreditable."[87]

William Ware replied to these strictures with dignity and with even more firmness than Chandler Robbins had shown under a similar attack. He insisted that the *Examiner's* moderate course had been the correct one. He could not agree, he said, either that Unitarians had been negligent in combating the current heresies, or that any significant number of American Transcendentalists had accepted the skeptical conclusions of foreign philosophers. Four or five, he admitted, may have gone beyond the pale of Christian belief; but he knew of only two members of the Boston Association who had done so (a reference probably to Parker and Ripley); and the other members of the Association had made plain their rejection of the ideas of these two.

Ware, while acknowledging that Peabody's review had contained a lower estimate of miracles than Norton himself would agree to, contended that the article "was certainly a Christian one." The *Examiner*, in fact, had been exercising such caution about accepting radically transcendental pieces that the editors had been charged with "exclusiveness" by no less a Unitarian leader than Dr. Channing. "You will acknowledge the difficulty of my

86. This brother of Henry Ware, Jr., had been the pioneer Unitarian minister in New York City (1821–36), and was proprietor and editor of the *Examiner* from 1838 to 1844. He died in 1852. Eliot, 2, 250–58.

87. Norton to W. Ware, February 24, 1840, NC.

position," Ware ventured. But he added, after some thought about that doubtful proposition, "I cannot suppose that I have satisfied you." [88] Norton indeed was far from satisfied, and he wrote William Ware again to suggest that when the *Examiner* should get around to reviewing the whole Ripley-Norton controversy, he would be glad to "furnish the reviewer with some facts, that he might not else observe or be aware of." [89]

When this accommodating proposal produced nothing, Norton attempted to step around the editor and supply a reviewer as well as material. In April 1840 he asked Professor Palfrey to write an article refuting Ripley's second pamphlet. If Palfrey would undertake this work in the *Examiner*, it would, he said, "go far to settle the vacillating character of that publication," and would encourage those "who think rightly" to speak out. Norton explained that he hesitated to write the review himself, lest this be taken as "the pleading of an advocate in his own cause."

To forestall Palfrey from arguing lack of time, Norton assured him of "such assistance as would bring the labor within a narrow compass." He then added several pages of detailed instructions as to what ought to be in the review, and concluded by promising that "if you will give me any encouragement, I will go on with my comments." [90] Whether or not the good Doctor gave encouragement, the projected article did not appear, and the *Examiner* continued to represent a counsel of moderation.

While Norton was making these somewhat frenetic final efforts behind the scenes, George Ripley, too, was moving off the stage of controversy, and was issuing the last proposals of his career as a church reformer.

88. W. Ware to Norton, February 25, 1840, NC.
89. Norton to W. Ware, March 10, 1840, NC.
90. Norton to Palfrey, April 13, 1840, NC.

Ripley's final break with the Unitarian ministry was not lightly undertaken or rapidly effected. His first move was a letter to the "proprietors" of his church in May 1840, in which he spoke of the poor financial condition of the society and suggested his own resignation as a remedy.[91] The proprietors would not hear of his resigning on these grounds, but Ripley then expressed more basic reasons for his proposal. He felt, as he told the parish in October 1840, that the relationship between pastor and people had become strained. Some of his parishioners had been complaining about his liberal theological and social opinions. He had tried to minimize the friction by preaching on traditional, noncontroversial subjects, but this had become a burden to himself. He could continue to minister to them, he said, only if they would consent to reforms in pastoral duties and church organization.

The first of Ripley's demands was that the congregation must allow him to preach on all subjects of human concern. He proposed, secondly, that the pew-ownership system should be abolished, or should at least be modified in such a way that parishioners would no longer have reason to continue as members after they had ceased to sympathize with the views of the minister.[92]

Negotiations continued until the beginning of 1841, by which time Ripley had concluded that the society would not accept his reform proposals. On the first of January he tendered his resignation, and this was accepted with expressions of great and undoubtedly sincere regret.[93]

In Ripley's *Farewell Discourse*, which was filled with kindly sentiments toward the congregation as a whole, the one harsh note was a bitter commentary on the pres-

91. Frothingham, *Ripley*, pp. 61–63.
92. George Ripley, *A Letter Addressed to the Congregational Church in Purchase St. by Its Pastor* (Boston, 1840), pp. 3–10, 20–24.
93. Frothingham, *Ripley*, pp. 61–91.

sures which had been exerted upon him by some members of the society and by his critics in the recent public controversy. Ripley told his parishioners that their pastor would not have had to leave the ministry if he had been

> more inclined to conform to ancient usage; if he were willing to work in the yoke of popular customs, to take his views of truth from his elders . . . if he would acquiesce more readily in prevalent errors and abuses; if he would take the social standard of Boston at this moment as the everlasting standard of right . . . in short, if it were his aim to be more of a priest and less of a man.

He had always been, he said, and would continue to be "a peace man, a temperance man, an abolitionist, a transcendentalist, a friend of radical reform in our social institutions." If Unitarians could not bear to hear discussion of those subjects from their ministers, then he must cease to be a minister.[94]

Despite the acerbity of these remarks, neither the church nor the Unitarian community judged harshly of Ripley. The society's "farewell Resolutions" were warmly eulogistic. The *Register* praised Ripley's "Christian attainments." And Gannett's *Monthly Miscellany*, after expressing the regret of the community about Ripley's departure, wished him success in his projected "educational experiment" at Brook Farm which, as Gannett remarked acutely enough, did not sound at all "transcendental." [95] With the launching

94. George Ripley, *A Farewell Discourse Delivered to the Congregational Church in Purchase Street, March 28, 1841* (Boston, 1841), pp. 17–18.

95. Appendix to ibid., pp. 22–24; *Register*, April 3, 1841; *Monthly Miscellany*, 4 (1840), 293–95. For accounts of Brook Farm see Lindsay Swift, *Brook Farm: Its Members, Scholars, and Visitors*, New York, 1900; Frothingham, *Ripley*, pp. 108–98. Although Ripley,

of the new utopian community on November 1, 1841, Ripley passed permanently from the role of church reformer.[96]

The first stage of the Transcendentalist controversy had ended in a stalemate which gave no clear indication of the direction which Unitarianism would take in dealing with the Transcendentalist challenge. The conservatives had achieved some unanimity in defining their stand on the miracles question. They had taken a position clearly favoring a supernatural interpretation of Christianity, an interpretation to which many of them thought belief in miracles was an essential corollary. But no significant amount of support had appeared as yet for Norton's proposal to anathematize transcendental speculations and deny the Christian name to those who doubted supernaturalist doctrines.

Despite the traditional conception of this early phase of the controversy as one in which intolerance and exclusiveness reigned on the conservative side, it is questionable whether more than two individuals could justly be accused of doing violence to Unitarian principles of free expression in their opposition to Emerson and Ripley. These two are Norton and the author of the proposed ban on nonconform-

---

W. H. Channing, and others occasionally led religious services at Brook Farm, no formal church organization was attempted, and the famous agricultural experiment of the Transcendentalists is therefore not part of the story of Transcendental church reform. Brook Farmers attended services in Boston and at Theodore Parker's church in West Roxbury. Swift, pp. 55, 221; Frothingham, *Ripley*, p. 119.

96. Ripley's Purchase St. society moved to a new location in 1848, taking the name "Thirteenth Congregational Church." The latter expired in 1860. Ibid., p. 93.

ing speakers at Harvard Divinity School. The School faculty did exercise their right to approve graduation speakers after 1838, and there were many whose personal attitude toward the Transcendentalists showed something bordering on exclusiveness. But official pronouncements, and also influential private opinion, leaned heavily on the side of moderation. The Unitarian tradition of liberality had not, as yet, given way to the exigencies of doctrinal defense.

Norton, whose efforts to bring a different result had put him in such an unfavorable light, must nonetheless be credited with having discerned the radical implications of Transcendentalism more acutely than either his hesitant colleagues or the Transcendentalists themselves. Leaders on both sides were sufficiently attuned to the movements of contemporary thought to know that a debate over Christian supernaturalism was no mere teapot tempest; and their repeated references to the foundations of "popular faith" showed a common awareness of the extent to which such questions as that of the miracles were the stuff of ordinary discourse in nineteenth-century New England. Neither party was quibbling over a few loaves and fishes. But Norton, in addition to recognizing the deeper issue, plotted a future course for Transcendentalist logic and found it ending not in the worship of Christ but, at most, in the veneration of Jesus. The later struggle over christology in liberal Protestantism showed the cogency of this projection.

Norton, however, was dealing with men as well as abstractions, and men have a right to their inconsistencies. There is real injustice, as well as futility, in assuming that one's opponents will be utterly logical, and in denouncing conclusions which they have not admitted. With the notable exception of Theodore Parker, the Transcendentalists were to stop short of an explicit rejection of revealed

Christianity. In this perspective the failure of Norton's enterprise in the 1830's stemmed not merely from the infelicities of his debating methods but even more from the fact that he was combating Theodore Parker several years before the latter's appearance in the conflict.

Chapter 4

Theodore Parker and the

Confessional Question

THE phase of controversy which began in 1841 and which centered in the person of Theodore Parker was the great trauma of mid-nineteenth-century Unitarianism. It brought out in bold relief the fundamental issues of supernaturalism, of church "discipline," and of the definition of Christianity which had been involved in the earlier discussion. Parker's ideas of religious reform were similar to those of other Transcendentalists, but his advocacy had a singular impact, first because he refused to allow his opinions or the objections raised against them to separate him from the Unitarian ministry, and secondly because he boldly voiced the denial, always latent in Transcendentalist theology, that Christianity is based on a special revelation of God. The Parkerite attack, unlike the earlier one, forced the denomination to rediscover and define its theological position. Though Unitarianism after the 1850's was still beset by the conflicting demands of free inquiry and Christian confessionalism, that church has never, since the Parker experience, suffered from its early delusion that the two can exist together as absolute principles.

The village preacher whose transcendental heresies brought him into the full glare of public attention in 1841 was then just thirty-one years of age. In physical appearance Parker was not prepossessing. He was short and sturdy, with a large head and a massive forehead that was made more so by a thinness of hair which had become a predominant baldness before he was forty. His rather ordinary facial lineaments were set off in later years by a "more than current" gray beard; but in the 1840's it was the steel-blue eyes, partly obscured by gold-mounted spectacles, that were his most arresting feature. Simple dress and unassuming manner, together with a certain awkwardness of bearing and a lack of musical quality in the voice, suggested to some that a ploughman or schoolmaster, not a priest, was occupying the pulpit. The task of captivating audiences was left almost entirely to his rhetorical abilities, which were more than adequate for that purpose.[1]

One of the youngest members of the Transcendentalist circle when he began attending their meetings in 1837, Parker even then had boasted greater scholarly attainments than most of them, and this in spite of a meager formal education. Born in 1810, the youngest son of a Lexington farmer, he had attended grammar school eleven weeks each winter for a period of ten years, and then had spent less than a year at the Lexington Academy. Home study, however, had enabled him to pass the entrance examinations for Harvard College, and without attending classes he had

1. Roy C. McCall, "Theodore Parker," in William N. Brigance et al., eds., *A History and Criticism of American Public Address* (3 vols. New York, McGraw-Hill, 1943–55), *1*, 259–60; *DAB;* Chadwick, *Parker,* pp. 211–12.

subsequently fulfilled all except the monetary requirements for the B.A. degree.[2] He had then spent two years (1834–36) in the Divinity School and in June of 1837 had been ordained to the Unitarian pastorate at West Roxbury, Massachusetts.[3]

A competent work of self-education would have been laudable in itself, but Parker's acquirements were prodigious. At age twenty-one he had been able to read in six languages, and four years later he claimed some degree of facility in eleven more. While attending the Divinity School he had been called upon to teach classes in Hebrew, and he had entered the field of biblical criticism as an editor of the *Scriptural Interpreter*. In the year preceding his settlement at West Roxbury he had translated DeWette's *Introduction to the Old Testament*, which he published with his own notes and commentaries in 1843.[4]

Parker had made his anonymous entrance into the Transcendentalist controversy with the "Levi Blodgett" letter of 1840, (above, p. 86), but he had shown his allegiance to the New School before that time. He had told a former Divinity School classmate in 1837 that he was preaching "abundant heresies" to his congregation, including "the worst of all things, Transcendentalism . . ." He had greeted Emerson's Divinity School Address with enthusiasm, and had deplored the "illiberality" shown by some members of the Boston Association who debated whether Emerson could be called a Christian.[5]

2. Harvard awarded Parker an honorary Master of Arts degree in 1840. Frothingham, *Parker*, p. 27.

3. Ibid., pp. 41–87.

4. Goddard, p. 85; Weiss, *1*, 72; Frothingham, *Parker*, pp. 75–85, 177–78. The *Scriptural Interpreter* was "a small magazine designed for easy family instruction," begun in 1831 by Gannett and ceasing publication in 1836. Ibid. p. 55.

5. J. E. Dirks appears to believe that Parker has generally been considered a thoroughgoing disciple of Emerson (Dirks, *Critical*

The philosophical and theological basis of Parker's campaign against orthodox Unitarianism was stated in numerous forms over the period 1841–53, when that campaign was most intense. It is necessary to explain this theoretical structure in some detail, since Parker's was the most complete and important of the more radical Transcendental theologies.

Parker, though he gave various names to his own highly individual formulations, regarded his system as falling within the limits of the "transcendental" philosophy. It was his view that "in metaphysics there are and have long been two schools of philosophers," the "sensationalists" and the "transcendentalists." The principal tenet of the sensationalists, he said, is that "there is nothing in the intellect which was not first in the senses." That of the transcendentalists is the reverse:

> that there is in the intellect (or consciousness), something that never was in the senses, to wit, the intellect (or consciousness) itself; that man has faculties which transcend the senses; faculties which give him ideas and intuitions that transcend sensational experience; ideas whose origin is not from sensation, nor their proof from sensation.[6]

Although such a division of the philosophical world may seem vastly overgeneralized, it must be remembered that

Theology, p. 136). While superficial studies of Transcendentalism may have sometimes exaggerated the resemblance, biographers of both men have been aware of the differences between them: see Chadwick, Parker, p. 177; Commager, Parker, p. 141; Rusk, Life, p. 386; Cabot, Memoir, 2, 406. And Parker's "discipleship" in the practical area of church reform should not be minimized; he criticized the metaphysics of the Divinity School Address but was strongly in accord with its "picture of the faults of the Church." Weiss, 1, 113.

6. Parker, Works, 6, 7, 23.

an active controversy produces broad alignments which in the abstract would seem quite impossible. To a zealot like Parker, sensationalism and transcendentalism were two great armies in the field of thought. The names emblazoned on their respective banners represented sharply contrasting approaches to contemporary problems, even though the makeup of each contending force was heterogeneous.

Parker saw clear differences between the practical effects of the two philosophies. In physics, he said, sensationalism produces a lack of ultimate assurance about the facts of the universe, while transcendentalism leads to metaphysical certainty. In politics the sensational philosophy leads to a denial of immutable laws, while the transcendental proclaims natural justice. In ethics, the first denies eternal rules of morality and counsels expediency, while the second encourages an ethical system based upon the universal and immutable promptings of intuition. In religion the logical result of the sensational philosophy is either a denial of God or a complete deference to revelation, while transcendentalism affirms the reality of divine things by making a priori belief the basis for all formulations.[7]

Parker had misgivings about some of the foot soldiers in the Transcendental army. He deplored the tendency of some of them to scorn observation and neglect the lessons of the past, and he blamed others for confusing personal whims with universal laws. Some devotees, he thought, were "transcendental-mad" rather than "transcendental-wise."

His own form of the philosophy attempted to avoid such extravagances. His theory of knowledge emphasized induction as well as intuition. Like Cousin among European transcendentalists and Brownson and several others of the American group, Parker warned repeatedly that mere

7. Ibid., pp. 7–37.

awareness of an intuitive fact of consciousness is insufficient. If deductions from consciousness are to become usable ideas, they must be formulated with the help of empirical observation.[8]

It is possible to argue that this kind of interest in scientific demonstration vitiated the whole intuitionist idea, but Parker, however inconsistently, believed it did not. The reasoning process, he thought, confirms and actualizes intuition, but does not displace it as the basis of the knowing process. His account of the way men attain to a knowledge of God is a striking illustration of this epistemological approach—and also of the Transcendentalist tendency to mix the ingredients of the Kantian critiques into a theological *potpourri:*

> Our belief in God's existence does not depend on the *a posteriori* argument, on considerations drawn from the order, fitness and beauty discovered by observations made in the material world; nor yet on the *a priori* argument, on considerations drawn from the eternal nature of things, and observations made in the spiritual world. It depends primarily on no *argument* whatever, not on reasoning, but *Reason.* The fact is given outright, as it were, and comes to the man, as soon and as naturally, as the belief of his own existence . . . This intuitive perception of God is afterwards fundamentally and logically established by the *a priori* argument, and beautifully confirmed by the *a posteriori* argument; but we are not left without the Idea of God till we become metaphysicians and naturalists and so can discover it by much thinking. It comes spontaneously, by a law of whose actions we are, at first, not conscious. The belief always pre-

8. Ibid., pp. 25, 29, 31–36. Dirks, *Critical Theology,* p. 81.

cedes the proof; intuition gives the thing to be reasoned about. Unless this intuitive function be performed, it is not possible to attain a knowledge of God.[9]

The passion for "systematic ransacking of the facts of history" which has justly been attributed to Parker,[10] was not an outright rejection of intuitionism. The scholar who ransacks history to put together many instances of human intuitiveness is not constructing a denial of intuition, even though his method has been partly inductive. Until the investigator shifts his fundamental reliance in epistemology to scientific demonstration, the intuited fact remains basic, the inductive demonstration auxiliary. Parker did not reject the Transcendentalist belief in man's religious consciousness. Instead, like Cousin and many others, he sought by an inductive process to bolster the intuitionist argument and make it at least appear scientifically respectable. To the frequent criticism of transcendentalism as too abstruse, he answered that "the transcendental philosophy . . . does not neglect experience. In human history it finds *confirmations, illustrations,* of the ideas of human nature . . . It *illustrates* religion by facts of observation, facts of testimony." [11]

9. Parker, *Discourse of Religion,* pp. 22–23. See also *Works, 4,* 169; *6,* 32–34.

10. Henry S. Commager, "The Dilemma of Theodore Parker," *New England Quarterly, 6* (1933), 269.

11. Parker, *Works, 6,* 32. Italics supplied. Dirks argues that Parker's appetite for historical verification places him "near, but not within, New England transcendentalism" (*Critical Theology,* p. 136). But he rests the case almost entirely upon a comparsion of Parker with Emerson, whom he seems to take as sufficiently representative of the entire group (ibid., pp. 98, 110, 133, 135–36). Such a criterion would exclude many in the New England movement. For analyses and examples of the intense historical interest of other transcendentalists see A. Robert Caponigri, "Brownson and Emerson: Nature and His-

Parker was far enough from a primary reliance upon the "facts" of history to reject what he termed the "historical method" of theological construction. Theologians using this method, he said, "get the sum of the theological thinking of the human race, and out of this mass construct a system . . ." Such a procedure is useful, he said, for showing "what has been done," but can no more lead to the perfect theology than the eclectic method can lead to a perfect philosophy. "Former researches," he argued, "offer but a narrow and inadequate basis to rest on." The more desirable method, which he called the philosophical, looks to the facts of history and of natural science simply as confirmations of "the primitive gospel God wrote on the heart of his child," and in this way uses "both the reflective and the intuitive faculties of man" in theological construction. The time would come, Parker believed, when men would attain to a true system of Nature and theology "by observation and reasoning"; but that time was still far off, and "meantime . . . the great truths of morality and religion . . . are perceived intuitively, and by instinct . . ." [12]

Parker applied the "philosophical method" in a theological system which he was calling spiritualism in 1842 but was defining as theism a decade later. Its basic tenets were the infinitude and absolute perfection of God, and the immanence of God in man and nature. Parker held that though God is different in kind from both matter and man,

tory," New England Quarterly, 18 (1945), 368–90; Frederic H. Hedge, Conservatism and Reform, Boston, 1843; James Freeman Clarke, Ten Great Religions, 2 vols. Boston, 1883; W. H. Channing, The Christian Church and Social Reform, Boston, 1848. Emerson himself had a greater interest in history and practical affairs than is sometimes recognized. Perry Miller, "Jonathan Edwards to Emerson," New England Quarterly, 13 (1940), 594–95.

12. Parker, Works, 4, 169–70; A Discourse on the Transient and Permanent in Christianity . . . May 19, 1841 (Boston, 1841), p. 12.

he must nonetheless be recognized as immanent in both, since to deny this would be to say there are places where God is not, and thus to deny his infinitude. All that exists or occurs, therefore, is God's doing, and there can be no distinction of supernatural from natural, of clean from unclean, or of "special" revelation from God's constant revelation in the human soul.[13]

In accordance with this fundamental theism, Parker regarded Christ as a human being, though a religious genius and supreme teacher. Jesus taught some errors, said Parker, but he also taught "Absolute Religion." The basic teachings of Absolute Religion are "love of God and love of man"; and the Scriptures or the Church are wrong insofar as they suggest that Christ's teaching was more than this. The Incarnation, he argued, has been misconstrued by the Church, for God is incarnate in the entire human race, not simply in Jesus. Christ did not "redeem" mankind, as the Church teaches, or even live for mankind: "He lived for himself; died for himself; worked out his own salvation . . ."[14] Neither Jesus nor the Scriptures, Parker reasoned, can make any valid claim to infallibility, for the teachings of both are true only insofar as they conform to Absolute Religion.[15]

Parker called himself a Christian because he believed Jesus to have been the only man thus far in human history who actually discerned and taught Absolute Religion. In Parker's detailed rendering of this basically Emersonian theme, the Gospel teachings were reinterpreted to conform to a monistic and naturalistic system. The references

13. See Parker, *Discourse of Religion*, Bk. I, chaps, 1–3; Bk. II, ch. 1; *Sermons of Theism*, pp. 154–57, 166–70.

14. *Discourse of Religion*, p. 478.

15. Ibid., Bk. II, chaps. 3–5; Bk. III, chap. 3; Bk. IV. For other summaries of Parker's theology see *Works*, *13*, 52–61, 330–37; Chadwick, *Parker*, pp. 192–99; Dirks, *Critical Theology*.

of Jesus to human sinfulness, for example, were taken to mean that men are degraded by too low an opinion of their own powers. Though Christ is reported to have called himself the Way, the Truth, and the Life, he must have meant, Parker explained, that his teachings were these things. And when the Scriptures speak of Christ as the Son of God, they are merely asserting that Jesus achieved the communion with God which is possible to all men.[16]

Parker regarded the Church as an institution of entirely human origin. Although Jesus, he said, was the central figure or "model-man" of the institution founded by the Apostles, Jesus himself founded no Church. Even if he had done so, this would not have constituted a transmission of divine authority, since Jesus was no more than human.[17]

In applying these conceptions to the religion of his own time, Parker first of all acknowledged that the "popular theology," even in its Calvinist form, contained "some of the greatest truths of religion which man has attained thus far." And Unitarianism was given credit for having modified the worst features of the Calvinist creed, for attempting "to apply Good Sense to theology, to reconcile Knowledge with Belief, Reason with Revelation, to *humanize* the church." [18]

But Unitarianism, he argued, had not gone far enough. It had refused to "develop the truth it has borne, latent and unconscious in its bosom," and was therefore full of contradictions. Philosophically, Unitarianism was "too rational to go the full length of the supernatural theory," yet "too sensual to embrace the spiritual method." Unitarian theology, he said,

16. *Works, 4,* 79–81; *Discourse of Religion,* pp. 255–57.
17. Ibid., pp. 383–87.
18. *Sermons of Theism,* p. 85; *Discourse of Religion,* pp. 467–68; see also Dirks, *Critical Theology,* pp. 111–15.

humanizes the Bible, yet calls it miraculous; believes
in man's greatness . . . yet asks for a Mediator . . .
admits man can pray for himself . . . yet prays 'in
the name of Christ' . . . censures the traditionary
sects, yet sits itself among the tombs, and mourns . . .
believes the humanity of Christ . . . yet his miraculous birth likewise and miraculous powers . . . stops
[men's] ears with texts of the Old Testament, and
then asks them to listen to the voice of God in their
heart . . .[19]

Parker's remedy for these inconsistencies was a complete
rejection of the supernaturalist elements in the popular
faith. He made no effort, in his later writings at least, to
hide his contempt for supernaturalism, and implicitly for
the silliness of those who held to it. He stated a concise *non
credo* in a sermon of 1852:

Of course I do not believe in a devil, eternal torment,
nor in a particle of absolute evil in God's world or
in God. I do not believe there ever was a miracle, or
ever will be . . . I do not believe in the miraculous inspiration of the Old Testament or the New
Testament . . . I do not believe in the miraculous
origin of the Hebrew Church, or the Buddhist Church,
or the Christian Church; nor the miraculous character of Jesus. I take not the Bible for my master, nor
yet the Church; nor even Jesus of Nazareth for my
master . . . I try all things by the human faculties
. . . Has God given us anything better than our
nature? [20]

A sermon by Parker in 1841, *The Transient and Permanent in Christianity*, brought these various rejections of

19. *Discourse of Religion*, pp. 470–73.
20. *Works, 13,* 61–62.

traditional belief to public notice. The sermon was delivered on May 19 at the ordination of Charles Shackford in the Hawes Place Church of South Boston.

The public outcry which followed was a protest against the tone of the sermon as well as against its heresies. Parker's affirmation in it that Christian rites and doctrines are mutable expressions of eternal religious truths would in itself have caused little offense. What aroused anger was that he pronounced certain tenets of the common faith as not merely imperfect but vulgar and absurd. He stated that Christian doctrines in general owed more to heathenism, Judaism, and "the caprice of philosophers" than to the teachings of Jesus. Many of these doctrines, he said, are "the refuse of idol temples . . . wood, hay, and stubble, wherewith men have built on the cornerstone Christ laid." The pure stream of Christ's message had, he thought, been "polluted by man with mire and dirt." Men have "piled their own rubbish against the temple of Truth." [21] Whatever the substantive merits of such assertions, this was a kind of invective which had not been heard since Norton's trumpetings in the *Advertiser*.

As for the alleged authority of Jesus, Parker could not see "why the great truths of Christianity rest on the personal authority of Jesus, more than the axioms of geometry rest on the personal authority of Euclid, or Archimedes." The preacher stated his belief that Christ did actually exist, but added, in a phrase which conservatives took as an absolute rejection of Christian faith, that "if it could be proved . . . that Jesus of Nazareth had never lived, still Christianity would stand firm, and fear no evil." [22]

Parker's sermon, like nearly all of his controversial works, also contained positive elements—appreciations of the excellence of Christ and the truths of the Bible, elo-

21. *Transient and Permanent*, pp. 11–12.
22. Ibid., pp. 16, 18.

quent and lofty appeals to man's spiritual nature. Such
affirmations in Parker's writings should not go unrecog-
nized, since they formed the bulk of his noncontroversial
preaching and unquestionably accounted for much of his
popular influence. Some of Parker's opponents of 1841 can
be criticized for ignoring this more constructive side of
his doctrine, although the severity of the preacher's negative utterances made it natural that discussion should center
in that area.

The first opposition to the *Transient and Permanent*
came not from Unitarians but from the Orthodox churches
and newspapers. Even Parker's strongest partisans have
recognized that the Unitarian press, particularly in the early
days of the dispute "did their best . . . to be charitable,"
and "cultivated a generous spirit." [23] But the non-Unitarian
papers almost immediately were filled with such epithets as
"infidel," "scorner," and "blasphemer," and the Orthodox
began declaring somewhat pompously that the liberal faith
had ended in pure naturalism, just as they had always predicted it would.[24] The Unitarian clergy, to be sure, were
in no position to join immediately in this general hue and
cry; for, like it or not, they bore a degree of responsibility. Parker was one of their number, and Unitarians had
given him the opportunity to speak at an official ceremony
of ordination.

The invitation to Parker had been issued by a committee of the Hawes Place Church with the approval of their
minister-elect. A clerical "Ordaining Council," invited in

23. Frothingham, *Parker*, p. 158; Chadwick, *Parker*, p. 103.

24. Most of the non-Unitarian reaction appeared in the *Courier*,
the *Daily Advertiser*, the *Evening Transcript*, the *Recorder* (all of
Boston), and the *New England Puritan* (see issues of June–August
1841). Parker's own book of clippings is in the Boston Public Library, but a good portion of the newspaper exchange can be
found in an Orthodox booklet called *The South Boston Unitarian
Ordination*, Boston, 1841.

the same way, included, besides Parker, Chandler Robbins and Samuel K. Lothrop of Boston, Nathaniel Folsom of Haverhill, Dr. John Pierce of Brookline, and five others.[25] It was the members of this Council who came in for the most immediate criticism, since they had allowed the ordination to come to an end without expressing their disapproval of Parker's remarks.

The gage was thrown down in an open letter from three non-Unitarian ministers [26] who had attended the ordination service by special invitation from candidate Shackford. Their brief letter, which appeared in the *New England Puritan* on May 28, stated that they had found Parker's sentiments so contrary to their own religious conceptions that they felt constrained to ask whether the Unitarian clergy, and the Council in particular, considered Parker a preacher of Christianity. They expressed surprise that no member of the Council had asked Shackford to disavow Parker's opinions as a condition to continuation of the ordination service.[27]

The first reply to the Orthodox questions came from Nathaniel Folsom, who denied that any formal disavowal of Parker had been necessary. All of the other participants in the service, he said, had expressed their Christian faith so strongly as to make their position perfectly clear; and Shackford had been preaching "the Gospel of the New Testament" in that very pulpit for the seven months preceding his ordination.[28] But this answer satisfied neither the Orthodox clergyman nor the non-Unitarian press, and

25. Samuel Barrett, Cyrus Bartol, and John Sargent of Boston, Joseph Angier of Milton, George Putnam of Roxbury. Ibid., pp. 3–8; *Monthly Miscellany* (June 1841), p. 351.

26. J. H. Fairchild of Phillips Church (Trinitarian Congregational), Thomas Driver of South Baptist Church, and Z. B. C. Dunham of the Fifth Methodist Society. *Unitarian Ordination*, p. 4.

27. Ibid., pp. 3–4.

28. Ibid., pp. 6–7.

the liberal ministers were kept on the defensive. Samuel K. Lothrop, of the Ordaining Council, outlined his position in two extended letters to J. H. Fairchild, one of the Orthodox complainants. He refused to speak for other members of the Council, but declared that for his own part he could no longer consider Parker a Christian minister, or at least could have no "intimate sympathy and fellowship" with him. However, if Mr. Parker thought himself a Christian, Lothrop said, and could find "a people willing to hear him, and ministers willing to exchange with him, that is his affair and their affair."

The "official statement" desired by non-Unitarians apparently was not to be had. "No Unitarian clergyman," as Lothrop explained, "feels himself responsible for his brethren, or authorized to speak for them. We recognize no creed, covenant, or union of any kind, that interferes with individual liberty and independence." [29] Parker was, however, reprimanded publicly in the *Register* for having expounded his heresies on an occasion when he was acting in association with other ministers. The editors, while conceding that the sermon had contained "many good things and many beautiful things, that came home to our hearts," thought that its tone of "sneer and ridicule" had been inexcusable.[30]

Parker's angry reply accused the *Register* of distorting the meaning of his sermon. He did not mind being harshly dealt with, he said—"it is a very small thing that I should be judged of you"—but he wished to be told more precisely

29. Ibid., pp. 14–15, 39–40.
30. *Register*, June 12, 26, 1841. The editors at this time were Samuel K. Lothrop and Samuel Barrett, both of whom had been on the Ordaining Council. Parker himself believed the *Transient and Permanent* to be one of his poorest productions, and Ripley agreed. Chadwick, *Parker*, p. 96.

what the "sneering" passages had been. He desired, he said, to have "the very head and front of my offending made manifest." And since the *Register* had disclaimed responsibility for his opinions, he wanted its editors to "tell me *for whose sentiments you are responsible*—always excepting your own." The *Register* gave its rebuttal in the same issue, by quoting a number of the passages in the *Transient and Permanent* which seemed to them to be "sneering" denials of the inspiration of Scripture or the authority of Christ, or to throw ridicule on particular beliefs cherished by many Christians.[31]

The *Monthly Miscellany* also took Parker to task. The reviewer (probably Gannett) prefaced his remarks with a hope that Parker would not "consider the open and fair expression of dissent from his opinions an act of injustice to him," as he had apparently done in the case of the *Register's* review. Parker's irreverent opinions about Christ and the Bible, said the *Miscellany*, had occasioned grief and surprise among Unitarians; but a more fundamental difficulty was that Parker's principles, if adhered to logically, would leave no ground for believing any part of the Christian Gospel, even those parts to which Parker assented. "Here—on the matter of *authority*," the writer asserted, "is the essential difference between Mr. Parker and others who value the Gospel." It was not necessary, he said, to question Parker's faith "in Christianity, viewed merely in its internal character. But on his principles *we* should have no faith in Christianity." [32]

In September the highly respected *Examiner* came out with the most thorough denunciation of the South Boston sermon that was to be given in the Unitarian press. The writer was A. P. Peabody, the conservative whom Norton

31. *Register*, July 3, 1841.
32. *Monthly Miscellany*, 5 (July 1841), pp. 45-47.

had thought too lenient toward the Transcendentalists in 1839. Peabody now atoned for his earlier moderation. His strongly worded article attempted to "follow Mr. Parker, as he passes with his besom among the time-hallowed furniture of the Christian Temple," but professed to find the iconoclast almost too erratic to follow. The basic inconsistency, Peabody thought, was in Parker's wish to give the Christian name to a system of "absolute religion" which admittedly "is so entirely independent of Christ, as to stand equally well without him." It seemed, he said, that the term "Christian" was in danger of becoming "a mere name of courtesy."

Parker had stated the requirements of Absolute Religion as "love to God and man." Its only creed, he had said, is belief in a perfect God, its only "form" a "divine life," its sole rule of morality, that one should do "the best thing, in the best way, from the highest motives." All of this, said Peabody, is very fine, "but why call it *Christianity?* It was all known before Christ; and, as Mr. Parker justly deems, is known independently of Christ. . . . To give it one name rather than another, is a mere matter of fancy."

Peabody discussed in detail Parker's assertion that the traditional forms and doctrines of Christianity had not been initiated by Jesus himself, and adduced scriptural and theological proofs to the contrary. He dealt in the same way with Parker's statement that the scriptural writers never had claimed special inspiration. The reviewer denied that the canonical books had been assembled by "caprice or accident." And he ridiculed Parker's assertion that traditional Christianity had always regarded Jesus as speaking on his own rather than God's authority. He knew of few sects which had ever believed such a thing. The true question, Peabody concluded, was not "whether truth is to be received on the authority of God or on that of Jesus. It is, whether truth is to be taken on any authority higher or other than our own." [33]

During the following winter Parker was given an opportunity to answer such criticisms. In June 1841 he had declined an invitation from "several gentlemen of Boston" [34] to give a course of lectures there late in the same year; but when the invitation was renewed several months later Parker accepted, very probably with the thought of vindicating his position before the Boston public.

The five lectures he delivered at the Old Masonic Temple on Tremont Street were enthusiastically received by the public. The hall (capacity 750) was filled nearly every time. His biographer Weiss later recalled that "all the earnest thinkers" were there; and Gannett's magazine, which could scarcely be accused of predisposition in Parker's favor, reported that his audiences sat through the learned two-hour discourses without showing "the least impatience." [35] The success of the series gave Parker his first definite assurance that he could find a ready audience in Boston if the Unitarian clergy should shut him out of their pulpits, as indeed they were already beginning to do.[36]

The lectures of 1841–42 were published, in expanded and heavily annotated form, as the *Discourse of Matters Pertaining to Religion*. The Rev. John H. Morison, of Milton, Mass., reviewing this work for the *Examiner*, found Parker's attitude and modes of expression more dogmatic than the popular theology which Parker so deplored. A more serious charge was that Parker's great show

33. *Examiner, 31* (1841), 99–109, 111–14.
34. S. E. Brackett, Charles Ellis, William Larned, and Charles L. Thayer. Weiss, *1*, 176–77.
35. Ibid., p. 177; *Monthly Miscellany, 5* (December 1841), pp. 352–53.
36. Frothingham, *Parker*, pp. 158–59.

of learning, which might seem to justify his assertiveness, was too full of inaccuracies to merit the reader's trust. Morison cited and documented some of the most flagrant examples of Parker's carelessness, and stated that he had found many more.

As for the cry of "persecution" which was being raised against the conservatives for questioning Parker's standing as a Christian minister, Morison suggested that "the terms bigot, superstitious, fanatic, pharisee, and hypocrite" which Parker was accustomed to apply to those "whose crime consists in differing from himself," were as unpleasant and could be quite as unjust as the epithets of which Parker was complaining.[37]

Another comment on the *Discourse of Religion* was written by Samuel Osgood, who still considered himself a Transcendentalist but believed that Parker had gone beyond what any of the other theologians in the New School could accept. "As the Strauss of our American theology," he said, Parker had come to occupy a position "almost alone." There had been some apprehension, Osgood remarked, that the radical preacher would gain a following among the Unitarian clergy; but "not a single voice has been raised by any of our preachers, or pen wielded by our writers" in support of the *Discourse of Religion*. It could be said, in fact, that "he is not now in any way identified with the Unitarian body." It was Osgood's position that Parker, having slurred the institutions valued by Unitarians, should not now feel grieved if the clergy "are not

37. *Examiner*, 32 (1842), 388–89, 392–94. Morison's original manuscript, as submitted to the *Examiner*, had added that "we do not feel called upon to cast him out or deny to him the Christian name." The editors, however, deleted this passage, and Morison thereupon published it in the daily papers. Chadwick, *Parker*, p. 127.

disposed to offer him the position of a champion of those institutions" by inviting him to address their congregations. Parker should of course be free to express his opinion, but his opponents must be allowed to exclude non-Christian preaching from their pulpits.[38]

Parker's intense and constant feeling that he was being "persecuted"[39] was based upon genuine inability to believe that his attitudes could cause pain or indignation to others. When close friends warned him about his impulsiveness or his scornful language, he received their criticism gracefully but remained utterly unconvinced. "While I thank you for your frankness," he told Mrs. Caroline Dall on one such occasion, "I by no means admit the justice of what you say. I am by no means conscious of giving utterance to 'an unchristlike sneer or an unkind accusation' in any of my writings, preachings, or prayings."[40] Since this was always his attitude toward his own behavior and motives, one is not surprised to find him expressing ever-greater shock and indignation as the churches of Boston gradually cease to extend the customary invitations to him. The de-

38. *Monthly Miscellany*, 7 (August 1842), pp. 145–50.

39. See Chadwick, *Parker*, p. 95; Frothingham, *Parker*, pp. 173–75.

40. Mrs. Dall had been especially critical of Parker's use, in the *Discourse of Religion*, of the following lines from Alexander Pope to illustrate his opinion of those who value the sacrament of Communion:

> Behold the child, by Nature's kindly law,
> Pleased with a rattle, tickled with a straw;
> Some livelier plaything gives his youth delight—
> A little louder, but as empty quite.

Parker said he had only meant "that at God's table there was milk for the maidens, meat for the men"; and he professed amazement that anyone should find this insulting. Weiss, *1*, 182. See also ibid., pp. 175–76.

cline in Parker's pulpit exchanges had begun in 1840, and by late 1842 only eight of the local ministers remained on his list of "probables." [41]

A crisis in the development of this exclusion policy was marked by a special meeting of the Boston Association in January 1843. The purpose of the session was to discuss Parker's relation to the Unitarian clergy, which had become strained not only because of the South Boston Sermon and the *Discourse of Religion* but also because of accusations which Parker had brought against some members of the Association for the part they had played in a dispute between the Rev. John Pierpont and his society.

Pierpont, who had been minister of the Hollis Street Church since 1819, had displeased some of his parishioners by his advocacy in the pulpit of prison reform, the peace and temperance movements, and antislavery. Since some of his more influential pew-holders had acquired their wealth in the distilling business, and for some years had stored New England rum in the cellar of the church, Pierpont's sermon against "Rum-making, Rum-selling, and Rum-drinking" met with particular disfavor, and an attempt was made to force his resignation. Pierpont, however, held his ground, and a "mutual ecclesiastical council" was agreed upon by the contending parties. Under the chairmanship of Dr. Francis Parkman, and with S. K. Lothrop as secretary, the Council eventually, in August of 1841, advised against dismissal of Pierpont. The decision was widely hailed as a triumph for freedom of the pulpit.[42]

41. Clarke, John Pierpont, J. L. Russell, John Sargent, Shackford, Stetson, Samuel Robbins of Chelsea, and G. A. Briggs of Plymouth. Chadwick, *Parker*, pp. 103–4.

42. Samuel K. Lothrop, *Proceedings of an Ecclesiastical Council in the Case of the Proprietors of Hollis-Street Meeting-House and the Rev. John Pierpont, Their Pastor* . . . Boston, 1841. Eliot, *2*, 188–89.

An Ecclesiastical Council, however, was something of an anomaly in the liberal church, even if agreed to by both parties, and Parker protested against its having been called in the first place. He was indignant also because the Council, while clearing Pierpont, had reprimanded the Hollis Street pastor for some of his conduct during the dispute. Finally, to Parker's way of thinking the procedures of the Council had been inexcusably dilatory and unsystematic.

Parker's strictures were about as severe as they could have been had the Council decided unfavorably to Pierpont. Writing in the *Dial*, he damned all ecclesiastical tribunals and inquisitions, without leaving any doubt that he considered the Hollis Street Council to be one of the genre. He denounced their report as a "piece of diplomacy worthy of a college of Jesuits." [43] To other Unitarians, who believed that the Council had performed an unpleasant duty conscientiously—and courageously, some said, considering the final stand against the vested interests—this utter disparagement seemed out of order. By stretching the point a bit, Parker's opponents managed to construe his article as an attack upon the Boston Association itself.[44]

The ministerial group determined upon a full-scale discussion of this issue and of the *Discourse of Religion*. But they wished Parker to be present to defend himself, and so sent a carefully worded notice to him particularly urging his attendance on January 23, 1842. When the session was convened in the home of the Rev. Robert C. Waterston,[45] tension and embarrassment were apparent on both sides. It became clear almost immediately that the most influ-

43. *Dial*, *3*, No. 10, 201–21.

44. Chadwick, *Parker*, p. 116; Frothingham, *Parker*, p. 165; Eliot, *2*, 188–89.

45. Pastor at this time of the Pitts Street Chapel of the Benevolent Fraternity of Churches; after 1845 pastor of the Church of the Saviour. Eliot, *2*, 112.

ential members of the Association were hoping to persuade Parker that he ought to withdraw voluntarily. Gannett argued that the Hollis Street Council article had compromised and injured Parker's fellow ministers, and Dr. Nathaniel Frothingham, chairman of the meeting, explained that the *Discourse of Religion,* which he called a "vehemently deistical book," had made it impossible for normal ministerial relations with Parker to continue, even though personal and scholarly associations need not cease. Chandler Robbins, putting the question directly, asked Parker whether he did not feel, in view of his lack of sympathy with the opinions of the other members, that it was his duty to withdraw.

Parker answered that, on the contrary, he believed that differences of theological opinion ought to exist and had always existed within the Boston Association; and when Frothingham countered by asserting that in this case the difference was one "between Christianity and no Christianity," Parker desired to know "the precise quiddity" which must be added to his Absolute Religion to make it "Christian."

When Gannett explained that "the miracles" and "the authority of Christ" must be added, the doctrinal line had been drawn, with Parker on one side and the rest of the Association at least nominally on the other. Neither party, however, was willing to regard adherence to this doctrinal standard as an absolute condition of membership. Parker had been asked to withdraw and had refused. In a body committed to free inquiry nothing more could be done unless dissolution of the Association itself were decided upon.[46] The meeting ended in anticlimax when personal

46. This was proposed, but rejected on the ground that it would appear as a victory for Parker: Chadwick, *Parker,* p. 115. A motion for expulsion of Parker received only two affirmative votes: ibid., pp. 173–74.

tributes to Parker by Gannett, Robbins, and Cyrus Bartol caused the accused man to break into tears and leave the room.[47]

Ezra Stiles Gannett   Samuel Kirkland Lothrop

A hiatus of nearly two years followed this indecisive encounter. In the summer of 1843 Parker completed his edition of DeWette's *Introduction to the Old Testament;* in September, exhausted by the work and controversy of the previous three years, he sailed for a year in Europe. Ezra Gannett told readers of the *Examiner* that the Parker controversy was over. Transcendentalism as a philosophical movement, he said, would continue to have its beneficial "spiritualizing" effect upon Unitarian thought, but "as one of the religious vagaries of the times," attacking the authority of Christ and the Gospels, it had ceased to be a danger. Since reaching full expression in Parker's *Discourse of Religion,* the "assailant movement" had lost the support of most of those who at first had thought it consistent with piety.

47. The best account of this meeting is Parker's own, in Weiss, *1,* 188–93. Weiss, however, edited out the names, and a list of these must be pieced together from the Parker biographies by Frothingham (pp. 161–68), Commager (pp. 88–90), and Chadwick (pp. 115–21).

Gannett continued by attempting a vindication of the Boston Association against those who thought Parker ought to have been expelled. The Unitarian clergy, he said, had taken the strongest stand that was possible or necessary. Under Congregational polity Parker could be "deposed" as a minister only by the West Roxbury congregation which had elected him; and to have expelled him from the Boston Association because his opinions were "not Christian" would have been to beg the very question in dispute.

> All that they could consistently do, was to express to Mr. Parker their individual views, and set before him in free and friendly conversation the inconsistency of his course in continuing to exercise the functions of a Christian minister while he rejected the main facts of the Christian Scriptures. And this they did. They had no authority to depose him from his place or cast him out from their company.[48]

Gannett's announcement that the Parker controversy had ended was, as it turned out, premature. The danger of Parker's obtaining a following among the established Boston clergy may indeed have been past, but it soon became clear that the fight within the denomination had only begun. Parker returned from Europe in September 1844, and the next seven months were full of new incidents. In November the Rev. John Sargent, whose mission chapel on Suffolk Street was supervised by the Benevolent Fraternity of Churches, exchanged with Parker and was thereupon reprimanded so severely by his superiors that he saw no course but to resign. Then, at the end of December, Parker took his turn preaching the traditional "Great and Thursday Lecture" in the First Church of Boston. His discourse

48. *Examiner*, *36* (1844), 406–8. Gannett's *Monthly Miscellany* had been discontinued at the end of 1843, and Gannett had become an editor of the *Examiner*, along with the Rev. Alvan Lamson.

on that occasion, "The Relation of Jesus to His Age and the Ages," [49] brought his heresies again into public notice, and the Boston Association moved to exclude him from further participation in the lecture series. In January, James Freeman Clarke also exchanged with Parker and by this action provoked the secession of fifteen leading families from his Church of the Disciples.[50]

All these incidents were brought under a general head of discussion in an open letter which Parker addressed to the Boston Association in March 1845. Parker's most immediate complaint was against the action excluding him from the Thursday Lecture; for, unlike the refusal of pulpit exchanges, this was a concerted move on the part of the Association. It had, moreover, been accomplished by a device which Parker considered underhanded—namely returning the right of invitation to the incumbent at First Church, in whose hands it had originally resided.[51]

The excluded preacher had always suspected that some who were nominally in opposition to him actually shared his heresies and were simply giving way to conformist pressures. The open letter of 1845 was an attempt to implant this same suspicion in the public mind by asking the Association as a body for a detailed statement of belief. "I shall take it for granted," he wrote, "that you have, each and all, thoroughly, carefully, and profoundly examined the matters at issue between us; that you have made up your minds thereon, and are all entirely agreed in your conclusions, and that, on all points . . ." It would not be charitable, Parker said, to suppose that the clergy would undertake to "censure and virtually condemn" one of their

49. In Parker, *Works*, 4, 40–57.
50. Chadwick, *Parker*, pp. 141–45; Weiss, *1*, 249–54.
51. A committee of the Association had been unable to persuade Parker to abdicate his right to preach the lecture in his turn. See Weiss, *1*, 251.

number if this were not the case. He then put twenty-eight questions to the Association, asking for their definitions of such terms as "miracle," "salvation," "inspiration," and "revelation," and posing particular questions in the areas of christology and biblical criticism.[52]

Parker's letter, which preserved an entirely cordial tone, was more than a little disingenuous. Its major queries had long since been answered, and no association of Unitarians had ever pretended to agree in detail on points of biblical interpretation. Although no "official" answer was forthcoming, Gannett probably expressed the predominant conservative reaction when he wrote that "though Mr. Parker professes to expect he shall find agreement among the members of the Association, he must know that any half dozen men, who are in the habit of thinking for themselves, would probably differ." It was well known, he said, that Parker's opponents were agreed on the essential point at issue, namely the defining of Christianity as a unique revelation.[53]

After Parker's *Letter to the Boston Association*, Unitarian writers abandoned the amenities of reserved statement and seemed fairly well settled in the conviction that Parker was neither a Unitarian nor a Christian.[54] Gannett, who had

52. *Works, 14*, 108–15.

53. *Examiner, 38* (1845), 423.

54. John Sargent's dismissal from the employ of the Benevolent Fraternity for exchanging with Parker provoked a heated exchange between Sargent and his conservative colleague Waterston. This was reproduced with editorial comment in the *Register*, January 18, February 15, March 1, 1845. See also the following pamphlets, all published in Boston in 1845: *Answers to Questions Not Contained in Mr. Parker's Letter . . .* by "One Not of the Association"; *Questions Addressed to Rev. T. Parker and His Friends* (anon.); *An Answer to "Questions Addressed to the Rev. T. Parker and His Friends,"* by "A Friend Indeed"; and John Sargent, *The True Position of Rev. Theodore Parker, Being a Review of Rev. R. C. Waterston's Letter . . .*

objected on principle to excluding Parker from the Boston Association in 1843, had no scruples about the technically different measures which had been taken since Parker's return from Europe. He had no doubt, he said, about the right of a minister to refuse to invite a colleague into his pulpit if he was personally convinced that the other's views were "unscriptural, unsound, and mischievous." To the question whether this was not a recession from ground taken by Unitarians when they themselves had been "excluded" from Boston churches, Gannett answered that possibly it was, but that he himself had never complained about being kept from Trinitarian pulpits, and that he would not invite Unitarians to preach in his church if he were a member of the Orthodox party. The correct policy, whatever might have been done or said in the past, was to withhold exchanges from Parker without trying to prevent his speaking elsewhere.[55]

The Rev. Orville Dewey of New York, addressing the Berry Street Conference in May of 1845, put the case for "exclusion" in even stronger terms. Showing some impatience with his Boston brethren for their constant soul-searchings about free expression, he attempted to set the record straight on the meaning of such terms as "liberality" and "persecution." Freedom of thought, he argued, does not imply an inalienable right to utter, without any risk of censure, what others regard as pernicious untruth. Nor does Christian liberality mean that the opinions of anyone who happens to call himself a "Christian" are *ipso facto* beyond reproach. Parker and his friends, therefore, must get over their tenderness and hurt feelings. "Reformers—as they consider themselves—must somewhat sturdily take their

---

55. *Examiner, 38* (1845), 267–71. Gannett did continue to refer to Parker, in a strictly qualified way, as a "Christian believer," and was taken to task by a fellow conservative for so doing. See the *Register*, March 1, 8, 1845; Gannett to George E. Ellis, February 28, 1845. Ellis Papers, Massachusetts Historical Society.

ground. They must not wonder at resistance nor rejection. They must let other people think too, and say what they think."

The real reason for Parker's feeling of persecution, Dewey believed, was his inability to understand how opinions opposite to his own could be held strongly and sincerely. "He has passed into another hemisphere of thought and feeling with regard to Christianity, and he does not know what is thought and felt in ours." The ideal of unlimited ministerial fellowship, he said, is an amiable one; but sometimes, as in the present case, it simply does not work. "We preach an authoritative and miracle-sanctioned Christianity. How can we unite in teaching with him who abjures all this . . . ?" [56]

Opposition to the exclusionist policy, however, had not been entirely stilled. William H. Furness, who had wavered in his support of Transcendentalism during the Ripley-Norton debate, was aroused by the treatment of Parker to print two sermons denouncing the "exclusive principle." William Ware, former editor of the *Examiner*, brought the traditional Unitarian prescription of "righteousness before doctrine" to Parker's defense. And a prominent layman told the Boston ministers that, though their right to exclude Parker from their pulpits was undeniable, it was "un-Christian" of them to exercise it. [57]

56. "Rights, Claims, and Duties of Opinion," *Examiner*, *39* (1845), 82–102. For further support of this position by Ellis and Gannett see the *Examiner*, *40* (1846), 77–94, and 459–71; for Dr. Frothingham's position see *Deism or Christianity, Four Discourses* . . . Boston, 1845.

57. Furness, *The Exclusive Principle Considered: Two Sermons on Christian Union and the Truth of the Gospels*, Boston, 1845; W. Ware, *Righteousness before Doctrine: Two Sermons* . . . Boston, 1845; William P. Atkinson, *Remarks on an Article from the "Christian Examiner" Entitled "Mr. Parker and His Views,"* Boston, 1845.

Despite such dissenting voices, it was clear by late 1845 that Unitarian clergymen were going to stand by the exclusion policy. It was plain, also, as Gannett had admitted, that the liberal tradition as once expounded by Unitarians had been considerably modified. The tortured attempt to find a middle way had failed, and in order to preserve their doctrinal tradition the conservatives had been forced to adopt measures which bore a painful resemblance to Orthodox maneuvers of thirty years before.

Parker's generally acknowledged right to "speak elsewhere" than in Unitarian pulpits was one which could not have been withheld from him even if his opponents had wished to do so. In February 1845 Parker had accepted an invitation from several Unitarian laymen to preach regularly at the Melodeon Theatre in Washington Street. His first year of preaching in that place had been so successful that in December he was persuaded to leave his pastorate in West Roxbury and give full time to the new group, which had organized itself in November as the Twenty-Eighth Congregational Society.[58]

Both parties to the intense dispute of the early 1840's had thus settled into fairly secure positions. Conservatives had their policy, Parker had his audience, and neither was likely to be moved by further argument. The conflict passed from an acute to a chronic stage, in which, for some seven years, a kind of strained cordiality was the dominant note. The Unitarian press began to refer to Parker as a "lecturer . . . formerly recognized as a Unitarian preacher." His writings and speeches were reviewed in a tone of detached and on the whole not unfriendly interest.[59]

A number of circumstances contributed to bringing this

58. For a full discussion of this society as an experiment in church reform see below, Chap. 5.

59. *Monthly Religious Magazine*, 2 (1845), 143–44; *Examiner*, 42, 149, 303; 43, 150; 44, 474; 48, 330–31; 52, 160.

cold war to an end in 1853. The most important was that
the security of the conservative position was being undermined by the continuance of Parker's influence within the
Unitarian body. Though the older ministers were showing
no movement toward Parker's opinions, young and devoted
Parkerites were coming up from the Divinity School and
being elected to Unitarian pulpits. O. B. Frothingham, a
graduate in 1846, was pastor of the North Church in Salem.
His classmate Samuel Longfellow was preaching for the
Second Unitarian Society in Brooklyn.[60] Samuel Johnson,
Thomas Wentworth Higginson, and many others of less
note were spreading the gospel of Parkerism. Parker himself was gaining a greater public reputation through his
increasing antislavery efforts, and the size of his audiences
at the Melodeon had necessitated a move in 1852 to the
new Music Hall, whose seating capacity of 2,700 was
frequently taxed to the limit.[61] Parker's *Massachusetts
Quarterly Review*, a robust journal dealing with all public
questions—"the *Dial* with a beard," Parker called it—had
appeared in 1847, and had provided him with an additional
forum during the three years following.[62] The Unitarian
conservatives felt a growing apprehension, therefore, that
the *modus vivendi* of the previous several years was becoming unsatisfactory.

In the summer of 1853 occurred the last serious clash
between Parker and his opponents. For the first time in the
history of their long debate, the immediate provocation
came from the conservative side. The Executive Committee
of the American Unitarian Association, in the professed
belief that the taint of Parkerite radicalism was compromis-
ing the liberal party and discouraging public support of
their projects, secured the adoption of an elaborate "dec-

60. Eliot, *3*, 121, 219.
61. Weiss, *1*, 412–13.
62. Gohdes, *Periodicals*, chap. 8; Frothingham, *Parker*, p. 398.

laration of opinion" that strongly resembled a creed.[63]

This declaration was significant in showing the uncharacteristically assertive position into which the denomination had been driven. Never before or since have Unitarians in any official statement come so close to creed-making. It is true that the declaration contained no hint of formal excommunication. It implicitly recognized that Parker was still a member of the denomination, since he had not been barred formally from the local ministerial association or barred in any way from the state and national groups.[64] Defenders of the declaration insisted that the document could not be construed as a "creed" or as an act of exclusion. The Association, as they said, was nonrepresentative, and could not make the declaration binding on any but the individuals who approved it.[65] But despite such disclaimers, it was obvious to many that the Unitarians had legislated a "creed" that was as official as any concerted action could be in this denomination. The most nearly representative Unitarian group in the eastern United States was on record as "basing its united action" upon belief in the supernatural origin of Christianity.[66] Leaders of the Association might deny that this was a creed, but they did expect the declaration to reassure Unitarians and influence the general public in their favor; and such hopes, after all, had meaning only if the Association had more actual power to "bind and loose" than it had in theory.

Under the leadership of Dr. Lothrop, who had been president of the Association since 1851, the Executive

63. *The Twenty-Eighth Report of the American Unitarian Association, with the Addresses at the Anniversary*, Boston, 1853.

64. Chadwick, *Parker*, pp. 267–68.

65. Debates on the Declaration are recorded in the *Register*, June 4, July 16, 1853.

66. The Western Unitarian Conference adopted a similar platform the following year. Wilbur, *History*, p. 463.

Committee [67] presented its controversial report on May 24, 1853. The report began with an account of the historical development of Unitarianism, and of the current crisis which the declaration was intended to meet. The slow growth of the liberal church was attributed to five major causes. The first four of these [68] did not involve Parker or radicalism; but the fifth was expressed in such a way as to suggest that it had been the main provocation to the creed-making activity which was being undertaken:

> One of the chief clogs impeding our numerical advance, one of the principal sources of the odium with which we are regarded . . . has been what is considered the excessive radicalism and irreverence of some who have nominally stood within our own circle . . . They have seemed to treat the holy oracles and the endeared forms of our common religion with contempt. They have offensively assailed and denied all traces of the supernatural in the history of Christianity and in the life of its august Founder. In this way, shocking many pious hearts, and alarming many sensitive minds, they have brought an unwarranted and injurious suspicion and prejudice against the men and views that stood in apparent support of them and theirs, and have caused an influential reaction of fear against liberal opinions in theology. It seems to us that the time has arrived when, by a proclamation of our general thought on

67. Other members of the Executive Committee were William R. Alger, Isaiah Banks, George W. Briggs, Albert Fearing, Calvin Lincoln, and Henry A. Miles. Parker, *Works*, *14*, 466.

68. These were (1) the negative character of the main Unitarian emphases in the early period, (2) the characteristic placing of intellect above piety, (3) Orthodox prejudices in the community, and (4) the social pressure toward Orthodox conformity. *Twenty-Eighth Report*, pp. 18–21.

this matter, we should relieve ourselves from the embarrassments with which we as a body are thus unjustly entangled by the peculiarities of a few . . ."[69]

There was no intention, the Report continued, of "dogmatizing" about such people, "their opinions, or their position." The Association ought simply to "state what our own position is, leaving every individual perfectly free to think, decide, and act for himself." It should assert, "in a denominational capacity . . . our profound belief in the Divine origin, the Divine authority, and the Divine sanctions, of the religion of Jesus Christ." The liberal party, "so far as it can be officially represented by the American Unitarian Association," should go on record as believing "that God . . . did raise up Jesus to aid in our redemption from sin, did by him pour a fresh flood of purifying life through the withered veins of humanity and along the corrupted channels of the world, and is, by his religion, for ever sweeping the nations with renovating gales from heaven, and visiting the hearts of men with celestial solicitations."[70]

Such language, it was recognized, would suggest to many a reversion to Orthodox views of human sinfulness. The Committee tried to forestall inferences of this kind by reiterating Unitarian disbelief in Original Sin, as well as in the Deity of Christ and other "current dogmas" of the Calvinist system. And the more affirmative portions of the declaration did contain strong assertions of human ability. There was, nonetheless, an unmistakable emphasis upon the need of a revelation, upon "the existence and influence of hereditary evil," and on man's need of a Redeemer.[71]

69. Ibid., pp. 21–22.
70. Ibid., pp. 22–23.
71. Ibid., pp. 24–29.

Such explicit affirmations of traditional beliefs were bound
to cause some surprise, even though individual conservatives had been stating similar positions throughout the
Transcendentalist Controversy.

The essential meaning of the entire document was
expressed in the first of three "resolutions" which were
voted upon separately from the Report as a whole. This
first resolution stated "that the Divine authority of the
Gospel, as founded on a special and miraculous interposition
of God for the redemption of mankind, is the basis of the
action of this Association." [72] While the full report, with
its detailed treatment of theological issues, aroused vigorous
discussion and was not passed unanimously, this statement
of the essential Unitarian position was agreed to "without
a dissenting voice." [73]

In October, Parker took up the challenge with his
*Friendly Letter to the Executive Committee of the Ameri-
can Unitarian Association*.[74] He made it clear in this

72. The second and third resolutions expressed the denominational sense of having "a distinct work" to do, and promised a
"new zeal" in the promotion of liberal Christianity. Ibid., p. 30.

73. *Register*, June 4, 1853; *Twenty-Eighth Report*, p. 50. Among
those speaking in favor of the *Report*, besides the Executive Committee, were George E. Ellis, E. B. Hall, John H. Morison, Samuel
Osgood, and Samuel Hoar. The strongest arguments against it
were given by Caleb Stetson, Henry W. Bellows, John Pierpont,
and John Sargent. *Register*, May 28, 1853. The opposition of Bellows is of special interest in view of his later emergence as a
leader and symbol of Unitarian denominationalism. Letters in the
Bellows Papers reveal an ambivalent attitude toward transcendentalism similar to that which he later adopted toward "free religion."
Bellows to William Silsbee, December 28, 1841; March 29, 1842;
February 11, 1845; Bellows to Orville Dewey, January 10, 1843.
Henry W. Bellows Papers, Massachusetts Historical Society. See
also Chap. 6, below.

74. *A Friendly Letter . . . Touching Their New Unitarian
Creed or General Proclamation of Unitarian Views*, Boston, 1853.
References here are to the same in Parker, *Works, 14*.

pamphlet that whatever others might think he considered himself still a Unitarian. "As a life-member in long standing in the Association," he said, he felt called upon to ask some clarifications of the recent Report. He wanted to know what persons were referred to as having "nominally stood within" the denomination and having brought disgrace upon it. He asked, further, what the "offensive doctrines" were that had been alluded to, and what the Association proposed to do about those who held them—whether it was planned to expel them from the denomination or just to "give them a bad name, and let them go." He asked precise definitions, as he had in writing to the Boston Association in 1843, of such terms as "supernatural" and "Divine Authority." He desired to know what was meant by "renovating gales from Heaven," "celestial solicitations," and "the withered veins of humanity." [75]

Again, as in 1845, Parker's questions were chiefly rhetorical, and this time they seemed even more so, since most of them had just been answered, in full and rather tiresome detail, in a formally approved public document. Parker could have stopped any intelligent Bostonian in the street and learned whether his antagonists "individually as men, and professionally as the executive committee, believe that the religion of Jesus had a miraculous origin." Anyone who had watched the movement and expressions of conservative opinion knew whether Unitarians believed "that God did raise up Jesus miraculously, in a manner different from that by which he raises up other great and good men"; and whether they believed doctrines are "any more divinely announced, when taught by Jesus, than when taught by another person of the same purity of character." [76] The Unitarian Association clearly had answered all of these questions in the affirmative.

75. Ibid., pp. 117, 123–26.
76. Ibid., pp. 125, 131.

A number of Parker's questions, such as those which pointed out the unresolved tensions in Unitarian thought between trust and distrust of human nature, or which deflated the Report's sometimes pompous phrasing, were perfectly legitimate. The criticisms they implied were well taken. But Parker unfortunately vitiated the effect of these questions by the general tone of his writing, and opponents were justified in feeling that the *Letter*, having served the polemical purpose for which it was intended, scarcely required an answer. The *Register* remarked that "some of Mr. Parker's inquiries have . . . the appearance of ungenerous and unwarrantable assumptions, that the clergymen and laymen he so extensively catechises, do not really believe, what they deliberately say they do believe." Why, they asked, must Mr. Parker always accuse others of insincerity and false pretenses the moment they disagree with him? [77] No further answer, apparently, was forthcoming.[78]

Parker's *Sermons of Theism, Atheism, and the Popular Theology*, his most thorough indictment of the conservative position since the *Discourse of Religion*, appeared later in the autumn of 1853. The *Examiner's* review, written by Rufus Ellis of the First Church, showed neither the hot resentment nor the chilly cordiality which had characterized the Unitarian reaction at various earlier stages. His article, which probably was an accurate reflection of conservative feeling at this time, was a three-page sigh of weariness—an oblique and somewhat caustic admission that further argument with this man would be futile. Ellis said he had found nothing new in Parker's latest book. "The

77. *Register*, October 15, 1853.

78. Neither the *Quarterly Journal* of the Association nor the *Christian Examiner* took notice of the *Friendly Letter*, and Charles W. Wendte searched manuscript minutes of the Executive Committee without finding any mention of the affair. See Parker, *Works, 14,* 466.

only wonder is that we have not more repetition. The variety in sermons is an admirable illustration of the doctrine of permutations and combinations." And he added, in the tone of one who had argued for the recent Unitarian declaration and who now considered matters quite settled: "We have read the volume through, every word of it. Whether from prejudice or some better cause, we are still believers in the Gospel of Jesus Christ . . . and we apprehend that Christianity will survive *Theism* as well as Deism." [79]

By late 1853 the great Transcendentalist Controversy had resulted in very much the kind of denominational retrenchment which Norton had demanded so vehemently in the early years. The Unitarian leaders of the 1830's had been timid and recalcitrant, in Norton's opinion, but the work of Gannett, Lothrop, Dewey, and George Ellis in the 1840's must have nearly satisfied him. It is worth remembering, however, that the methods of these later leaders were not those of Norton himself. The conservatives were firm, and from the point of view of anyone who disagrees with their theology they were also reactionary; but they acted on the whole with a fairness and restraint at least equal to that of their antagonist. Hardly an instance of so-called conservative intolerance can be found which was not provoked by intolerance or insult on the part of Parker himself.

It has sometimes been argued, justly enough, that Parker could not have had his immense influence in the enlivening of American religion and the remedying of social evils had he been more sensitive to the feelings of others and more indulgent toward what he found to be their shortcomings. But it should be possible to acknowledge the reformer's

79. *Examiner*, 55 (1853), 465–68. For Parker's subsequent relations with the Unitarians see Chap. 6 below.

contributions without adopting his rather distorted view of the opposition. Though Parker seems to have believed that his opponents were dogmatic and illiberal, the record shows that they were acutely conscious of the liberal tradition in which they had been trained, and that they made a strenuous effort to preserve what they could of it.

But they had to choose, and the choice could not please everyone. As Hedge later observed, "a movement is strong by what it includes, an organism by what it excludes." [80] Unitarians by 1853 had come reluctantly to the decision that some ideals of the Movement must be sacrificed in order to preserve the organic integrity of the Church. They had therefore made their affirmative beliefs explicit, and had declared that whatever the consequences for traditions of "free inquiry," a Christian church must take its stand with the Christian confession.

80. Quoted in Allen, "Historical Sketch," p. 230.

Chapter 5

"The Church of the Future":

Prophets and Experimenters

ANDREW PEABODY's mental image of Parker, as a kind of busybody heedlessly sweeping away the "time-hallowed furniture of the Temple," was one which had wide currency even among persons basically in sympathy with Transcendentalist aims. Samuel Osgood, for example, complained in 1842 that reformers of the Parker variety were showing themselves to be little more than "eloquent destructives." "It requires very little talent," he observed, "to say smart things against the cherished opinions of the Church." [1] Emerson and Ripley, as well as Parker, were frequently accused of concentrating their efforts exclusively upon the negative part of the reformer's task. It was said of these men, and sometimes of the Transcendentalists in general, that they lacked constructive ideas about

1. *Monthly Miscellany*, 7 (1842), 155.

the erecting of new institutions to replace those of which they were so critical.

In defense of Parker and Emerson on this score, it should be noted that both were fundamentally interested in a reform of preaching, and expected the new gospel of "man's infinitude" to remake ecclesiastical institutions in an almost automatic fashion. They did not see that any further prescription was needed; a properly spiritualized religious philosophy would bring about the needed reforms as a matter of course, preserving, as Parker said, "all the old which is good," [2] and destroying only what was unspiritual and useless.

As a group, moreover, the Transcendentalists were not guilty of shirking their responsibilities as constructive reformers. A majority of the clerical members of the original group continued as ministers to Unitarian congregations, doing what they could to bring new life into "the forms already existing." A number of them not only elaborated concrete schemes for a "Church of the Future" but also committed themselves to the difficult task of realizing such schemes in the spheres of denominational and parish activity.

This more positive side of Transcendentalist reform efforts can best be seen in the work of such mediators as Frederic Henry Hedge and James Freeman Clarke, both of whom laid out detailed plans for the Church of the Future and eventually gave practical expression to their ideas through their work as denominational leaders. The constructive approach is also illustrated, on a smaller scale, in the experimental efforts of Orestes Brownson, W. H. Channing, Clarke, and Parker, all of whom established new religious societies which were, to a greater or lesser extent, attempts to apply Transcendentalist principles to parish organization.

2. *Sermons of Theism*, p. 203.

Hedge, during the most active years of the Transcendental Movement, was pastor of the Independent Congregational Society in Bangor, Maine (1835–50), and of the Westminster Congregational Church in Providence (1850–56). So far as is known, he attempted no radical innovations in these societies, nor was he as yet a major denominational figure, but his writings influenced Unitarian thinking during this period. In his anthology *Prose Writers of Germany* [3] he continued the championing of foreign speculations which had brought him into prominence in the early 1830's. In such sermons and tracts as *Gospel Invitations, The Leaven of the Word,* and *Practical Goodness the True Religion,*[4] he set forth his own synthesis of Transcendental idealism with Christian supernaturalism. In *Conservatism and Reform,* an oration first delivered at Harvard in 1841, he urged the Unitarian conservatives to meet radical ideas with discussion instead of with demagogic appeals to popular fears.[5] And in articles for the *Examiner* Hedge drew upon an exceptional knowledge of ecclesiastical history to explain the possibility of a "Broad Church" that would make use of the Transcendentalist emphasis upon natural religion without forfeiting distinctly Christian characteristics.[6]

As a mediator between Transcendentalism and the traditional faith, Hedge occupied a position which to extremists on either side seemed highly illogical. In later years, reminiscing about the Transcendental Club, he explained

3. Philadelphia, 1848.
4. Published in Boston, 1846, 1849, and 1840.
5. Hedge, *Conservatism and Reform* (Boston, 1843), pp. 19–22.
6. *Examiner,* 41 (1846), 193–204; 51 (1851), 112–34; 52 (1852), 117–36. The best discussion of Hedge's ideals for the Christian Church and for Unitarianism is George H. Williams, *Rethinking the Unitarian Relationship with Protestantism: An Examination of the Thought of Frederic Henry Hedge (1805–1890),* Boston, Beacon Press, 1949.

that, "though I hugely enjoyed the sessions, and shared many of the ideas which ruled the conclave, and the ferment they engendered, I had no belief in ecclesiastical revolutions. . . . My historical conscience, then as since, balanced my neology, and kept me ecclesiastically conservative, though intellectually radical." [7]

To Hedge these two positions seemed compatible. Unlike Parker, he conceived of the Christian Church as the living expression of the faith of centuries, an organism whose historical forms must be venerated if one purports to accept Christianity at all. The mistake of some Transcendentalists, Hedge thought, and of such European writers as Constant, was their notion that each age constructs its own religious institutions and therefore can, if necessary, discard the historic Church and substitute a set of the latest theological speculations in its place. Freedom of speculation within the Church should be as wide as possible, he said, but theories and interpretations of Christianity are only commentaries by mortal men on God's revelation; they are not a new revelation, and therefore cannot fulfill the function, which the Church does fulfill, of giving concrete expression to God's will for society. [8]

Hedge's position on the specific questions which arose between Transcendentalists and conservatives in their period of controversy may be summarized as follows: He agreed with the conservatives in holding to the special and supernatural mission of Christ, and in insisting that the confession of Christ's uniqueness makes the Christian Church what it is. But he agreed with the Transcendentalists in their protest against Lockean sensationalism, accepted the distinction made by Kant and Schelling between Reason and Understanding, asserted the one-ness

7. "The Destinies of Ecclesiastical Religion," *Examiner*, *82* (1867), 12.

8. Ibid., pp. 14–15.

of nature and spirit, and believed with Channing and the Transcendentalists that good as well as evil is a natural tendency of human behavior.

In the New School's protest against Unitarianism, he approved what he called their critique of religious institutions. This critique, as he saw it, consisted of examining religious institutions to discover which of their fundamental ideas are innate in the human mind and which are dependent upon special revelation. Hedge thought this a valuable procedure, even though he could not agree with some Transcendentalists in their tendency to value the innate ideas above the revealed ones.

Finally, Hedge shared the Transcendentalist confidence in the perfectibility of man and society, and more than shared their appreciation of German scholarship.[9]

Basing his judgment on these criteria, Hedge aligned himself with the Transcendentalists on the miracles question. "I am far from maintaining," he wrote, "that Christianity must stand or fall with the belief in miracles." But he could not go along with Parker in the latter's definition of Christian belief. "I do maintain," said Hedge,

> that Christian churches, as organized bodies of believers, must stand or fall with the Christian confession,—that is, the confession of Christ as divinely human Master and Head. . . . The scope of the Liberal Church is large; but everything and everybody cannot be embraced in it. . . . The distinction involved in the Christian confession is organic and vital; its abolition would be the dissolution of the ecclesiastical world and the end of Christendom.[10]

9. See his *Conservatism and Reform*, p. 33; "Natural Religion," *Examiner*, 52 (1852), 133–36; and Wells, pp. 147–50.

10. *Reason in Religion* (Boston, 1867), pp. 218–19.

Hedge's proposals for the improvement of Unitarianism all presupposed this fundamental acceptance of the Church. The "Church of the Future" would, however, have no creed other than the acceptance of Christ as Saviour. Beyond this, its common basis of action would be a commitment to practical reform—"the regeneration of society in the image of Christ." No attempt would be made, in this future Church, to bring members together on detailed points of doctrine; for "when men begin to speculate, they fly asunder in every direction; but when they come to act, they are drawn nearer together." [11]

Another characteristic of the Church of the Future would be its rejection of artificial divisions between ministers and other believers, and between the various Christian sects. There would be "but one order of priesthood—the hierarchy of the wise and good. . . ." The "petty barriers" of sect and creed would be swept away by "the tide of humanity." [12]

Hedge also believed, however, that this ideal Church was still a great way off, and that Christians must work through sects and denominations while striving for its realization. Mystics might hold themselves aloof if they could be convinced that they felt a direct commission from Christ, but "for those of us who can hardly claim an apostolic commission in this sense," churches are still necessary. Hedge's words justifying denominationalism could be read as the manifesto of his own vigorous program of participation in Unitarianism:

> The action and success of Christianity, at any given time, must depend on the vigor, the soundness, and prosperity of the various sects which represent Christianity at that time. Such being the case, it seems to me

11. "The Churches and the Church," *Examiner, 41* (1846), 203.
12. Ibid., p. 204.

the duty of every one, who has the cause of Christianity at heart, to throw the weight of his influence into that denomination of Christians with which he can best adjust himself . . .[13]

For Hedge as for other Transcendentalists, Unitarianism represented "the Protestant idea in its last development and fullest extent," the penultimate institutional form out of which the Church of the Future must evolve.[14]

The church reform ideas of James Freeman Clarke were strikingly similar to those of Hedge, but Clarke's case is of even greater interest because he formed a religious society conforming to his transcendental principles. He, too, had wide-ranging theories of what the Church of the Future would be, and eventually applied them in positions of general denominational leadership, but Clarke had a zeal for practical experimentation which Hedge lacked. A sermon preached before his society in 1845 contains this typical statement:

In order to realize this [ideal] Church, what is needed is not a new theory. . . . We want an *instance*. We want a real example, an actual specimen, a church itself. We want something actual, which, if nothing more, may be a seed out of which the future church may grow. Imperfect and humble, as all beginnings are, it may be; but the germ of the future may be in it.[15]

Because of this combination of prophetic idealism and practicality, Clarke's career as a church reformer has an extra dimension. And because his society was the only one

13. *Examiner*, 51 (1851), 132–33.
14. Ibid., p. 132.
15. James F. Clarke, *A Sermon on the Principles and Methods of the Church of the Disciples* (Boston, 1846), p. 33.

established by a Transcendentalist which achieved permanence and stability,[16] it shows especially well how the New School's ideas could be made to work in the context of ordinary parish organization.

Clarke's period of greatest influence as a denominational leader came after the Transcendentalist era, as did the bulk of his writings on doctrinal and ecclesiastical subjects. To be sure, his election in 1845 to the Board of Directors of the American Unitarian Association testified to his high standing at that time—especially so since this honor came to him just after his controversial exchange of pulpits with Parker.[17] But Clarke concentrated mainly upon his parish work in these years; and his most significant utterances as a Church reformer were the sermons and brochures in which he explained the functions of his society.

Clarke settled permanently in his native Boston in January 1841, at the end of a seven-year pastorate in Louisville. Dissatisfied with his experience in the West, he had stayed there after 1836 mainly out of a sense of duty. In 1841, having finally made the break, he was determined to find a new situation that would give him an opportunity to experiment with the reform ideas which he had been developing. He returned to Boston because his family and closest friends were there and, more particularly, because he expected to find an audience there for the Christian Transcendentalism he wished to preach.

Clarke gave numerous definitions of the particular brand of Transcendental philosophy which underlay his programs of reform. The most succinct was one which he stated in 1877, when he declared: "I am a Transcendentalist. I do not believe that man's senses tell him all he

16. Clarke's Church of the Disciples continued its separate existence until 1942, when it was merged with the Arlington Street Church (the former Federal Street Church of Channing and Gannett).

17. Chadwick, *Parker*, p. 145.

knows." [18] Another, which indicates that in the Transcendentalist Controversy his position was similar to that of Hedge, was offered in 1848. The valid teachings of Transcendentalism, he then said, are

> That God is now in the world, that he is now in our hearts, that he is ready now to inspire us by his spirit, that he is uniformly near, the light within us, the life of our life,—these are the teachings of Transcendentalism, for the sake of which we can easily overlook its extravagant opposition to miracles and what seems to me its unreasonable denial of the supernatural element in history. [19]

It was characteristic of Clarke to look upon any system of philosophy, as he looks here upon Transcendentalism, as an ore from which the pure metal of truth is to be extracted. His conception of the Church of the Future (which he also called the Comprehensive Church) was that it must combine the best elements from all former religious systems. These would include, as "independent but harmonizing elements," the Catholic principle of universality, the Orthodox Protestant understanding of sin and the supernatural, Unitarian liberality, and the Transcendentalist emphasis upon Divine immanence. Within the Comprehensive Church, he said, radical movements would no longer be looked on as heresies but instead would be welcomed in the belief that they carry "Providential meanings" —that is, that they indicate some need which God wishes his Church to fulfill. [20]

The forms of organization within the Comprehensive

18. *Essentials and Non-Essentials in Religion: Six Lectures Delivered in the Music Hall, Boston* (Boston, 1878), p. 19.

19. *The Church as It Was, as It Is, as It Ought to Be: A Discourse Delivered . . . March 15, 1845* (Boston, George H. Ellis, 1909), p. 17.

20. Ibid., pp. 15–17; Clarke, *Church of the Disciples*, p. 33.

Church could be "various," Clarke said, but all of its sub-divisions must be united by a common faith in Christ as Saviour and by the common activity of humanitarian re-form. And he asserted—echoing Hedge—that eventually distinctions between Clergy and Laity would disappear. "The clergy-church must be changed into the Church of the People." [21]

In the establishment of his experimental society, which was to be the "specimen" or model for the Comprehensive Church, Clarke molded his theories into three principles of practical organization—the voluntary principle, the social principle, and the principle of congregational wor-ship.

The meaning of the voluntary principle was that the "proprietary system" was to be excluded; pews were not to be rented or sold. This was a reform which Orestes Brownson had instituted in his experimental society as early as 1836 and which Ripley had suggested to his congrega-tion in 1840; but Clarke constructed a more elaborate theory in its support than had either of these predecessors. The basic objective of the voluntary system was to end the distinction between church members and "proprietors." In most Boston churches, the church members as a body had no function except to meet regularly for Communion, business affairs being regulated by the larger group of pew-holders. Clarke believed that the core of regular church members ought to do the work of the society and carry on its business. There would, as before, be a large number who would attend services without becoming communicants, but after the abolition of the proprietary pew system there would no longer be any reason for putting parish affairs in the hands of such persons.[22]

Under the social principle, meetings were to be organized

21. *Church as It Was*, p. 20.
22. *Church of the Disciples*, pp. 5–6, 21–24.

in which members and friends of the Church could take a more active part than they could take in the actual service of worship. Clarke designed these various social meetings to stimulate each of the three faculties of the human mind— discussion groups for the intellectual faculty, prayer meetings for the spiritual, community service to stimulate the will or moral faculty.[23]

The principle of congregational worship meant that, contrary to current Unitarian practice, the people would take active part in the Scripture readings and prayers and would sing the hymns, which in most churches were rendered by organist and choir alone.[24] Clarke, in his hopeful attempt to provide an example of the "Church of the People" which was to come, carried this Principle a step further. Election and ordination, he said, ought not to set the pastor apart as the only member capable of leading a service of worship, and he therefore proposed that lay members should also lead services and preach sermons.[25]

None of these three principles was entirely original with Clarke. All of them had precedents in the customs of Congregationalism at other times and were paralleled by current practices among the Quakers, Methodists, and frontier religious societies, as well as among certain other Transcendentalists. The voluntary system of church support was common in Unitarian and Orthodox Congregational churches outside of Boston.[26] Orestes Brownson, besides introducing free pews in his church, had caused a stir in the community in 1840 by advocating abolition of the "priesthood" throughout Christendom. Charles Follen had

23. Ibid., pp. 18–21.
24. Ibid., p. 24; Edward E. Hale, ed., *James Freeman Clarke: Autobiography, Diary, and Correspondence* (Boston, 1891), pp. 145, 158.
25. Clarke, *Church of the Disciples*, pp. 24–28; Hale, p. 146.
26. *Register*, July 30, 1836.

tried the experiment of discussion meetings with the congregation at East Lexington, and John Dwight had instituted the same practice at Northampton.[27] Bronson Alcott and Margaret Fuller had been strong for the conversational method of religious instruction. And all of Clarke's three principles drew inspiration from the protest central to Transcendentalist thinking on ecclesiastical matters, against all things priestly or pontifical, against all second-hand religious teaching.

The significance of Clarke's proposals, therefore, lay not in their originality but in their systematic and forceful application in a society that was distinctly Christian. He took Transcendentalist reforms—which up to then had made little progress because so often advocated by religious enthusiasts of allegedly infidel tendencies—and brought these reforms to mature respectability.

In the Boston community of 1841, divided and confused by the contrary preachings of the Transcendentalists and their opponents, Clarke readily found an audience for his reform ideas. Some fifty individualists, in despair of finding a church home that would promise both the security of a positive faith and a guarantee against the dogmatism which they saw in conservative Unitarianism, had been gathering in private homes each Sunday through most of the year 1840. These people were without a minister, but had been carrying out most of the functions of traditional worship. After some preliminary discussions with them, Clarke announced a series of three sermons to be preached "with the purpose of forming a new religious society." The response was gratifying, and by the end of April the group had taken permanent form as the Church of the Disciples. The charter membership was forty-eight.[28]

27. Cooke, *Dwight*, p. 39.
28. Clarke, *Church of the Disciples*, pp. 28–31; Arthur S. Bolster, Jr., *James Freeman Clarke: Disciple to Advancing Truth* (Boston, Beacon Press, 1954), p. 131; Hale, pp. 157–61.

The "statement of faith and purpose" to which members of the new church subscribed reflected both the desire for "comprehensiveness" and the wish for a distinctly Christian commitment:

> Our faith is in Jesus, as the Christ, the Son of God;
> And we do hereby form ourselves into a Church of his
>   Disciples, that we may cooperate together in the
>   study and practice of Christianity.[29]

Dr. Channing, whom Clarke consulted about this statement, thought it too conservative. The Unitarian leader suggested that Jesus be designated "the divinely appointed teacher of truth" instead of "the Christ, the Son of God"; but Clarke, believing that Christianity rests upon the messianic claims of Jesus as much as upon his moral teachings, rejected Channing's advice. "We wished," he said later, "to connect ourselves, not only with one another, but with the whole church of Christ, the only way of doing which was to adopt a universal confession . . ." [30]

The statement of faith and purpose was, however, interpreted so liberally that few were likely to be excluded by it. Clarke believed that the right of church membership must be extended to seekers and doubters as well as to those who were already settled in their beliefs. To become a member, one had only to notify the pastor or the pastoral committee, then be introduced to the congregation and sign the statement. The articles of organization, formally adopted in 1844, provided no method for rejecting an applicant for membership, since it was considered "highly improbable" than anyone desiring membership would meet congregational opposition.

Individuals who wished to make a public confession of faith when joining the church were specially accom-

29. Clarke, *Church of the Disciples*, p. 4.
30. Hale, p. 160.

modated, as were those who wished to be baptized, by im-
mersion or otherwise. The sacrament of Holy Communion
was offered on a similar plan; members could participate
or not, as they preferred, and non-members were free to
partake.[31]

The conciseness of the Disciples' church covenant was
in the tradition of the New England churches, and its
articles of faith were not far removed from the essentials
of current Unitarianism. But the established churches in
both wings of Congregationalism had been moving toward
more elaborate statements of belief, and toward more
literal interpretations of their original covenants. So Clarke's
church was clearly in the progressive ranks. The flexibility
of its arrangements for membership, Communion, and
Baptism no doubt was partly a matter of necessity; for
Clarke had the problem of satisfying some widely divergent
individual requirements. But it was the Transcendentalists'
eclectic approach to religious practices which enabled him
even to attempt such a feat of comprehensiveness.

The eclectic spirit was nowhere more strikingly illustrated than in Clarke's modernization of the traditional
Christian system of Feast Days. Every Communion Sunday
was dedicated to a particular religious purpose or idea, and
he appointed "festival days" to commemorate such diverse
events as the birth of Swedenborg, Washington, or Dr.
Channing, the death of Joan of Arc or John Brown, the
laying of the Atlantic cable, and the Hegira.[32]

The Church of the Disciples enjoyed a reasonably steady
growth. The loss of some fifteen leading families at the time
of Clarke's pulpit exchange with Parker in 1845 was a
severe setback, but membership reached 200 in the 1840's,

31. Clarke, *Church of the Disciples*, pp. 6–10; *Articles of Organization and Rules of the Church of the Disciples* (rev. ed.
Boston, 1868), pp. 5–8, 12–13.

32. Ibid., pp. 22–23.

and weekly attendance averaged 700 at the end of that decade. In 1848 and again in 1869, new and larger buildings were constructed for the society. Membership and attendance continued to increase in the post-Civil War period.[33]

As for the three principles of organization which Clarke had instituted, all were continued with varying success throughout the period of Clarke's pastorate. The system of voluntary financial support was maintained even through times of financial distress; pews were eventually designated for particular persons or families, but never were sold or rented. The other principles, involving discussion meetings and greater congregational participation in services, succeeded so well that a portion of the congregation was able to carry on without a pastor during a sick-leave of three years which Clarke was forced to take in the 1850's. Although, as Edward Everett Hale remarked, Clarke was much more necessary to his congregation than he affected to be, he did have lay members leading the biblical discussion groups and prayer meetings, helping to make policy decisions which in many churches were the sole responsibility of the minister, and occasionally assisting him in the regular services of worship.[34]

Clarke's radical reforms of 1841 had ceased to seem unusual some fifty years later. Boston churches by the end of the century had adopted most of his expedients in their parish activities and services of worship.[35] It would of course be a mistake to give sole credit to Clarke or to Transcendentalism for bringing about these changes. His principles were essentially common-sense reforms, demanded by the "liberated" portions of the community in the 1840's and merely articulated for them by such Tran-

---

33. Bolster, pp. 145, 298–302; Hale, pp. 167, 211.
34. *Articles of Organization*, pp. 3, 13–15; Bolster, pp. 147, 206; Hale, p. 146.
35. Hale, pp. 145–46.

scendentalist preachers as Ripley, Brownson, and Clarke. But the Church of the Disciples was what he had intended it to be—an instance, and a pioneer instance, of the revitalizing effect which Transcendentalism could have upon Christian congregations.

Hedge and Clarke have been considered first in this discussion because their ideals for the Church of the Future form the best groundwork for treatment of the Transcendentalists' practical reform efforts. Clarke's Church of the Disciples, however, was not the earliest of the Transcendental religious societies. The distinction of being first in the field belongs to the Society for Christian Union and Progress, founded in 1836 by that brilliant and eccentric reformer Orestes Brownson.

Brownson's philosophy of Church reform had many points of contact with the ideas of Hedge and Clarke. It had a similar intuitionist basis, and proceeded on the same optimistic assumptions about the possibility of unlimited progress. Brownson, like the others, thought that the religion of the future would combine the best features of all existing religions, and would therefore make a successful appeal to all of humanity. A final and most important similarity was the emphasis of all of these men upon social reform as the common purpose which would outweigh doctrinal differences.

Brownson's church reform ideas are difficult to summarize, since he was constantly changing them. If consistency is, as Emerson said, the hobgoblin of little minds, Brownson deserves a high rank among Transcendentalist thinkers, for he had little compunction about making complete reversals of opinion and exceeded most of the New School in his readiness to embrace totally a "new truth." During his period of greatest activity as a reformer of Unitarianism, however—from 1836 to 1842—his reversals and contradictions do fit into a general pattern. His persistent objective in those years was to find a formula that would make Protestantism workable, and his search, during most of that period, was guided by a conviction that the Transcendental faith, expressing itself through Unitarianism, would bring about the necessary reforms.

Brownson was much like Theodore Parker in his attitude toward transcendental philosophy. He saw the same basic division in the world of thought, and contended that "whoever is not a transcendentalist, must . . . needs be a skeptic, or a materialist and an atheist." [36] But, like Parker again, he deplored the tendency of some members of the New School to disregard facts of observation. "So far as Transcendentalism is understood to be the recognition in man of the capacity of knowing truth intuitively," he said, "or of attaining to a scientific knowledge of an order of existence transcending the reach of the senses . . . we are Transcendentalists"; but he had little sympathy for those "who disregard experience, ask no aid of facts, and who deem themselves competent to construct a true philosophy of man and the universe by means of speculation alone." [37] Cousin's philosophy, more than any other, inspired Brownson to emphasize this distinction, and it was Brownson who persistently urged that the New School in America should be called the Eclectic.

In his attempts to apply his transcendentalism to religious reform, Brownson made use of specific ideas from Schleiermacher, Constant, Saint-Simon, Heinrich Heine, the Abbé Lamennais, and Dr. Charles Follen, in addition to taking the general approach of Cousin. Schleiermacher and Constant both had stressed the importance of the human "re-

36. *Boston Quarterly Review*, *4* (1841), 300.
37. Ibid., *3* (1840), 322–23; *Examiner*, *22* (1837), 188.

ligious sentiment" as the originator of creeds and churches, and Constant in particular had pointed out the necessity of adjusting the "forms" of religion to the needs of a given age. Saint-Simon, in his *Nouveau Christianisme*, had translated the biblical command "love thy neighbor" into a call for "the quickest possible amelioration of the poorest and most numerous class." Heinrich Heine, German poet and follower of St. Simon, had deplored the Church's exclusive interest in the spiritual needs of mankind, and had demanded "the rehabilitation of the material." Lamennais, priest, essayist, and quondam Church reformer, had insisted upon the necessity of a religious approach to social reform; and his writings had helped, in the early 1830's, to win Brownson away from the opposite position as held by the Owenites. Dr. Follen's *Religion and the Church* had been impressive to Brownson as a first attempt to apply the theories of Schleiermacher and Constant to American conditions.[38]

All of these influences were present in Brownson's most complete statement of Church reform philosophy, the *New Views* of 1836. In the preface to this little book, the author assured readers that his title said just what he intended; he was proposing not a new religion, like Saint-Simon, but rather reforms in the old one. "It is not a new Christianity,"

38. For Brownson's acknowledgments of debt to these writers see his *The Convert*, p. 182; also *Works, 4,* 2; and *Boston Quarterly Review, 3,* 432. Saint-Simon's *Nouveau Christianisme* (1825) is translated in F. M. H. Markham, ed., *Henri Comte de Saint-Simon (1760–1825): Selected Writings*, New York, Macmillan, 1952; see also E. M. Butler, *The Saint-Simonian Religion in Germany* (Cambridge, England, Cambridge University Press, 1926), pp. 7–10. For Heine see Frederic Ewen, *The Poetry and Prose of Heinrich Heine*, New York, Citadel Press, 1948. The relevant work by Lamennais is his *Paroles d'un croyant* (1834), which marked the renunciation of his former royalist and ultramontane beliefs and the beginning of his career as a democratic publicist.

he explained, "but a new church that is required." The watchwords of this new Church, he said, must be Union and Progress.[39]

The emphasis upon union was something more than the plea of Hedge and Clarke for a broad and comprehensive Church. Its more exact meaning in Brownson's system was "the reconciliation of spirit and matter." His synonym for union was "atonement" or "at-one-ment," and he attempted by this terminology to emphasize the relationship between his own reform ideas and traditional Christian doctrine.[40] According to Brownson, Jesus, the God-Man, had announced an atonement between the divine and the human, and had taught the essential unity of flesh and spirit. The early Church, however, had caught only a part of Christ's message, and had begun to preach that Jesus came not to reconcile but to "redeem." The Catholic Church, he said, had become thoroughly and dogmatically committed to a rejection of all things material, and the impulses of the Renaissance, denied complete expression within Catholicism, had brought about the Protestant schism.

Brownson went on to define the Protestant tradition as one of exclusive materialism. As a critical movement, he said, Protestantism had performed a vital service; but it had never been truly a Church. The Protestant form of belief, when consistently adhered to, exalts fleshly interests above spiritual ones, and is therefore essentially irreligious. Brownson admitted that Protestants have, in fact, managed to maintain a valid religious tradition; but he claimed that this

39. *Works, 4,* 1, 45.

40. Brownson's definition of "atonement," also that of some other Transcendentalists, was faithful to the etymology of the term; but the accepted usage by the nineteenth century suggested propitiation and redemption, not simply reconciliation. Contemporaries, therefore, criticized Brownson for distorting the accepted meaning. See *Examiner, 22,* 128; *Western Messenger, 3, 531.*

had been done only by inconsistently retaining Catholic traits of spirituality and dependence on authority. Where religion exists among Protestants, he said, it is merely "as a reminiscence, a tradition." [41]

Brownson saw Unitarianism as the end-point of this advance of materialism, "the last word of Protestantism, before Protestantism breaks entirely with the Past." The principle of progress was already established in this sect, and only the principle of union, or atonement, was required to overcome the materialistic emphasis and produce the true Church. With an unbounded optimism typical of the reform enthusiasms of his day, Brownson found announcements of the new order in all of the "signs of the times." "Unitarians are every day breaking away more and more from tradition," he noted. "Mind at this moment is extremely active among them." Both in and out of Unitarianism he saw a strong popular desire for a new philosophy that would unite matter and spirit, and he likened the providential appearance of Cousin's eclectic philosophy at such a time to the appearance of Alexandrian eclecticism in the earliest period of Christian history. In the popular mania for "associations" Brownson saw the beginnings of a practical spirit of tolerance—a willingness to forget theoretical differences for the sake of joint social endeavors—which would characterize the Church of the Future. These signs seemed unmistakable to Brownson, whose intense and almost millennialist fervor had given him a sense of mystical identification with all of humanity, leading him to believe himself the voice of the universal mind. In words that were later to have a special pathos for him, he asserted, "I do not misread the age. I have not looked upon the world only out from the window of my closet; I have mingled in its busy scenes . . . I am but what it has made me. I cannot misread it." [42]

41. *Works,* 4, 4–24, esp. 22.
42. Ibid., pp. 39–44, 55–56.

The concrete problem to which Brownson's broad recommendations were applied in the later 1830's was that of
the amelioration of the working classes. He proposed to
take a middle, or "reconciling," course between the two
most common methods of social reform. The Owenites and
Abner Kneeland, on the one hand, were concerned solely
with the material needs of the workers; Christian ministers,
on the other, appeared to care about nothing but the saving
of souls. Brownson intended to minister to both material
and spiritual needs. He proposed to preach "spiritual"
Christianity to the workers and the social reformers, and
to enlist the clergy in the "material" cause of social reform.

Brownson's Society for Christian Union and Progress
began its meetings in May 1836, in the Lyceum Hall on
Hanover Street, Boston. Early notices used the title Social
Reform Society, but Brownson shortly adopted the longer
and more explicit name, by which the experiment was
known until its demise in 1843. Formal organization was
effected on May 29, when Brownson explained the principles of the society in a sermon, The Wants of the Times.[43]
In July a new place of worship was obtained at the Masonic
Temple on Tremont Street.[44]

Details of the history of Brownson's society are difficult
to uncover.[45] One reason, probably, is the very casual way
in which the church was organized. Brownson's preaching
was so much the center of interest that the meetings had
more the aspect of weekly lectures than of religious services.
When the preacher discontinued his ministry, during the

43. *A Discourse on the Wants of the Times* . . . Boston, 1836.
44. Brownson, *Orestes A. Brownson*, *1*, 138–40.
45. The Brownson Papers, in the archives at the University of
Notre Dame, contain abundant materials on the content of Brownson's preaching but almost no descriptions of the Society. The four
major biographies of Brownson (see below, Bibliography) have
had to draw upon the recollections of Henry Brownson and a few
scattered details given by such observers as Miss Martineau and
Isaac Hecker.

period 1839–42, there was no attempt, so far as is recorded, to continue meeting without him.[46] Brownson's son recalled that membership in the Society was permitted to anyone "who held to the Christian morality, allowed free inquiry, and was desirous of promoting social progress." [47] It is unlikely that there was any formal procedure for receiving "members," although a Church Registry of some sort may have existed.

Estimates of the size of Brownson's weekly audiences have varied, but a compilation of the guesses would suggest that Brownson normally drew about 300, and sometimes attracted as many as 750.[48] Henry Brownson records that "the majority . . . belonged to the laboring class"; and Isaac Hecker, Brownson's disciple of the 1830's who later founded the Roman Catholic Paulist Order, recalled that "most of the radical minds of Boston sat under Dr. Brownson in those times." They were persons, Hecker said, "with whom religion had run off into pure intellectuality," and he remembered the proportion of men to women in the usual Brownson audience as three to one.[49]

46. The Society apparently held meetings from July 1836 until the end of 1839 (although Hecker implies that Brownson continued preaching during the early part of 1840), and from April 1842 to late 1843. *Review*, 5 (1842), 366–71; Isaac Hecker, "Dr. Brownson in Boston," *Catholic World*, 45 (1887), 468 ff.; *Orestes A. Brownson*, 2, 1.

47. Ibid., 1, 145.

48. Hecker put the average attendance at 300, Henry Brownson at 500. A clipping in the Brownson Papers from the Boston *Daily Advertiser* (no date, but probably late 1836), contains the statement that "Mr. Brownson has collected an overflowing audience." If, as one assumes, the meetings were held in the lecture room of the Masonic Temple, this last observation puts the figure at over 750. Hecker, "Dr. Brownson," p. 470; Brownson, *Orestes A. Brownson*, 1, 140. For the size of the hall: *Boston Almanac*, 1837.

49. *Orestes A. Brownson*, 1, 141; Hecker, "Dr. Brownson," p. 471.

The one feature of the Society's form of organization which is adequately chronicled in Brownson's writings is the system of free pews. His arguments for this plan bring out a working-class orientation which was not prominent in the similar reforms of Clarke and Ripley. Brownson railed against proprietary pew-holding as creating an "aristocracy" within the churches,[50] and it was to emphasize the Society's welcome to the poorer classes that the system was abolished.

Services were held at the usual time on Sunday mornings. Even though the sermon was the central attraction, the other traditional forms of worship were observed. "The music," Hecker recalled, "consisted of a harmonium played by a young man accompanying three or four male and female singers. The hymns, if I remember rightly, were those of the Unitarians. A collection was taken up every Sunday . . ." In his prayers Brownson maintained "the posture and style of any Protestant clergyman." [51] It was the content of the preacher's message, rather than the form of church organization and worship, which constituted the radicalism of his experimental society.

Brownson's overwhelming interest in the years just following 1836 was the preaching of Christian social reform, but he also aided specific projects which were not directly related to his Society. He supported the temperance and ten-hour movements, and favored a nonextremist approach to the abolition of slavery. In the field of popular education he became an advocate of manual-labor schools which would be designed to meet the needs of the working class by providing instruction in both academic and vocational subjects.[52]

Besides the Society, Brownson had the *Boston Reformer* as a sounding board for these reform objectives. He had

50. Brownson, *Wants of the Times*, pp. 7–8.
51. Hecker, "Dr. Brownson," p. 470.
52. *Orestes A. Brownson, 1,* 91–95, 190–204.

secured appointment as editor of this weekly journal, "a medium for free discussion on all topics connected with religion, morality, literature, and politics," in June 1836, and had immediately begun to fill its columns with his own sermons and writings on the Christianizing of reform. Old subscribers complained that the paper now had "too much religion," but the journal's proprietors apparently were satisfied with his work. After Brownson, finding the editorial duties burdensome, had resigned at the end of 1836, they prevailed upon him to begin again in the summer of the following year. In late 1837 he resigned once more, this time with the purpose of founding his own journal, the *Boston Quarterly Review*.

Although the *Review* during its four-year existence carried articles by Ripley, Parker, Alcott, Margaret Fuller, George Bancroft, Elizabeth Peabody, and many others, it was, like the *Reformer*, primarily a vehicle for Brownson's own ideas. In its pages the most significant of his own frequent changes in attitude were chronicled.[53]

One such change was his increasing adherence to the Democratic party. By 1838 he had become enough of a party man to win a political appointment as steward of the marine hospital at Chelsea.[54]

In this same period, influenced partly by his observations of working-class misery during the Panic of 1837, Brownson was losing his faith in Channing's "individual regeneration" as the basis for social reform, and he began to advocate a more radical approach. "In laboring to perfect the indi-

53. Ibid., pp. 161, 171, 183, 213–14; Gohdes, *Periodicals*, pp. 46–48.

54. George Bancroft, appointed by Van Buren as Collector of the Port of Boston, secured the Chelsea position for Brownson. The duties were light, involving mainly tours of inspection and superintendence of supply orders. Brownson was ejected from the post after the Whig victory of 1840. Brownson, *Orestes A. Brownson*, *1*, 211–12.

vidual," he told readers of the *Review* in 1838, "we are laboring for but an insignificant unit of an innumerable multitude." Even if individual perfection is possible, he now asserted, "still the perfection of the social state is a means to attain it." [55] This line of thought, encouraged by his reading of the French radical writers Dupuis and Potter and by a renewed interest in the doctrines of Saint-Simon and Fanny Wright,[56] led him by 1840 to adopt the view that social salvation could come only through such sweeping reforms as the abolition of the "priesthood," the strict limitation of the activities of government, the elimination of banks and monopolies, and the abolition of hereditary property. Brownson's famous essay "The Laboring Classes," which has been called "perhaps the best study of the workings of society written by an American before the Civil War," [57] put all of these radical proposals before the public. That public, as Brownson later put it, responded with "one universal scream of horror." [58]

Brownson's virulent attack upon the "priesthood," which was in effect an attack upon all organized religion, arose out of more complex motivations than were apparent on the surface. His theological writings just before the appearance of the controversial essay had revealed not a growing radicalism but a renewed interest in traditional Christian forms. In July 1839, for example, he had told *Review* readers that he was becoming less disdainful of Orthodox symbols and institutions: "We have ceased . . .

55. *Review*, *1* (1838), 471.

56. *Orestes A. Brownson*, *1*, 440; Schlesinger, p. 93. C.-F. Dupuis's *Origine de tous les cultes* was first published at Paris in 1795, L.-J.-A. de Potter's *Histoire du Christianisme* at Paris in 1836–37.

57. Schlesinger, p. 96. The essay, a review of Carlyle's *Chartism*, appeared in *Review*, *3* (July, 1840), 358–95. A sequel and rebuttal is in ibid. (October, 1840), pp. 420–510.

58. Brownson, *Convert*, p. 228.

to deny, and have commenced an examination" of these formulations, "not to reject them, nor even to modify them, but to comprehend them." He said that he had come to appreciate the depth of meaning in such Orthodox doctrines as the Trinity and Original Sin, and would readily choose Calvinism over Unitarianism if forced to accept either system in its entirety.[59]

In view of this renewed appreciation of Christian "forms," the only apparent explanation for the diametrically opposed antiformalism of "The Laboring Classes" is that Brownson, subconsciously at least, was trying to show the absurdity of the conclusions to which antiformalist principles can lead when fully and logically expounded. It is true that Brownson was unusually susceptible to persuasion by whatever authors he happened to be reading sympathetically at a given time, and that the "Laboring Classes" represented a momentary enthusiasm for the anticlerical writings of Dupuis and Potter. But the author's statements both during and after this intellectual crisis suggest strongly that he felt he had come to the end of the line in both his democratic and his Protestant faith, and that the essay was a kind of purgation for him. The "Laboring Classes," he later said, "marked the crisis in my mental disease. In it I had made my confession to the public; I had made . . . a clean breast of it, and had no further concealment. I had thrown off a heavy load . . . and felt relieved." [60] Even while writing the essay, Brownson had been perfectly sure that his radical ideas would not be accepted. He predicted, and seemed almost to desire "condemnation . . . contumely, and abuse." In a postscript to the article he somewhat sententiously begged the public to be lenient with those who had loved him or agreed with him in the past, and not

59. *Review,* 2 (1839), 381–84.
60. *Convert,* p. 265.

to hold such persons responsible for the aberrations of their friend.[61]

When the expected reaction came, in the summer of 1840, Brownson defended the essay's doctrines with his usual vigor, but within a few months he had come to the conclusion that the public would never accept the logical consequences of either Protestantism or democracy. They would not hear of abolition of the clerical profession, nor of the abolition of private property. The Whig victory in the "hard cider" election of 1840 seemed to him to confirm that the voters were more interested in the trappings of democracy than in its substance, and the shock of that election virtually ended Brownson's long-standing faith in the intuitions of the people. "I became henceforth a conservative in politics," he declared in *The Convert*, "and through political conservatism I advanced rapidly towards religious conservatism." [62]

The anti-clerical doctrines of "The Laboring Classes" are therefore significant as a kind of jumping-off place for one type of reforming Transcendentalism. Much of Brownson's essay was simply a more strenuous expression of ideas previously expressed by Emerson and Ripley. Emersonian doctrines were particularly evident in the distinctions which Brownson tried to make between the "priesthood" and true religious teachers. The first he condemned, whether Catholic or Protestant, as hirelings devoted to the enslavement of mankind and the perpetuation of human misery.[63] The true religious teachers, on the other hand, were those who preach not for hire but out of an overwhelming personal sense of the presence of God. Ordinary forms of worship, Brownson complained, force a minister to preach and pray when the

61. *Review*, 3, 393–95.
62. *Convert*, pp. 266–67.
63. *Review*, 3, 378–87.

spirit is not upon him. "We hold," he said, "that no man has a right to preach unless called by the Holy Ghost, and only when he is moved by the spirit of God." [64] The complaint reminds one not only of the Divinity School Address, but also of the personal struggles of both Emerson and Ripley against the binding force of conventional pastoral duties.

It was some time before the full effects of Brownson's intellectual turning of 1840 worked themselves out, and for almost four years after this he remained, nominally at least, a Protestant and a reformer of Unitarianism. His faith in Transcendentalism, however, disappeared rapidly. During the year 1841, when the movement entered a new phase of controversy under Parker's leadership, Brownson suddenly found the area of his agreement with the New School seriously diminished. His first reaction to Parker's *Transient and Permanent* had been highly favorable; he had called it "rich . . . appropriate . . . striking . . . and reverent." [65] But when he heard Parker lecture on the same themes during the following winter, he experienced a sharp reaction. Those lectures, as he later said,

> contained nothing except a learned and eloquent state-
> ment of the doctrine I had long defended, and which I
> have called the Religion of Humanity. But strange as it
> may seem, the moment I heard that doctrine from his
> lips, I felt an invincible repugnance to it, and saw, or
> thought I saw at a glance, that it was unphilosophical
> and anti-religious.[66]

One source of this antipathy to Transcendentalism, and of Brownson's later rejection of the Unitarian faith, was his new acquaintance with the philosophy of Pierre Leroux.

64. Ibid., p. 447.
65. *Review, 4* (1841), 436–37.
66. *Convert*, p. 343.

Leroux's chief message for him at this time was that the human spirit is not self-sufficient, as the Transcendentalists urged—that man, as Brownson put it, "cannot lift himself, but must be lifted, by placing him in communion with a higher, and elevating object." "Communion" became the dominant theme in his writings,[67] and he renounced both the "imbecile eclecticism" of Cousin, and Constant's premise that religious institutions are of human origin. By mid-1842 he had become a foe of transcendental philosophy in all of its forms.[68]

Loss of confidence both in Unitarianism and in the possibility of church reform followed rapidly after this recanting of Transcendentalist ideas. As late as April 1842 he continued to believe the Unitarian Church "the truest Christian Church now on earth,[69] but a practical apostasy from Unitarian principles was apparent in the open letter to Dr. Channing, called *The Mediatorial Life of Jesus*, which he published two months later. In this communication he told Channing that the latter's doctrines of human self-sufficiency and human likeness to God were untenable. The Calvinists had been right all along, he said: men by nature are not good but evil, and if they attain to any God-like qualities, they do so by virtue of Divine Grace, which is bestowed by supernatural means and is transmitted through all of humanity by the mystical process of Communion.[70]

67. Ibid., p. 286. "Communion" signified a mode of spiritual communication by which humanity becomes the vehicle of Divine Grace. Leroux's term for this mystical interrelationship of all humanity—borrowed by him from legal usage and in turn donated to the sociologists—was "solidarity." Leroux, formerly a Saint-Simonian, published *De l'Humanité* in 1840 (2d ed. 1845). See Maxine Leroy, "Leroux," in *Encyclopedia of the Social Sciences*.

68. *Review*, 5, 60–84, 149–83.

69. Ibid., p. 199.

70. Brownson, *The Mediatorial Life of Jesus: a Letter to Rev. William Ellery Channing, D.D.*, Boston, 1842.

Just as Cousin had been Brownson's main link to the transcendental philosophy, Dr. Channing had been his hero among the Unitarian thinkers, and this rejection of Channing's central faith in human nature was therefore a major step toward wholesale repudiation of Unitarianism. During the next two years Brownson was struggling to avoid the conclusion that the Roman Catholic Church is the true agent of that communion by which God's grace is passed on to humanity. His lectures of 1843–44 abounded in admiration of medieval Catholicism. The "priesthood," which in 1840 he had condemned as the enslaver of mankind, he began to regard as the opponent of wealth and tyranny in all ages except the modern. His church-reform objective became "a new Catholic church," and his new slogan was "Catholicity without the Papacy." [71]

In October 1844, after several months of discussions with Bishop Fenwick of Boston and his coadjutor, John B. Fitzpatrick, Brownson became a convert to Catholicism.[72] This step of course meant the final abandonment of the outposts of Unitarianism and Church reform which he had been defending. The tendency of Unitarianism toward naturalism and atheism, of which he had expressed some fear in his letter to Channing of 1842, he now saw as much more than a tendency. "The God it professes to recognize," he asserted, "is only an abstraction." [73] As for Church reform, Brownson wrote a fitting epitaph for his efforts of the previous eight years when he told the Fourierist Parke Godwin that "instead . . . of looking for a church to come, I accept the Church that is." [74]

71. Brownson, *Social Reform: An Address Delivered . . . in the Wesleyan University* (Boston, 1844), pp. 31–36; Schlesinger, p. 173; *Orestes A. Brownson, 1,* 382–85; Brownson, *Convert,* p. 352. See also Brownson, "The Present State of Society," *United States Magazine and Democratic Review, 13* (1843), 25–26, 35–36.

72. *Orestes A. Brownson, 1,* 472–77.

73. Brownson, *Works, 3,* 470. See also *4,* 560–61.

74. Quoted in Schlesinger, p. 175.

Brownson's contemporaries, both among the conservative Unitarians and among the Transcendentalists, followed his turbulent career with interest and a marked apprehensiveness. Occasionally his meanderings amused them, but in general he was far too formidable to be taken lightly. The most general attitude toward him at the time of his first entrance upon the Boston scene was one of cautious approval. The Unitarian clergy were aware of the young radical's unusual powers, and at the same time anxious to keep his activities from intruding directly into the established order. They encouraged the formation of his experimental church partly because of a sincere desire that the poor should have the Gospel preached to them, but also because they were pleased to have the radicals spending their energies outside of the regular churches.[75] Dr. Walker, who welcomed Brownson's contributions to the *Examiner*, nonetheless warned him about the dangers of unduly exciting the workers against the "capitalists and accumulators." [76]

Dr. Channing, who more than any other had been the inspiration for Brownson's efforts, at first expressed gratification that this "gifted spirit" had been won over to Unitarianism, but by 1837 believed that Brownson's criticisms of the clergy (for ignoring social questions) were too extreme and vitriolic. "I did hope," he told Miss Peabody, "that the study of great truths . . . would give calmness and stability to his mind." [77] And when "The Laboring Classes" appeared in 1840, Channing asserted that though he still sympathized with Brownson's "feelings towards what he calls the 'masses,'" he considered the proposals in that essay "shocking, or absurd." [78]

During the last tortured phase of Brownson's career as a Protestant, Unitarians looked on with puzzlement but gen-

75. *Orestes A. Brownson*, 1, 126–34.
76. Quoted in ibid., pp. 120–21.
77. Peabody, *Reminiscences*, p. 395.
78. Ibid., p. 416.

erally with patience. Dr. Channing, near death when he wrote his answer to *The Mediatorial Life of Jesus* in 1842, appeared to be more relieved about Brownson's growing conservatism than cognizant of its implications for Unitarian principles. "You have found new light," he wrote, "and I am disposed to look upon your changes, not as fluctuations, but as steps of rational progress. . . . God made you for something more than to scatter random shot . . ." [79]

The *Christian Register* in this same period recognized Brownson's leaning toward Orthodoxy and deplored it, but also stated with evident sincerity that they were pleased if Brownson's latest wrong opinions had really, as he claimed, produced good effects on his character. And Gannett's *Monthly Miscellany* took a similar line, noting that the *Mediatorial Life* manifested the radical writer's usual keenness and "in addition, what he has not so often manifested—the earnestness of an affirmative faith." [80]

This new appreciation was, of course, short-lived. Immediately after his conversion to Catholicism in late 1844, Brownson's vehemence against his former co-religionists prompted this analysis, in the *Register*, of his attacks upon Protestantism:

> We must confess he goes to the work in good earnest. It is no boy's play with him. One can hardly help supposing that it is something more than zeal which prompts him . . . that it is a sort of desperation which seems to say, "all other systems have been tried and rejected; this is my last resource; and if I cannot maintain my ground here, all indeed is lost." [81]

79. Quoted in *Orestes A. Brownson*, *1*, 443–44.

80. *Register*, June 25, 1842; *Monthly Miscellany*, 7 (1842), 42. See also *Examiner*, 36 (1844), 141. For other contemporary comments on Brownson as a radical see *Examiner*, 22 (1837), 127–30; *Register*, June 25, July 2, 9, 30, August 6, December 3, 1836, April 29, 1837, January 13, October 20, 1838; *Messenger*, 3, 529–39.

81. *Register*, March 22, 1845.

James Russell Lowell's *Fable for Critics* (1848) put the Boston reaction in less prosaic terms:

> The worst of it is, that his logic's so strong,
> That of two sides he commonly chooses the wrong;
> If there *is* only one, why he'll split it in two,
> And first pummel this half, then that, black and blue.

It was somewhat safer to laugh at Brownson once he had put himself firmly on the "wrong" side.

A Transcendentalist who approached Brownson in changeability, if not in the ability to defend each change with logical acumen, was William Henry Channing, nephew and protégé of the great Unitarian leader.

Channing was perhaps the most extreme embodiment, among the Church reformers, of the misty, ill-defined Transcendentalism which the public came to associate with the entire "New School." The transcendental philosophy, however, was only one of the prominent elements in his thought. In the intellectual history of the 1840's Channing is at least equally important as a preacher of associationism, the American version of the doctrines of Charles Fourier. His ideas and projects as a reformer grew out of an attempted integration of transcendental principles with the system, and in particular the vocabulary, of Fourier and the American associationists.

O. B. Frothingham, who had heard Channing speak on many occasions, found it difficult to recall, in later years, exactly what the orator's opinions had been. "The warmth of Channing's utterance," he said, "lingers lovingly about the heart, but all except the glory is departed. He was an atmosphere, life-giving but impalpable." [82] Since transcendental doctrines rivaled Channing's own in "impalpability," one does not expect to find a systematic appraisal of that

82. Frothingham, *Channing*, p. 8.

philosophy in his writings; but he did make enough statements about Transcendentalism to indicate which of its emphases were present in his reform program. Channing agreed with the Transcendentalists "that human nature in its primitive affections is good, that man has innately a love of the right, an adaptation to the true, a desire of the morally beautiful, and, most of all, an inward oracle of duty and a power of self-command." But he also concurred in his uncle's oft-expressed dislike of transcendental "ego-theism." Members of the New School, he said, too often failed to perceive that man is good only because his nature is derivative—dependent upon God. He deplored the Transcendentalist tendency toward "forgetfulness . . . of the great mystery of our spiritual existence." He accused some of them of self-complacency, excessive individualism, and exaggerated self-reliance.[83] The Church of the Future, or "New Church," as he called it, would avoid these errors; it would accept the Transcendentalist idea of Divine immanence, but would stress the divinity of the human race rather than that of the individual soul.[84]

Channing made use of the doctrines of Fourier to bridge the gap between his own mystical conception of human divinity and the practical objectives of social reform. The central idea in Fourier's system was that of a divinely ordered harmony of human interests. Dividing the passions of men into three categories—the senses, the "affective passions," and the "distributive passions"—he proposed a

83. W. H. Channing, *The Gospel of Today: A Discourse Delivered at the Ordination of T. W. Higginson* . . . (Boston, 1847), p. 9. See also "Oneness of God and Man," *The Present, 1* (1843), 153.

84. "The New Church," *The Spirit of the Age, 2* (1850), 73–74. Channing's first magazine, *The Present*, was published in New York from September 1843 to April 1844. *The Spirit of the Age*, also issued at New York, and superintended by George Ripley when Channing was in Boston, ran from July 1849 to April 1850.

scheme of society in which all men would serve the common interest by following exactly the dictates of each one of these sets of impulses. The ideal form of social organization was the "phalange," a highly regulated community of 1,620 persons among whom duties would be divided according to individual skills and inclinations. Human society, Fourier said, if organized in this entirely rational way, would reflect the harmony of the Divine mind.[85]

The American disciples of Fourier, led by Albert Brisbane and Horace Greeley, pruned his recommendations to meet conditions in this country; and one special characteristic of the American movement from its inception in 1840 was its Christian emphasis. Albert Brisbane "sugar-coated" it, as a recent analyst has said, "with a secularized Christianity"; and adherents like Channing, Ripley, and John S. Dwight, who were or had been Christian ministers, brought with them an even more pronounced, if still undogmatic, Christian perspective.[86]

Channing's version of associationism was set forth in numerous "Confessions of Faith" and "Statements of Principle" which, though they convey few precise ideas, do show the influence of both the Fourierist and the transcendental vocabulary. In the first number of the *Present* (1843) he gave this explanation of his idea of God:

> I believe, 1. That the Infinite, Eternal, all-blessed Being, who alone is God, from essential love, through ideas of truth, puts forth benign and beautiful creative power from everlasting to everlasting; 2. That in harmonious series of existences, endless in numbers and varieties, and sublimely related by successive growths, mutual de-

85. Edward S. Mason, "Fourier," in *Encyclopedia of the Social Sciences.*

86. T. D. Seymour Bassett, "The Secular Utopian Socialists," in Donald D. Egbert and Stow Persons, eds., *Socialism and American Life* (Princeton, Princeton University Press, 1952), *1*, 176–80.

pendence and analogy, he manifests his perfections in forever brighter glory; 3. That, through systems on systems, and worlds on worlds, he crowns his creations by giving birth to hosts of spirits, destined originally, through revelations, for ever brightening, to grow up in his likeness, and, by interchanges of good, to be united into families of immortal children, imaging in the heavens their holy Father . . .[87]

In a discourse on reform, given in 1848, he listed seven "Principles of Social Science," among which were the following:

1. The One God . . . lives in three modes; of which Love is the Principle,—Beautiful Joy the End, and Wisdom the harmonizing Medium . . . 2. The Divine Idea of Man is of Many men made One . . . 3. The Life of Man is Love . . . 4. The Form of this Unitary Life is the Law of Series . . . 6. The aim of a community should be to form a Collective Man . . .[88]

One is faced with cacophonies of half-expressed meanings in nearly all of Channing's *credos*. A general survey of his writings, however, indicates that the most important of his Church reform principles were: (1) that religious institutions are human creations, brought into being by the action of inspired individuals of whom Christ is the highest but by no means sole example; (2) that the succession of these religious institutions has always been in the direction of greater progress; (3) that the "true" Church will embody the best from all preceding forms of religious exercise, and for that reason will be the *final* church, not subject to the ills and dissensions of all earlier ones; (4) that the Church of

87. *Present*, *1* (1843), 6.
88. *The Christian Church and Social Reform* (Boston, 1848), pp. 22–23.

the present must be remade into an instrument of social reform; (5) that since all men are capable of direct religious experience, the distinctions between "priesthood" and people must be broken down.[89]

The first of Channing's experiments in reform was a free chapel which he established during a brief settlement as Unitarian minister-at-large to the poor of New York City. Frothingham relates, with unkind but possibly unintended humor, that the attendance at the first service in this chapel, in May 1837, was "twenty, including those that went out," [90] and the young preacher had despaired of the entire New York project by August of the same year. He supplied various pulpits until March 1839, when he accepted the Unitarian pastorate in Cincinnati.

Within two years, Channing had left the Cincinnati church, and was thinking of retiring permanently from the ministry, because of doubts about the truth of Christianity. By 1842, however, he had reinstated himself in the Christian faith, this time as an apostle of a "religion of humanity" much like the one which Brownson was then preaching.[91]

Another Channing experiment had its beginning in the autumn of 1842, when the young preacher, determined to establish a "free religious society," conducted services for a small company of malcontents in a Brooklyn schoolhouse. While preaching in this place Channing showed his distaste for religious formalism by removing the pulpit which had

89. See *Present*, *1* (1843), 148–49; *Christian Church and Social Reform*, pp. 8–15, 22–24 and passim; *Spirit of the Age*, *1* (1849), 264–65, 280–81, 297, 344–45; ibid., *2* (1850), 72–75; Channing, *Gospel of Today*, pp. 34–36; Frothingham, *Channing*, pp. 174–75, 231–36.

90. Frothingham, *Channing*, p. 137.

91. Ibid., pp. 150–64, 171–73. Channing, like Brownson, had been influenced by Leroux's *L'Humanité*. In 1842 he proposed to Theodore Parker the establishment of a new sect, an "Order of the Sons of God," based upon the divinity of the human race. Ibid., 173–76.

been provided for him, and by inviting free discussion of the sermon topic at each meeting.[92]

Early in 1843 Channing moved the meetings into New York City, first to the Stuyvesant Institute on Broadway and then to a hall on Crosby St., where a society called the "Christian Union" was formally organized in April. In a *Statement of the Principles of the Christian Union*, the minister explained that the watchwords of the new society would be Humanity, Wisdom, and Holiness. Beyond this, he said, "we have no creed. . . . We are learners, not teachers; we set up no limits: and cordially invite all to join us who have affinity for our principles." The society was called "Christian," he said, because "we reverently acknowledge Jesus the Christ, as a Saviour from sin, and an annointed messenger of God." [93]

According to the original plan, three types of religious meetings were to be sponsored by the Christian Union—a service of worship on Sunday morning; a second meeting on the Sabbath for the presenting of "testimonies" by members of the group, and a week-night session for "conversation." Channing emphasized that although he had been designated to preside at the services of worship, he was to be called "leader" rather than "minister." "We recognize . . . no peculiar priesthood set apart by human ordination for official ministrations." The true priesthood, he said, is "the innumerable company of earnest, upright, loving souls, whom God forever consecrates anew with the annointing of goodness." In the Christian Union, "pure and sincere persons" might perform any rite which they felt called to perform. "We wish to see a holy nation, a people of priests." [94]

92. Ibid., pp. 184–85.
93. *A Statement of the Principles of The Christian Union* (New York, 1843), pp. 10–11.
94. Ibid., pp. 11–12.

Little is recorded about the extent to which these principles and arrangements were carried through, but attendance and membership apparently remained quite small.[95] Channing abandoned the New York ministry in the autumn of 1845 in order to spend a few months at Brook Farm. In early 1846, after Theodore Parker's removal to Boston, he preached for the congregation at West Roxbury; but for reasons that are not entirely clear, Channing was not invited to settle in that church, and in late 1846 he was planning a new independent society, to be organized this time in Boston.[96]

The new society, called the "Religious Union of Associationists," was an illustration of the attempt to give a sugar-coating of Christianity to Fourierist ideals. The group, despite their rejection of traditional religious practices, showed a desire for the forms and symbolism of an ecclesiastical body. A distinct religious creed they could hardly have agreed upon, since the core of the congregation included "eleven Unitarians, three Orthodox Congregationalists, one Presbyterian, one Baptist, one Methodist, one Roman Catholic, three Universalists, two Rationalists, one Come-Outer, one Jew, one Swedenborgian, one Transcendentalist, and two Skeptics." The statement of the society merely asserted a common faith in "Universal Unity" as the will and purpose of God, a hope of the Kingdom of God upon Earth as "announced by Jesus Christ," and a reliance upon the inspiration of the Holy Spirit in seeking "the perfect at-one-ment." [97] But permeating all of the activities of

95. Frothingham, *Channing*, p. 194. Frothingham notes that Henry James, Sr., Christopher Cranch, Horace Greeley, and Margaret Fuller (then Greeley's associate on the *Tribune*) were among the regular attendants at Channing's meetings. Ibid., pp. 185, 191–92.

96. Ibid., pp. 197–99.

97. Ibid., pp. 221, 236.

the Christian Union was a certain groping for a religious symbolism which would satisfy these devout natures without obvious concessions to traditionalism.

A curious example of this was their form of Communion. The elements used were bread, water, and fruit, to symbolize Wisdom, Love, and Joy. On the altar was a Cross formed of evergreen and violets, behind the altar an empty chair to signify "the unseen Presence." As in their other services, the members prayed, heard the Scriptures and sacred music, and had an address from Channing. They then joined hands and repeated the statement of association, after which the elements were distributed—"during the repast conversation being carried on of a religious character." A small singing group rendered the "He Shall Feed His Flock" from Handel's *Messiah*.

When a missionary was sent by the group to Cincinnati, where he was to labor "in the cause of association, laying special emphasis on its religious aspects," the services of Ordination and Communion were combined. After partaking of the elements, the group joined hands; the minister then laid his own hand on the head of the missionary, so that the "divine Fullness" could flow from members to candidate.[98]

The music on such occasions was Christian sacred music (though only of the more sophisticated sort); the prayers and Scripture were Christian; and the minister preached upon orthodox topics quite as much as upon distinctly Fourierist doctrines. Channing, indeed, was showing an increasing interest in traditional Christian ideas during this period. His sermons, many of which were published in the *Harbinger* [99] and the *Spirit of the Age*, stressed the universal-

98. Ibid., pp. 225–27.

99. The *Harbinger*, which first appeared on June 14, 1845, was successor to Albert Brisbane's *Phalanx* as the chief Associationist

ity of evil nearly to the point of dualism, and gave a spiritualized but essentially conservative interpretation of the resurrection, the divinity of Christ, the communion of saints, and the Trinity. In 1847 he was writing sympathetically of the current religious revivals, and of their emphasis on man's need of regeneration.[100]

The tinge of traditionalism, and even of Orthodoxy, in the services of the Religious Union was one expression of the shift of emphasis, mainly in the direction of a transcendentalized Christianity, which characterized the efforts of the American Fourierists in the latter part of the 1840's. Brook Farm and most of the other communitarian experiments having ended in disappointment, the Union represented the hope that a saving remnant, by banding together, could stimulate new missionary zeal. Channing, whose cosmic enthusiasm was seemingly too far removed from the practical to be dampened by the failures which had disheartened Brisbane and Ripley, was peculiarly fitted to lead this child of despair. But by 1849 it was clear that even such ardor as his could have little reviving effect upon the rapidly declining fortunes of associationism. Few attended the meetings of the Religious Union; the original membership of thirty-three was not increased; and no encouraging word was returned by the apostle to Cincinnati. By 1850 Channing was longing for a regular pastorate, and in the summer of that year he accepted one in the Unitarian Church of Rochester, New York. There he remained until 1854, still active in social reform movements and interested in associationist

organ. Until 1847 it was edited by Ripley, Dwight, and Charles A. Dana at Brook Farm; from 1847 to 1849 by Ripley and Parke Godwin in New York. Gohdes, *Periodicals*, pp. 102–5.

100. *Harbinger*, May 22, 1847; *Spirit of The Age*, 2 (1850), 72–75; Channing, *Gospel of Today*, pp. 8–11; *Examiner*, 43 (1847), 374–94.

struggles, but finished with his career as an experimentalist in church organization.[101]

Of all the Transcendentalist religious reformers, Theodore Parker was perhaps the one least given to formulating grandiose plans for the Church of the Future. In his *Discourse of Religion* in 1842, after discussing the entirely human origin of the Christian Church, he closed a chapter with the following rather pallid definition: "The Christian Church may be defined as a body of men and women assembling for the purposes of worship and religious instruction. It has the powers delegated by the individuals who compose it." [102]

In a later sermon, *The Idea of a Christian Church*, Parker expanded upon this definition by saying that the members of a Christian Church should be united by "a common regard for Jesus of Nazareth, regarding him as the noblest example of morality and religion,—as the model, therefore, in this respect for us." [103]

In other writings, though Parker dwelt far more upon matters of speculative theology than upon details of church organization, one does find frequent hints of what he believed the Church should be and do. The duty of the Church and its ministers, he believed, is to teach "the true Idea of God, Man, and their relations," to kindle religious feelings by social communion, to encourage men to translate their religious intuitions into practical secular action, and above all to help all men to become Christ's equal—"sons of God as much as he . . . incarnations of God, as much

101. Frothingham, *Channing;* pp. 221, 227, 237–40, and chap. 11; Bassett, "Secular Utopian Socialists," pp. 180–85.

102. Parker, *Discourse of Religion,* p. 387.

103. Parker, *The Idea of a Christian Church: A Discourse at the Installation of Theodore Parker as Minister of the Twenty-Eighth Congregational Society* . . . (Boston, 1846), p. 3.

and as far as Jesus was one with God, and an incarnation thereof." In doing these things the Church should not ask its members to observe all of the forms that Christ himself "complied with," but "only such forms as help you."

A church, to implement these ideas, Parker said, must have unity of purpose and at the same time allow "entire freedom for the individual." It should encourage "the spirit of devotion" in all its people, teach the young to respect their own natures, and provide a medium through which members can aid each other both spiritually and in material need. The Church must be outspoken on all social issues, encourage education and the culture of the people, and denounce unsparingly the sins of society. Its only sacraments, Parker said, should be "great works of reform" and "institutions for the comfort and culture of men." [104]

Such innovations in church organization as Parker made were, on the whole, far less radical than the doctrines with which he supported them. There was nothing boldly experimental about the Twenty-Eighth Society. Its significance lies, first, in its contribution to the spread of Parker's influence, and secondly in what it reveals about Parker as a reformer—to what extent he had definite and viable ideas for reforming the Christian Church, and to what extent the true effect of his doctrines was, as his opponents charged, to make ecclesiastical organization impossible.

On January 22, 1845, a group of Boston laymen met at Marlboro Chapel to form an organization called "The Friends of Liberal Religious Thought." Incensed at the recent action of the Boston Association in excluding Parker from the Great and Thursday Lecture, they resolved "that the Rev. Theodore Parker shall have a chance to be heard in Boston." Two weeks later, Parker met with a committee

104. Parker, *Sermons of Theism*, pp. 203–5; *Christian Church*, pp. 6–28. See also Parker, "The Position and Duty of a Minister," *Works*, 13, 83–108.

appointed to secure his services and to arrange for a place of worship. He consented to preach the following two Sunday mornings, and "if it is possible," to continue with them for a year, preaching once each Sunday. He gained permission from his West Roxbury congregation to divide his time between the two parishes. By November, Parker's Boston followers had organized as the Twenty-Eighth Congregational Society. In December of 1845, Parker, encouraged by the success of his preaching and aware that the burden of two active parishes was excessive, accepted an invitation to become their full-time minister.[105]

The Melodeon, which the committee had procured in 1845 for Parker's preaching, and which the society continued to use until 1852, stood on the west side of Washington Street, near Boylston Street and just south of the site of the later Boston Theatre.[106] This hall, which seated 1,500, was sometimes inadequate for the crowds who came to hear Parker, and furthermore was hardly conducive to an atmosphere of worship. In the last sermon which he preached in that building Parker told his parishioners that "as I have stood here, I have often seen the spangles of opera-dancers, who beguiled the previous night, lying on the floor beside me

105. *The Twenty-Eighth Congregational Society of Boston: Its Services, Organization, Officers, and Principles*, Boston, 1883; Weiss, *1*, 259–60; Chadwick, *Parker*, pp. 202–4; Frothingham, *Parker*, p. 230.

106. Commager, *Parker*, p. 101; Frothingham, *Parker*, p. 216. The Melodeon building, formerly the Lion Tavern, had become the Lion Theatre, a hall for "dramatic and equestrian performances" in 1836, and then, in 1839, had been reconverted into a lecture and concert hall, called first the "Mechanics Institute" and then, when leased to the Handel and Haydn Society, the "Melodeon." From this period until construction of the Music Hall in 1852, it was known as "the leading concert and exhibition hall in Boston." Samuel A. Drake, *Old Landmarks and Historic Personages of Boston* (5th ed. Boston, 1876), p. 394. Winsor, *Memorial History of Boston, 4*, 371.

. . . Dancing monkeys and 'Ethiopian serenaders' . . . have occupied this spot during the week, and left their marks, their instruments, and their breath behind them on Sunday." [107]

The Music Hall, Boston

The Music Hall, newly constructed when the Twenty-Eighth Society moved into it in November 1852, made up in spaciousness and beauty for the loss of the intimacy of the smaller building. This elegant new home, which stood at the corner of Winter Street and Bumstead Place several blocks

107. A. A. Burrage, "Theodore Parker's Society," *Register*, February 14, 1889; Parker, "Some Account of My Ministry," *Works*, *13*, 81.

northeast of the Melodeon, normally seated 2,700—700 of whom sat in the galleries and 500 on the stage and steps behind the speaker. The hall was 130 feet long, with two balconies and no fewer than forty-two exit doors.

The character of the audiences as well as the nature of the place of worship determined the atmosphere in which Parker worked. Although the acoustics in the Music Hall were planned according to "all that was then knowable" in that science, Weiss recalled that Parker's voice was frequently drowned out by the noise of belated entrances and impatient departures through the forty-two doors. Parker also found it necessary to ask his hearers not to applaud during the sermon, and not to read books and newspapers while waiting for the service to begin.[108]

The Twenty-Eighth at one period had 7,000 names on its "Parish Register," [109] and Parker sometimes preached to overflow audiences of 3,000. As the sole pastor of this numerous flock he had little chance of establishing with them the normal relations between minister and people. It is probable, however, that most of his hearers had little desire for the usual relationships of a church. "It was his preaching," as Commager remarks, "that men wanted to hear." His hearers were "a crowd of unknown persons," and Chadwick remarked on the "erratic photosphere of iconoclasts and fanatics and Adullamites" which was always discernible. Parker's congregation, in short, was nearly as much a mere lecture-hall assemblage as the sanctuary of the Twenty-Eighth was a lecture and concert hall.[110]

108. Weiss, *1*, 407–9, 417.

109. Chadwick, *Parker*, p. 201. The statement at the head of the Parish Register read: "We, the undersigned, hereby signify our desire to join the society worshipping in the Melodeon [later "Music Hall"] under the instruction of Rev. Theodore Parker." *Christian Register*, February 14, 1889.

110. Chadwick, *Parker*, pp. 201–2, 210, 218; Commager, *Parker*, p. 116; Weiss, *1*, 415.

To Parker, who for all of his criticism of religious institutions was a great lover of decorum and order,[111] all of this might have seemed an intolerable price to pay for being "heard in Boston," had there been no parishioners of a more substantial sort. But there was a nucleus of some 200 persons [112] who regarded Parker as more than a stirring iconoclast and anti-slavery lecturer, who desired most of the traditional forms in a service of worship, and who wished to participate in parish activities of the usual sort.[113]

Parker knew the advantages of a large hall, and of a preaching style that appealed to many besides the pious. Indeed, his success in drawing crowds of 3,000 constituted part of the vindication which he desired both for himself and for Absolute Religion. But his inclusion of traditional exercises in the Sunday services shows how determined he

111. He always considered the clergyman's traditional black the only suitable garb for the pulpit. Weiss, *1*, 417.

112. An unidentified clipping, dated 1853, in the Parker collection at the Boston Public Library, puts the number of "paying members" at 230. John T. Sargent estimated that the nucleus of the Society numbered "not more than 200," and remarked that most of these were former members of the Suffolk Street Chapel which he himself had led until 1845, or were former parishioners of John Pierpont, who had left the Hollis Street Church in the same year. Sargent, *The Crisis of Unitarianism in Boston, as Connected with the Twenty-Eighth Congregational Society, with Some Account of the Origin and Decline of That Organization* (Boston, 1859), p. 23. These and other remarks in Sargent's little-known pamphlet reveal the deep resentment which that radical had come to feel against Parker and his Society. Sargent credited Clarke, Pierpont, and himself with having sacrificed to gain Parker a hearing in Boston, and implied that none of them had had much thanks for it. Ibid., p. 12.

113. Among the more prominent of such persons were Robert and Eliza Apthorp, Ednah D. Cheyney, Caroline Dall, Charles M. Ellis, William Lloyd Garrison, John C. Haynes, Julia Ward Howe, Samuel Gridley Howe, Rufus Leighton, Samuel May, and Franklin B. Sanborn. Chadwick, *Parker*, p. 203.

was to provide the full experience of worship for those who desired it—even if this should provoke a raising of newspapers and slamming of doors among those who had come for a lecture. The service is described as "of the plainest kind of the New England Puritan usage." Included were hymns, pastoral prayers, and the reading of Scripture.[114]

The form of the service, however, was traditional only in a limited sense. Following out the logic of his theological principles, Parker read the Bible "with such amendments or omissions as his moral sense required," and he gave occasional readings from the "inspired books" of other religions. He also extended the "voluntary principle" pioneered by Brownson and Clarke, ruling out the taking of a collection as well as the pew-ownership system. He took the marriage ceremony seriously, but had no personal use for the rites of Baptism and Holy Communion. Like Emerson, he was content that the latter two rites should be made available to those who found them helpful, but there is no record of his having administered either sacrament in his Boston parish.[115]

The formal organization of the Society was of the simplest kind. The pastor was assisted in parish affairs by a Clerk, a Treasurer, and a Standing Committee of nine members.[116]

Subsidiary parish organizations were formed, and had varying success. That which most nearly fulfilled Parker's expectations was the Committee of Benevolent Action, which collected and dispersed contributions for the poor; but the record of other ventures makes melancholy reading, as do the efforts of Parker and his biographers to excuse the failures.

114. Ibid., p. 211.
115. Ibid., p. 211; Weiss, *1*, 420; Parker, *Discourse of Religion*, p. 504. He did administer both Communion and Baptism at West Roxbury: Weiss, *1*, 182.
116. Parker, *Christian Church*, appendix, p. 37.

Parker had hoped to organize committees to represent the society in each of the great reform movements of the day. Nothing could have been more in harmony with his conception of a Christian Church, but he was forced to admit, in 1849, that "I have not time for all things of that sort." Individual members were active in reforms, Parker said, and it would have to be left at that.[117]

A Sunday School for poor children was tried, but this failed, according to Weiss, because of "the preponderating influence of the Catholic priests over our foreign population"; and the foreigners, it was thought, were "the only class needing this charity." Another attempt at forming a Sunday School, this time for the children of the parish, foundered because the young adults of the church, though willing to teach in the school, showed themselves "incredulous of its value or necessity." Parker himself acted as superintendent, but a few months' experiment convinced him, as Weiss records, "that the teachers were right, and that this class of children had sufficient direct instruction from other sources." [118]

Also designed to actualize Parker's notions of the true functions of a church were the Sunday afternoon meetings "for free discussion of what pertains to religion." Parker blamed "outsiders, who talked much, while they had little or nothing to say" for the short duration of this scheme. Details are not given, but apparently the announcement of public meetings for "free discussion" was taken at face value, and Parker as chairman was unable to cope with what resulted.

117. Frothingham, *Parker*, pp. 236–37.
118. Weiss, *1*, 418. Frothingham excused this failure by noting that "Sunday schools rarely prosper in cities; never, probably, in intelligent congregations that choose to teach their own children, and improve their Sunday leisure in their own way." Frothingham, *Parker*, p. 237.

Next, Parker tried a Sunday afternoon course on the history and interpretation of the Bible. But this did not succeed; few were attracted, a parishioner recalled later, by "the dry and methodical form of a critical analysis," and the idea was abandoned when the society moved to the Music Hall in 1852. A Saturday afternoon class for young women fared better and was continued for several years. Finally, just before Parker's last illness and departure in 1858, members of the church, without his help, organized a "fraternity," which sponsored lectures on "the great humane subjects of the day," and which later broadened into an organization for charitable works and social reform.[119]

The financial stability of the society was never assured. The reason given by Frothingham for this was that radicalism and riches do not go together. Chadwick goes a little deeper in noting that the extreme application of the voluntary principle meant that most of Parker's hearers gave nothing at all. But Parker, pinpointing the trouble still more exactly, protested that he was not much of a businessman, and bore this out repeatedly by proposing cuts in his own salary instead of calling upon his congregation for support of a reliable system of subscriptions.[120] Such a system does, however, appear to have been instituted after the society's removal to the Music Hall in 1852. A newspaper report of 1853 indicated that the 230 paying members, contributing from $1 to $100 each, had enabled the society to show a surplus for that year of $170 over expenditures of $3,500.[121]

119. Parker, "Experience as a Minister," *Works, 13,* 402–3. See also Frothingham, *Parker,* p. 238; Weiss, *1,* 417–19; and *The Parker Fraternity: Its Constitution and By-Laws, Officers, Donors, Past and Present Members, etc.,* Boston, 1864.

120. Frothingham, *Parker,* p. 239; Chadwick, *Parker,* p. 211.

121. Unidentified clipping, Parker Collection, Boston Public Library.

After its founder's final departure in 1858 the Twenty-Eighth was continued in one form or another for over thirty years. Though David A. Wasson was their regular minister for a short time in the 1860's,[122] the group depended mainly upon outside speakers, including laymen and occasionally women. As early as 1858, observers noted that the church was degenerating into a mere vehicle for the lecture-sponsoring activities of the Parker Fraternity. In 1863 the society moved back to the Melodeon, and three years later began to hold its meetings at the fraternity rooms on Washington Street. In 1873 a new Parker Memorial Meetinghouse was erected, but the society continued to decline, and in 1889 it was formally dissolved, the Parker Memorial being then transferred to the Benevolent Fraternity of Churches.[123]

The constructive reform ideas of all of these five Transcendentalists, and the experimental efforts of the last four who have been discussed, provide data for a fresh evaluation of that "practical religious interest" which has always been recognized as inherent in American Transcendentalism. A frequent observation about reformers is that they can unite in the work of destruction, but not in that of rebuilding. Emerson in 1844 thought it characteristic of the social and religious faddists of the preceding quarter century that "they defied each other, like a congress of kings, each of whom had a realm to rule, and a way of his own that made concert unprofitable." [124]

122. Wasson was a former Calvinist who in the 1850's had organized an "independent" society in Groveland, Mass. Ill health caused his resignation as pastor of the Twenty-Eighth in 1867, after two years of service there. He was a founder of the radical Free Religious Association in 1867. Persons, *Free Religion, an American Faith* (New Haven, Yale University Press, 1947), p. 27.

123. *The Twenty-Eighth Congregational Society*, pp. 2–3; Sargent, *The Crisis of Unitarianism*, p. 24; *Register*, February 14, 1889.

124. Emerson, "New England Reformers," *Works, 3,* 252.

Certainly Transcendentalism, with its varied prescriptions for social betterment, must fall generally under this indictment, and the Church-reforming wing of that movement cannot entirely escape from it. But underlying the diversities in religious program are striking resemblances. The long-range ideals of these reformers—the Church of the Future, the Broad Church, the Comprehensive Church, the Church of the People, the Order of the Sons of God, the New, True, and Final Churches—all partook of that supreme optimism which rode on the air of the 1830's and 1840's. Furthermore, all of these plans for the earthly Kingdom looked to the fulfillment of the Protestant principle in an actual "priesthood of all believers." And finally, in their common conception of social reform as the true basis for unity, they all proposed to carry the Unitarian axiom of "works before doctrine" to its logical conclusion. This reforming zeal, together with the interest in comprehensiveness which they shared, suggests at least a distant relationship to the ecumenical and social emphases in later Protestantism.

The experimental societies which were established as charter units in the Future Church also had much in common. They all attempted to reach classes of the community which were not welcomed in the older churches or were not attracted to them. Clarke's voluntary principle was used by each of these innovators, and this, together with the invitation which all of them extended to seekers and antiformalists, attracted intellectuals as well as the poorer classes. There was a marked common interest in spontaneity, expressed through their various plans for congregational participation or social and "conversational" meetings. And all of them made attempts, more or less fruitful, to minimize the distinction between pastor and people.

Only Clarke, among the Transcendentalist experimenters,

was able to establish a church organization that was strong
enough to continue effectively without its founder. Parker's
society degenerated into a kind of memorial lyceum association after his death, and the congregations of Brownson
and Channing made no efforts to stay together after their
pastors had gone on to other endeavors. What John T.
Sargent remarked about Parker's Twenty-Eighth Society
would apply equally well to the Channing and Brownson
experiments. The Twenty-Eighth, Sargent said, had never
had "a very fixed basis of association or consolidation. . . .
Its members gathered because of their sympathy with an
iconoclast." [125]

Clarke's more lasting success undoubtedly owed much
to his conception of his transcendentalized society as an
organic part of Unitarianism and of the Church Universal.
For, as Frederic Henry Hedge always warned, a school
of speculative theology cannot in itself fulfill the functions
of a Church. Still less can self-perpetuation be expected of
an organization which has the personality of one man as
its "basis of association." Brownson in the 1840's was so
completely won over to this view that he took refuge in
the supreme ecclesiastical continuity of the Church of
Rome. William Henry Channing, also gradually persuaded
of the values in a churchly tradition, became a zealous
promoter of Unitarian denominationalism. And most of
the other Transcendentalist reformers—Furness, Francis,
Bartol, and Osgood as well as Hedge and Clarke—had
from the start combined their radical idealism with a deep
awareness of the historical dimension of Christian experience.

125. Sargent, *The Crisis of Unitarianism*, p. 23.

Chapter 6

Transcendentalism and

American Liberal Religion

THE Unitarian denomination since the last years of the nineteenth century has officially defined Christianity, and
religion in general, very much as Theodore Parker defined
them. Parker's terminology appears in the modern by-laws
of the American Unitarian Association, where religion is
explained as "love to God and love to man," and where it
is suggested that this is the essence of Jesus' own teaching.[1]
Although no single statement of belief is accepted universally by Unitarian churches, the one which has been most
widely used in the present century proclaims "the Father-
hood of God, the Brotherhood of Man, the Leadership of
Jesus, Salvation by Character, and the Progress of Mankind Onward and Upward Forever." [2] The denomination

1. *Unitarian Year Book . . . and Annual Report* (Boston, American Unitarian Association, 1957), p. 13.

2. J. Paul Williams, *What Americans Believe and How They*

for over seventy years has declined to set any doctrinal standards for membership, and at present lists among its member churches a number of religious societies which have ceased to designate themselves as Christian.[3]

This withdrawal from the conservative confessional position of 1853 has been treated by most historians, and especially by Unitarian writers, as a vindication of the principles of Parker and the Transcendentalist reformers. But such an appraisal is justified only in part. While it is true that Parker's Absolute Religion was vindicated in these later developments, the victory of Parker in this respect was not a victory for Transcendentalism as a whole; it was, in fact, a repudiation of beliefs held by most Transcendentalists of Parker's generation. Furthermore, even the posthumous triumph of Parker himself was a strictly qualified one, for the final ascendency in Unitarianism of free religion over revealed Christianity was won by a radical generation in which intuitionist philosophy had failed to maintain itself, and for whom Parker's constant attempt to use traditional terminology in expressing radical ideas seemed unnecessary. The gradual acceptance of Transcendentalism after 1853, of which a brief account will be given here, should not, therefore, be looked upon as proof that Transcendentalist prescriptions were fully accepted by the new Unitarianism.

Worship (New York, Harper, 1952), p. 226. Further predominating beliefs of modern Unitarianism may be summarized as follows: The one-ness of God, the strict humanity of Jesus, the natural character of the Bible, the divine nature of man (and of Jesus as a man), entire freedom of opinion, and dependence upon the intellect and science in the search for truth. Frank S. Mead, *Handbook of Denominations* (New York, Abingdon–Cokesbury, 1951), p. 179; Charles Graves, "Unitarianism," *Encyclopedia Americana.*

3. Williams, *What Americans Believe*, pp. 228–31; Willard Sperry, *Religion in America* (New York, Macmillan, 1946), p. 89.

The process of *rapprochement* between the Transcendentalists and their opponents had no more striking illustration than in the changing attitude toward Emerson after that writer's final withdrawal from the ministry.

Cornelius Felton's review of the *Essays* in 1841 had been scornful to the point of personal insult. Transcendentalist opinions, he had said, were "ancient errors and sophistries, mistaken for new truths . . . high flying pretensions, set up by young ladies of both sexes." The author of the *Essays*, Felton had asserted, was neither a good Christian nor a good writer.

Within a few years, however, Emerson's growing literary reputation made this position of Felton's a difficult one to defend, and the *Examiner* in the later 1840's began to entrust most reviews of Emerson to the sympathetic hands of Hedge and Bartol, both of whom deplored the lack of any "recognition in his pages of the Christian faith," but otherwise were highly favorable. "We fear not even his errors," Bartol wrote in 1850; "we love his nobleness, we honor his integrity, we would emulate his candor. . . . He must speak benedictions to the world spite of his mistakes." [4]

By the 1860's, even the objections about Emerson's lack of religious faith began to be modified. Hedge, reviewing *The Conduct of Life* in 1861, remarked that the author "in all these years, has not ceased to preach. . . . Though his voice is no longer heard in Christian pulpits, yet what preaching can be more practical and evangelical than this?" The editor of the *Monthly Religious Magazine*, Rufus Ellis, in reviewing the same work, took a similar position,

---

4. Felton, in *Examiner*, *30* (1841), 257; Hedge, ibid., *38* (1845), 87–106; Bartol, ibid., *42* (1847), 255–62, and *48* (1850), 318. See also, for changes in the attitude toward Emerson, *Monthly Miscellany*, *5* (1841), 90–97, 346–47; *Register*, April 9, 1842 and April 27, 1850; *Examiner*, *47* (1849), 461.

and conceded that Emerson's doctrines had administered a necessary corrective to the "merely historical Christianity" preached by Unitarians in the 1830's.[5]

In the same decade, Harvard University, though not the Divinity School, ended its long boycotting of the former heresiarch, awarding him an honorary degree in 1866, electing him an Overseer and Phi Beta Kappa speaker in 1867, and sponsoring his lectures of 1870, "The Natural History of the Intellect." Finally, in 1874, the Divinity School also relaxed its proscription, and he spoke there in May 1874.[6]

The reinstatement of Parker, though just as complete as that of Emerson, did not begin until the 1860's. During the preceding decade, despite a growing respect for the radical preacher's antislavery leadership,[7] conservative Unitarians continued adamant against all that he stood for in the area of religion. In 1857, when a senior class at the Divinity School wished to invite Parker to be their graduation speaker, the faculty refused permission.[8] Parker's *Experience as a Minister*, written in 1859 during his voyage to Europe in search of health, was received coldly;[9] and the Association of Alumni of the Divinity School, at their annual meeting in 1859, refused to vote a resolution of sympathy to the dying man.[10] Even Parker's death, which

5. Hedge, in *Examiner*, 70 (1861), 149–50. Ellis, in *Monthly Religious Magazine*, 25 (1861), 65–66.

6. Rusk, *Life*, pp. 435, 488.

7. See *Examiner*, 68 (1860), 190; Chadwick, *Parker*, chap. 9.

8. Willard L. Sperry, " 'A Beautiful Enmity': the Student History in the 19th Century," in Williams, *Divinity School*, p. 163.

9. *Quarterly Journal of the American Unitarian Association*, 7, No. 1 (1859), 1–12; *Examiner*, 67 (1859), 282–86; ibid., 68 (1860), 189–91.

10. William H. Furness published a vigorous protest against this action (*A Word to Unitarians: A Discourse Delivered in the First Congregational Church* . . . Philadelphia, 1859), but Hedge

occurred at Florence in May 1860, brought no immediate change of attitude among Unitarian leaders. Of the almost numberless obituaries and memorials which were published in the succeeding few months, those which treated Parker as a perverse iconoclast and a non-Christian found most favor with the denominational journals.[11]

During the five years following, however, the official opinion was altered by several influences: by the natural effects of time, by the wartime growth of appreciation for a great leader of the antislavery cause, by John Weiss' biography of Parker (first published in 1863), and by a change in the editorship of the *Examiner*.[12] The Weiss biography, in particular, seemed to have a strong effect; most reviewers, including those in the *Examiner*, spoke of it as helping to correct the "harsh popular impression" of the man and his opinions.[13] By 1865 the trend toward acceptance of Parker had definitely set in. It was not to be reversed.

The less radical Transcendentalists, who had encountered little opposition even in the pre-1853 period, also extended their influence in these later years.

---

argued that since resolutions of sympathy had never been voted for members in good standing, it would have been impolitic to vote one for Parker. *Examiner*, 67 (1859), 435–39.

11. *The Monthly Journal of the American Unitarian Association* published extracts from sermons and articles on Parker by Bartol, W. H. Channing, O. B. Frothingham, Edmund H. Sears, George H. Hepworth, and several others. Bartol's, the most highly critical of Parker, was thought by the editors to be the most satisfactory: *Monthly Journal*, 1 (1860), 445–60. The *Register* and the *Monthly Religious Magazine* agreed: *Register*, July 14, 1860; *Religious Magazine*, 24 (1860), 73–88.

12. Joseph H. Allen replaced the more conservative team of Hedge and Hale in 1861.

13. *Examiner*, 76 (1864), 1–24; 77 (1864), 38; *Monthly Journal*, 5 (1864), 184–86. See also *Examiner*, 72 (1862), 297, 384–86; 79 (1865), 138. But cf. *Monthly Religious Magazine*, 31 (1864), 170–76.

Frederic Henry Hedge, after a pastorate in Providence (1850–56), accepted a call to the Unitarian church in Brookline, where he remained until 1872. While at Brookline, he was nonresident professor of Ecclesiastical History in Harvard Divinity School, and he continued in the latter position until 1878. He received honorary doctorates from Harvard in 1852 and 1886, served for a decade as professor of German in Harvard College, edited the *Examiner* for a period of four years, and was president of the American Unitarian Association between 1859 and 1862. Hedge's writings, which appeared in prodigious numbers in this later period, were important in providing a rationale for the work of denominational organization that was being led in the postwar period by Henry W. Bellows; and his *Reason in Religion* (1865) was a particularly influential statement of the Broad Church objectives which came to fruition under Bellows' vigorous leadership.[14]

The contributions of James Freeman Clarke were along similar lines. He was a Director of the American Unitarian Association, an Overseer of Harvard College (and recipient of a doctorate in 1863), a nonresident professor of Natural Religion and Christian Doctrine in the Divinity School (1867–71), and later a lecturer on Ethnic Religions in the same institution (1876-77). Of Clarke's 64 publications in this later period, the most important were his *Ten Great Religions* (1871–83), a pioneer comparative study, and *Self-Culture* (1880), which taught a combination of Emersonian self-reliance and Puritan God-reliance. In his *Manual of Unitarian Belief* (1884) he provided a general credal statement which was designed to satisfy both the Transcendental and the scientific schools in post-Civil War Unitarianism, and which succeeded so well in this mediating

14. Eliot, 3. Wells' bibliography lists 42 books, articles, and other writings by Hedge in the post-1853 period. Wells, pp. 220–22.

aim that it is still used, in the slightly revised edition of 1924, to set forth the doctrinal stand of the denomination.[15]

William Henry Channing, though he never attained the stature of Hedge or Clarke as a denominational leader, was another who helped to mediate between Transcendentalism and regular Unitarianism in the period after 1853. Spending his later years in England, he became something of an international figure in the denomination. In 1854 he accepted an invitation to become the minister at Renshaw Street

James Freeman Clarke

Chapel in Liverpool, and three years later he was chosen as James Martineau's successor at Hope Street Chapel in the same city. He returned to the United States during the Civil War to serve as pastor of the Unitarian society in Washington, D.C., and as chaplain of the House of Representatives. After the war he again held pastorates in England, but he was warmly received by Unitarians in America on his occasional visits to this country.

Channing's personal liking for churchly traditions, which had occasionally been evident even in his most radical period and had nearly made him a convert to Catholicism in 1835, became more marked during this later career.

15. Revised by Charles T. Billings, Boston, Beacon Press, 1924.

His biographer records that he "put on the gown, wore a high collar and a white cravat, [and] wanted a lofty pulpit." Always a preacher of social reform and a highly spiritualized theology, he came to surpass Hedge as a living example of the combination of "intellectual radicalism and ecclesiastical conservatism." [16]

The later influence of Convers Francis was exerted almost solely through his professorship in the Harvard Divinity School, which he held until his death in 1863. Francis was so "all-sided" in his opinions that his precise contribution to the spread of Transcendentalist ideas is difficult to assess. It has been estimated, however, that by 1860 some twenty-five Unitarian clergymen were adherents of Parkerite views; [17] and the number sympathetic to a milder form of Transcendentalist doctrine was undoubtedly much larger. Although Divinity School students imbibed their radicalism from many sources outside of the instruction of the School, former protégés of Francis remembered him as one whose receptivity to new ideas and constant encouragement of unfettered thought did much to inculcate a respect for Transcendentalist intuitionism.[18]

Several other members of the original New School helped to make Transcendentalism a respected point of view in the post-1853 period. Cyrus Bartol, pastor of the West Church until 1889, became increasingly radical in his later

16. Frothingham, *Channing*, pp. 113–14, 285–91, 348, 396–97.

17. Earl M. Wilbur, *Our Unitarian Heritage: An Introduction to the History of the Unitarian Movement* (Boston, Beacon Press, 1925), p. 443. The *Harvard Quinquennial Catalogue* shows that 158 men were graduated from the Divinity School between 1840 and 1860. Not all, of course, entered the Unitarian ministry.

18. Newell, "Memoir," pp. 245–48; Eliot *3*, 119; Persons, *Free Religion*, p. 22. For the gradual movement of the Divinity School toward intuitionist doctrine see Ahlstrom, in Williams, *Divinity School*, pp. 135–45.

years, and came to be regarded by some as the ideological successor of Parker, whom he had criticized so bitterly at an earlier time.[19] Samuel Osgood, who served from 1849 to 1869 in the New York pastorate formerly held by Orville Dewey, preached an intuitionism which, though moderate, contrasted strongly with the views of his predecessor.[20] William H. Furness continued as pastor of the First Unitarian Church in Philadelphia until 1896, influential through numerous books and pamphlets in promoting a naturalistic interpretation of the Gospels.[21]

A number of younger Unitarian ministers, converted to Transcendentalism during the 1840's and after, assisted in restoring the Transcendental position to respectability during the postwar period. Some of them, like O. B. Frothingham and John W. Chadwick, came to believe that scientific demonstration, rather than intuition, must form the basis of religious faith; but David Wasson, Samuel

19. Bartol, *Radical Problems*, Boston, 1872; *Harvard Graduates' Magazine*, 9 (1900–01), 421; *Lamb's Biographical Dictionary*.

20. Osgood became an Episcopal clergyman in 1869. Eliot, 3, 87.

21. Others of the early Transcendentalists whose pastorates continued into this period were Charles T. Brooks, Caleb Stetson, and Sylvester Judd: Eliot, 2, 3. A word may be added here about the several early Transcendentalists who had left the ministry by the 1850's. George Ripley, after the failure of Brook Farm in 1847, continued to edit the Fourierist *Harbinger* until 1849; in the latter year he assumed the position which he held until his death in 1880, as literary editor of Greeley's *Tribune*. Orestes Brownson, operating mainly through his rechristened *Brownson's Quarterly Review*, pursued a hectic career as a Catholic polemicist until his death in 1876. John S. Dwight, editor for thirty years of *Dwight's Journal of Music*, built a substantial reputation as a guide of the public's musical tastes. Christopher Cranch had a happy but relatively unproductive career as a painter and dilettante for some thirty years after leaving the ministry in 1841. Jones Very, the mystic poet, held Unitarian pastorates until the late 1850's; and then, at age 45, went into retirement for his last twenty years. For brief sketches of all of this latter group see *DAB*.

Johnson, Thomas Wentworth Higginson, and to some extent John Weiss, remained loyal to intuitionism.[22] And Frothingham and Chadwick, who between them produced most of the early biographies of Transcendentalists, retained a sentimental attachment to the older philosophy, looking upon it as the happy childhood phase of a free religion which since had matured to years of discretion and realism.

The cumulative effect of all of these forms of Transcendentalist infiltration can be seen in the Unitarian denominational histories which began to appear at the end of the nineteenth century. The important place given to Transcendentalism in these volumes shows how completely the former heresy had gained acceptance as "an inevitable step of intellectual advance." Dr. Channing and Theodore Parker were generally, by this time, accorded equal status as the great Unitarian leaders of their respective eras, and J. H. Allen cited the portraits of the two men "that serenely face each other" at the headquarters of the American Unitarian Association as proof that Parker had been fully installed in the Unitarian gallery of worthies.[23]

Unitarians of the late nineteenth century looked back upon this gradual acceptance of Parkerite Transcendentalism as a perfectly natural and inevitable development, the logical consequence of adherence to traditional Unitarian principles. But this is only half the story. The Unitarianism of earlier decades had had, after all, two major principles, not just one; the Unitarianism of Channing had coupled

22. Persons, *Free Religion*, pp. 22–31.

23. Joseph H. Allen, *Our Liberal Movement in Theology*, p. 66; "Historical Sketch," p. 215. See also Channing Hall Lectures, *Unitarianism: Its Origin and History* (Boston, 1895), chaps. 8–10 passim; Cooke, *Unitarianism*, pp. 197–201; Fenn, in *Religious History*, pp. 126–29; Wilbur, *History*, p. 464. The American Unitarian Association first sponsored an edition of Parker's writings in 1885 (Parker, *Views of Religion*, ed. James F. Clarke, Boston, 1885).

free inquiry with acceptance of revealed Christianity. The new Unitarianism of the 1890's, therefore, though perhaps a logical development of one set of historic ideals, was a virtually complete rejection of the other.

The history of the post-Civil War movement toward inclusiveness shows, moreover, that the gains of the anti-confessional party were not easily won. Proponents of revealed Christianity fought the radical movement bitterly at every step.

At the organizational meeting of the National Conference (the first truly representative Unitarian body) in 1865, Henry W. Bellows and other leaders resorted to deft parliamentary maneuvering to keep the phrase "Lord Jesus Christ," which offended some of the radicals, in the preamble of the proposed constitution.[24] And when the radicals tried again, in the annual meeting of 1866, to open the National Conference to those who did not believe in "the lordship of Jesus," Bellows, Clarke, and Hedge again defeated this move. The disaffected "free religionists" felt obliged to form a separate Association.[25]

24. Persons, *Free Religion*, pp. 15–16. Pursuing a middle course, Bellows also stifled conservative attempts to commit the Conference to the supernaturalist principles of the 1853 Declaration: Wilbur, *History*, p. 470.

25. Persons, *Free Religion*, pp. 39–54. The new group, called the Free Religious Association, was active from 1867 to 1897. Throughout that time it suffered from an internal division into Transcendentalist and "scientific theist" factions. Among its more prominent members, the second-generation Transcendentalists—such men as Weiss and Higginson—opposed the empirical approach championed by Francis E. Abbot, E. C. Towne, and the converted O. B. Frothingham. There was constant dissension, also, about the group's relationship to Unitarianism. As the credal stipulations of that denomination were gradually liberalized in the 1880's and after, the majority of the Free Religionists returned to the Unitarian fold, although Abbot and some others refused to do so. Ibid., pp. 35–38, 127, 155–56.

After this purging of the radical element in 1866, the defenders of revealed Christianity continued to dominate the National Conference for a period of sixteen years, although the controversial preamble was somewhat liberalized in 1872. In the 1880's, however, after many of the strongest advocates of a distinctly Christian confession had passed away (N. L. Frothingham in 1870, Gannett in 1871, Dewey and Bellows in 1882, Lothrop in 1886, Clarke in 1888), a new advance of radicalism overwhelmed the conservative position. A constitutional amendment in 1882 reopened the Conference to "any who, while differing from us in belief, are in general sympathy with our purposes and practical views," and the convention of 1894, reaffirming this invitation to the radicals, adopted the statement that "these churches accept the religion of Jesus, holding, in accordance with his teaching, that practical religion is summed up in love to God and love to man." [26] This use of Parker's definition of Christianity served to emphasize how completely the confessional dike of 1853 had been broken through by postwar currents of radicalism.

The Unitarian denomination could be said by the 1890's to have accepted the most extreme Parkerite conclusions about the "religion of Jesus." Unitarians had gone on record as believing that Jesus was a human teacher who happened to enunciate nearly all of the truths of Absolute Religion; and their statement of the denominational position made it plain also that the church welcomed those who could not accept even this minimal estimate. The radical faction which produced this result was partly "scientific theist" in religious philosophy and partly extreme Transcendentalist, with the believers in science holding an in-

26. Wilbur, *History*, p. 484. For progress of the same controversy in the West see Charles H. Lyttle, *Freedom Moves West: A History of the Western Unitarian Conference, 1852–1952*, Boston, Beacon Press, 1952.

creasing numerical superiority as the years passed. The most nearly precise statement, then, about the influence of Parkerism within the denomination, is that its definition of true religion was accepted, while the intuitionist rationale for the definition was not.

The less extreme Transcendentalist doctrines, which had been incorporated into Unitarianism long before the 1890's, eventually came to be accepted outside the denomination as well. A distinguished leader of Congregationalism, John W. Platner, in 1917 fittingly described the Unitarian Movement retrospectively as the "acute liberalization" of Christianity in nineteenth-century America.[27] Unitarianism, in other words, was a cutting edge for liberal religion. In the Transcendental period, biblical certainties, pulpit formalism, and the social traditionalism of the churches had been the prime objects of liberalization; and these were also the matters upon which liberals of all denominations were concentrating by the end of the century.

Outside of Unitarianism just as within it, "scientific" liberals rather than intuitionists presided over the formation of the New Theology of the 1880's and after. John Fiske and Lyman Abbott successfully summoned Christians to a Darwinian pilgrimage "from Nature to God";[28] and the typical starting-point in this kind of religion was not an idea in individual consciousness but rather a search for scientifically verifiable facts about the universe and man's relation to it. But the main outlines of the later liberalism were very much the same whether argued from a Platonic, Hegelian, or Darwinian premise. The New

27. "Congregationalists," in *Religious History*, p. 57.
28. Herbert W. Schneider, *Religion in Twentieth Century America* (Cambridge, Mass., Harvard University Press, 1952), pp. 117–26. Ira V. Brown, *Lyman Abbot, Christian Evolutionist: A Study in Religious Liberalism*, Cambridge, Harvard University Press, 1953.

Theology stressed tolerance, both toward differing sects within Christianity and toward non-Christian religions. It emphasized the continuity between the natural and the supernatural, the human and the divine. It expressed a marked optimism about the nature and the future earthly prospects of man, and trusted human faculties (though differing as to which ones) in the search for truth. Good character, according to this liberalism, was more to be desired than right opinion, and effectiveness in social action was regarded as a primary test of individual character. Whether scientific or intuitionist, the liberals found God immanent in man and nature.[29] Transcendental religious thought, along with frontier evangelicalism and the theologies of Nathaniel Taylor and Horace Bushnell, had been a forerunner and herald of these later Protestant formulations.[30]

29. John Dillenberger and Claude Welch, *Protestant Christianity Interpreted through Its Development* (New York, Scribner's, 1954), pp. 211–24; Henry P. Van Dusen, "The Liberal Movement in Theology," in Samuel McC. Cavert and H. P. Van Dusen, eds., *The Church through Half a Century* (New York, Scribner's, 1936), pp. 68–70; John C. Bennett, "After Liberalism–What?" *Christian Century* (November 8, 1933), pp. 1403–4.

30. For the similarities of emphasis in Transcendentalism and revivalism see Timothy L. Smith, *Revivalism and Social Reform in Mid-Nineteenth-Century America* (New York, Abingdon, 1957), pp. 141–43. Studies of Taylor and Bushnell are Sidney Mead, *Nathaniel William Taylor, 1786–1858: A Connecticut Liberal*, Chicago, University of Chicago Press, 1942; and Barbara M. Cross, *Horace Bushnell: Minister to a Changing America*, Chicago, University of Chicago Press, 1958. Transcendentalist influence in various areas of later liberal religion is attested in Schneider, *Religion in Twentieth Century America*, p. 117; Stow Persons, "Evolution and Theology in America," in Persons, ed., *Evolutionary Thought in America* (New York, Braziller, 1956), pp. 424, 439–40; Charles H. Hopkins, *The Rise of the Social Gospel in American Protestantism, 1865–1915* (New Haven, Yale University Press, 1940) pp. 4–5.

The idealistic philosophy championed by the Transcendentalists was by no means wholly submerged in this later period, despite the popularity of other systems. German idealism, in both its Kantian and its Hegelian forms, began to gain a solid footing in American academic curricula during the closing years of the nineteenth century.[31] As early as the 1870's, such champions of Lockean philosophy as Francis Bowen of Harvard and Noah Porter of Yale had begun to speak appreciatively of the Germanic contributions.[32] Idealism then came into its own as an academic philosophy in the speculative idealism promoted by J. E. Creighton, the dynamic idealism of George Sylvester Morris, the personalism of Borden Bowne, and the absolute idealism of Josiah Royce.

All of these idealistic systems owed basic insights to the romantic version of German philosophy which the Transcendentalists had helped to domesticate in this country. Absolute idealism, for example, shared and developed the emphasis of the Transcendentalists upon cosmic unity; Personalism reflected Transcendentalist concentration upon the self as basic to philosophical construction. And various forms of ethical intuitionism followed the earlier romantics in finding an immediately known moral imperative at the root of religious and philosophical knowledge.[33] Even the pragmatism of Peirce and James has been shown to owe a significant debt to the Transcendentalists.[34] Although

31. Harvey G. Townsend, *Philosophical Ideas in the United States* (New York, American Book Co., 1934), pp. 97, 115.

32. Bowen, *Modern Philosophy from Descartes to Schopenhauer and Hartmann* (New York, 1877), chaps. 10–14 and 17–20 passim; Porter, "The Kantian Centennial," *Princeton Review*, new ser. *8* (1881), 394–424.

33. Schneider, *American Philosophy*, pp. 466–90; Henry N. Wieman and B. E. Meland, *American Philosophies of Religion* (Chicago, Willett, Clark, 1936), pp. 99–211.

34. Frederic I. Carpenter, "William James and Emerson," *Ameri-*

German idealism never won the pre-eminent place its champions in Concord and St. Louis had expected it to gain, it did exert a powerful influence upon later American philosophical and religious thought.

As Parkerite radicalism was gaining its secure place in the structure of modern Unitarianism, there came to be fewer strong voices within the denomination to reiterate the warnings of the conservative Unitarians and moderate Transcendentalists of an earlier period. The most direct successors to the ideas of Hedge, Lothrop, and Dr. Channing, therefore, were Protestant liberals outside of Unitarianism, men whose theology was strikingly similar to the earlier Christian Unitarianism but whose commitment to the Christian Confession made it impossible for them to sympathize with the Parkerite Unitarianism of the 1890's.

George Angier Gordon, minister to the Old South Congregational Church, expressed the sentiments of such liberals in 1895 as he analyzed the apparent capitulation of the Christian Unitarians to free religion. Gordon argued that this capitulation had effectively isolated the Unitarians from the main forces of liberal Christianity, and he called upon the denomination to continue the work of Channing and Hedge, who had creatively reinterpreted the traditional Christian doctrines, instead of following the Parkerites who had discarded those doctrines. Unitarianism had been a power in American religion, he said, because of its role in the nineteenth-century re-evaluation of the sources of religious authority, and because its leaders, once their

can Literature, 11 (1939), 39–57; "Charles Sanders Peirce: Pragmatic Transcendentalist," New England Quarterly, 14 (1941), 34–48; "The Genteel Tradition: A Re-interpretation," New England Quarterly, 15 (1942), 427–43. Henry A. Pochmann, New England Transcendentalism and St. Louis Hegelianism: Phases in the History of American Idealism (Philadelphia, Carl Schurz Memorial Foundation, 1948), pp. 122–25.

critical work was done, had given thought to a possible "deeper return" to basic Christian affirmations. If the Unitarian Movement should "spend its force and run out," Gordon added, "it will be owing to this one thing, more than to all others, that its leaders today have given up this meditation of a deeper return to the past." [35] Such warnings, coupled with insistence upon what Hedge had called "the distinction involved in the Christian confession," were as often heard among adherents of the New Protestantism as they had been among the earlier Christian Unitarians.

This similarity of attitude in judging the requirements for a truly Christian liberalism does not necessarily indicate a clear line of influence from the Unitarian conservatives to the New Theology (although such influence can be shown in individual cases). The point is that the stand taken by Unitarians against Parker's views was not considered ridiculous by a later generation of liberal Christians.

35. George A. Gordon, *The Christ of Today* (Boston, 1895), pp. 143–46. Gordon's point of view has been reflected within Unitarianism in recent years by an influential minority group, known as the Unitarian Christian Fellowship, whose purpose is "to preserve and strengthen the Christian essence of Unitarianism." See their publication, the *Unitarian Christian*. A leader in this movement, George H. Williams of Harvard, contends that Unitarianism has "lost communication" with contemporary theology, and deplores the effects of Unitarian "isolation from the main Christian forces, combined with our stereotyped insistence that we are in the vanguard . . ." Williams, *Rethinking the Unitarian Relationship with Protestantism: An Examination of the Thought of Frederic Henry Hedge (1805–1890)* (Boston, Beacon Press, 1949), p. 11. The aims of the Christian Unitarian group received a setback, however, when the national Association voted in 1957 to substitute the word "Unitarian" for "Christian" in the title of the historic *Register*. See *Christian Century* (June 19, 1957), p. 173. A "resolution of clarification" was approved by the Association the following spring. This stated "that the delegates . . . cherish the historic Judaeo-Christian heritage of Unitarianism" and also "affirm the universal sources and inspiration of modern Unitarian faith . . ." *Unitarian Register*, *137* (1958), 6.

The record of Transcendentalist efforts in the field of religion makes it clear that their "spiritual principle" was actively and often constructively applied to the specific problems of the Church. Transcendental religion was not simply a general faith that found its expression in literary works and social reform; nor was the Church, for a significant group of Transcendentalists, merely a stopping-place on the way to other careers. While the work of several important adherents of the movement can be fully understood without reference to practical religious objectives, it is plain that Transcendentalism as a whole cannot be.

The evident variety of opinion among the Unitarian conservatives, considered along with the similar diversity in Transcendentalism itself, indicates that the religious discussions of the Transcendentalist period must be viewed as a spectrum rather than as a polarized field. On detailed matters there were many groupings, and even on the essentials at least four "parties" are clearly discernible. Among the conservatives, those who opposed all transcendental philosophy must be distinguished from their moderate brethren who feared only the more radical conclusions. The Transcendentalist reformers must be divided into those who worked within the framework of the Christian confession and those who did not.

The clarifying of these distinctions shows the weakness in the traditional, polarizing, epithets. That Unitarianism was "corpse-cold" may perhaps be suggested by Norton's *Latest Form of Infidelity*, but the slogan will not fit Ware's *Personality of the Deity*. The "warmth" of transcendental theology is much more evident in the writings of Clarke and W. H. Channing than in Parker's scheme of Absolute Religion or in Emerson's exposition of the self-executing spiritual laws.

It may seem that such distinctions and qualifications deprive the theological debate of its drama. But Norton and Parker remain in their places; the conflict between their extreme positions is still important and still dramatic. And the calmer discussions of the moderates make up for their lack of intensity by a provision of deeper insights into the perplexities of the liberal tradition. Men like Clarke and Gannett were not discussing the relatively clear-cut issues which arise between free expression and hide-bound reaction. They were struggling with a problem which makes far greater demands upon the liberal intellect—the problem of giving principles of freedom an institutional form. It was these men, not the Nortons and Parkers, who were sensitive to the real dilemma of their denomination.

The two moderate groups by the mid-1850's had resolved this dilemma in a way that was satisfactory at least to the majority in their immediate generation. Their agreement lay in the conviction that, just as a free government must define citizenship, so Unitarians must candidly define the difference between being in the Church and being out of it. For some forty years the moderates held the line with this assertion, successfully resisting the demands for stringent credal requirements on one hand and for complete inclusiveness on the other.

In the history of American Christianity, this attempt to solve a classic liberal dilemma is at least as important as the clash between radical Transcendentalism and extreme Unitarian traditionalism. The eventual breakdown of the moderate solution within Unitarianism could not nullify the contributions made by both the Transcendentalists and their opponents to that humanistic Protestantism which expressed the outlook and aspirations of so many nineteenth-century Americans, and which retains a respected place in the religious thought of today.

BIBLIOGRAPHICAL ESSAY

MANUSCRIPTS

Of the several manuscript collections consulted, that which proved of most value for this study was the Andrews Norton Collection at the Harvard University Library. The Henry W. Bellows Collection at the Massachusetts Historical Society is useful mainly for the post-1853 period, but did yield several items relating to the earlier controversy. Also consulted were the Cornelius C. Felton Papers at Harvard, the George E. Ellis Papers at the Massachusetts Historical Society, and the Emerson Papers, deposited by the Ralph Waldo Emerson Memorial Association at the Harvard University Library. The large Brownson Collection, in the Archives at the University of Notre Dame, includes two scrapbooks of clippings from the otherwise unavailable Boston *Reformer* and from various contemporary periodicals. The Parker Collection, deposited in the Boston Public Library, was consulted for information about the Twenty-Eighth Congregational Society.

NEWSPAPERS AND PERIODICALS

The most important Transcendentalist publications—the *Dial*, the *Western Messenger*, the *Boston Quarterly Review*, the *Harbinger*, the *Present*, the *Spirit of the Age*, and the *Massachusetts Quarterly Review*—have all been useful for this study, as have the less well-known Boston *Reformer*, edited by Orestes Brownson, and the Boston *Observer and Religious Intelligencer*, of which George Ripley was editor. The history and contents of all of these publications except the last two are treated in *The Periodicals of American Transcendentalism*, by Clarence L. F. Gohdes, Durham, N.C., Duke University Press, 1931.

Information on the reaction of Unitarian conservatives to Transcendentalism has been drawn mainly from the two most important Unitarian periodicals of the Transcendentalist period, the *Christian Examiner* and the *Christian Register*. Also of substantial value were the *Monthly Miscellany of Religion and Letters*, the *Monthly Religious Magazine and Theological Review*, and the *Quarterly Journal* (after 1859 the *Monthly Journal*) *of the American Unitarian Association*. Data on all of these Unitarian periodicals may be found in Frank Luther Mott's *History of American Magazines*, 4 vols. Cambridge, Mass., Harvard University Press, 1938–57. William Cushing's *Index to the Christian Examiner* (Boston, 1879) was invaluable for identification of authors of unsigned articles in that journal.

The following newspapers, all published in Boston, were consulted for materials on certain episodes in the Transcendentalist controversy: the *Daily Advertiser*, the *Morning Post*, the *Courier*, and the *New England Puritan*.

PUBLISHED WRITINGS OF
THE TRANSCENDENTALISTS

The best bibliography of writings by (as well as on) the Transcendentalists is in Vol. 3 of Robert E. Spiller et al., *Literary History of the United States*, 3 vols. New York, Macmillan, 1948. Another valuable bibliography is in Vol. 1

of the *Cambridge History of American Literature*, 3 vols. New York, G. P. Putnam, 1921. For the writings of individual Transcendentalists see George Willis Cooke, *A Bibliography of Ralph Waldo Emerson*, Boston, Houghton Mifflin, 1908; Edward Everett Hale, ed., *James Freeman Clarke: Autobiography, Diary, and Correspondence*, Boston, 1891; Ronald Vale Wells, *Three Christian Transcendentalists: James Marsh, Caleb Sprague Henry, Frederic Henry Hedge*, New York, Columbia University Press, 1943; William Newell, "Memoir of the Rev. Convers Francis, D.D.," *Proceedings of the Massachusetts Historical Society* (March 1865), pp. 252–53; and the bibliographies of Ripley, W. H. Channing, Furness, Parker, Bartol, and other Transcendentalists in Samuel A. Eliot, ed., *Heralds of a Liberal Faith*, 4 vols. Boston, American Unitarian Association, 1910–52.

The most widely used of the several editions of the writings of Emerson is the Centenary Edition, *The Complete Works of Ralph Waldo Emerson*, 12 vols. Boston, Houghton Mifflin, 1903–04. The *Journals of Ralph Waldo Emerson* were edited by Edward W. Emerson and Waldo E. Forbes, 10 vols. Boston, Houghton Mifflin, 1909–14, and *The Letters of Ralph Waldo Emerson* by Ralph L. Rusk, 6 vols. New York, Columbia University Press, 1939. For a collection of Emerson's sermons, with a useful introduction, see Arthur C. McGiffert, Jr., *Young Emerson Speaks: Unpublished Discourses on Many Subjects by Ralph Waldo Emerson*, Boston, Houghton Mifflin, 1938. Parker's works are in the Centenary Edition (15 vols., titles vary), Boston, American Unitarian Association, 1907–13. Brownson's are in 20 volumes, *The Works of Orestes A. Brownson*, Henry F. Brownson, ed., Detroit, 1882–88. Characteristic writings of Brownson have been assembled by Alvan S. Ryan in *The Brownson Reader*, New York, P. J. Kenedy, 1955. Perry Miller has presented a number of Transcendentalist pieces, including many previously available only in manuscript or pamphlet form, in *The Transcendentalists: An Anthology*, Cambridge, Mass., Harvard University Press, 1950. Most of the Transcendentalist writings which relate to their controversy with the Unitarians may be found in the periodicals listed above or in the various collected works. Those which are not to be found in these places, and which are not published in full in Miller's anthology, are the following: George Ripley's *Discourses on the Philosophy of Religion*, Boston, 1836; "*The Latest Form of Infidelity*" *Examined: A Letter to Mr. Andrews Norton* . . . Boston, 1839; *Defence of* " '*The Latest Form of Infidelity*' *Examined*": *A Second Letter to Mr. Andrews Norton* . . . Boston, 1840; *Defence of* " '*The Latest Form of Infidelity*' *Examined*": *A Third Letter* . . . Boston, 1840; and *A Letter Addressed to the Congregational Church in Purchase Street by its Pastor*, Boston, 1840. Also, Orestes A. Brownson, *A Discourse on the Wants of the Times* . . . Boston, 1836; Convers Francis, *Christianity as a Purely Internal Principle*, American Unitarian Association Tract Series, 105, Boston, 1836; and William H. Furness, *The Exclusive Principle Considered*, Boston, 1836. Significant pamphlet contributions by Transcendentalist sympathizers are *The True Position of Rev. Theodore Parker*, by John T. Sargent, Boston, 1845; *Remarks on an Article in the "Christian Examiner" Entitled "Mr. Parker and His Views,"* by William P. Atkinson, Boston, 1845; and *An Answer to "Questions Addressed to the Rev. Theodore Parker and His Friends,"* by "A Friend Indeed," Boston, 1845.

Information on the experimental religious societies of Clarke, Brownson, Channing, and Parker is contained in their respective biographies (cited below), and also in the following sources: James F. Clarke, *A Sermon on the Principles and Methods of the Church of the Disciples*, Boston, 1846; *Articles of Organization and Rules of the Church of the Disciples,* rev. ed. Boston, 1868; Isaac Hecker, "Dr. Brownson in Boston," *Catholic World, 45* (1887), 466–72; W. H. Channing, *A Statement of the Principles of the Christian Union,* New York, 1843; *The Twenty-Eighth Congregational Society of Boston; Its Services, Organization, Officers, and Principles,* Boston, 1883; and John T. Sargent, *The Crisis of Unitarianism in Boston, as Connected with the Twenty-Eighth Congregational Society* . . . Boston, 1859.

PUBLISHED WRITINGS OF
UNITARIAN CONSERVATIVES

William E. Channing's writings are available in a one-volume edition, *The Works of William E. Channing, D.D.,* Boston, 1877. Other collected writings are *The Works of Joseph Stevens Buckminster; with Memoirs of his Life,* 2 vols. Boston, 1839; *The Works of Charles Follen, with a Memoir of His Life,* 5 vols. Boston, 1841–42; and *The Works of Orville Dewey, D.D., with a Biographical Sketch,* Boston, 1883. The *Tracts of the American Unitarian Association* (Boston, 1825–60) supplement the *Examiner* as a general source for information about the conservative position. The following books and pamphlets have a particular bearing on the Transcendentalist controversy: Andrews Norton, *The Evidences of the Genuineness of the Gospels,* 3 vols. Boston, 1837–44; *A Statement of Reasons for Not Believing the Doctrines of Trinitarians Concerning the Nature of God and the Person of Christ,* Boston, 1819; *A Discourse on the Latest Form of Infidelity* . . . Cambridge, Mass., 1839; *Remarks on a Pamphlet Entitled* " 'The Latest Form of Infidelity' *Examined,*" Cambridge, Mass., 1839; *Two Articles from the "Princeton Review" Concerning the Transcendental Philosophy of the Germans and of Cousin, and Its Influence on Opinion in This Country,* Cambridge, Mass., 1840. Also Henry Ware, Jr., *The Personality of the Diety*, Boston, 1838; Nathaniel L. Frothingham, *Deism or Christianity?* Boston, 1845; *The South Boston Unitarian Ordination*, Boston, 1841; *Answers to Questions not Contained in Mr. Parker's Letter to the Boston Association of Congregational Ministers*, by "one not of the Association," Boston, 1845; and *The Twenty-Eighth Report of the American Unitarian Association, with the Addresses at the Anniversary*, Boston, 1853.

HISTORIES AND STUDIES
OF TRANSCENDENTALISM

The most recent general study of the Transcendental Movement, Alexander Kern's "The Rise of Transcendentalism," in *Transitions in American Literary History*, ed. Harry Hayden Clark (Durham, N.C., Duke University Press, 1953), is the most satisfactory account which has appeared to date, even though the spatial limitations of a general survey have prevented inclusion of desirable detail at many points; Kern's annotations provide an up-to-date guide to recent scholarship on Transcendentalism. Additional histories of the movement, in the order of their general usefulness to the scholar, are Harold C. Goddard's *Studies in New England Transcendentalism*, New York, Columbia University Press, 1908; and Octavius B. Frothingham's *Transcendentalism in New England: A History*, New York, 1876. Other studies of some value are *Transcendentalism in New England: A Lecture*, by Caroline W. H. Dall, Boston, 1897. *Transcendentalism, With Preludes on Current Events*, by Joseph Cook, Boston, 1878; Francis Tiffany's "Transcendentalism: the New England Renaissance," in Channing Hall Lectures, *Unitarianism: Its Origin and History*, Boston, 1890; and Thomas Wentworth Higginson's article, "The Sunny Side of the Transcendental Period," *Atlantic Monthly*, *93* (1904), 6–14. Special aspects of the movement are treated in *Brook Farm: Its Members, Scholars, and Visitors*, by Lindsay Swift, New York, 1900; in George W. Cooke's *An Historical and Biographical Introduction to accompany the "Dial,"* 2 vols. Cleveland, The Rowfant Club, 1902; and in F. DeWolfe Miller's *Christopher Pearse Cranch and His Caricatures of New England Transcendentalism*, Cambridge, Mass., Harvard University Press, 1951.

Studies of Transcendentalism in the context of literary history are plentiful. The most recent interpretations are those of Kern and the *Literary History of the United States* (both cited above), and F. O. Matthiessen's *American Renaissance: Art and Expression in the Age of Emerson and Whitman*, New York, Oxford University Press, 1941. The accounts in Charles F. Richardson's *American Literature, 1607–1885* (New York, 1886–88) and Barrett Wendell's *Literary History of America* (New York, 1900) are useful because of their authors' personal acquaintance with the persons involved. Other studies are Vernon L. Parrington's *Main Currents in American Thought*, 3 vols. New York, Harcourt, Brace, 1927–30; Van Wyck Brooks's *The Flowering of New England, 1815–1865*, New York, Dutton, 1936; Lewis Mumford's *The Golden Day: A Study in American Literature and Culture*, New York, Boni and Liveright, 1926; and an excellent recent contribution by R. W. B. Lewis, *The American Adam: Innocence, Tragedy and Tradition in the Nineteenth Century*, Chicago, University of Chicago Press, 1955.

For the philosophical context, see Herbert W. Schneider, *A History of American Philosophy*, New York, Columbia University Press, 1946; Harvey G. Townsend, *Philosophical Ideas in the United States*, New York, American Book Co., 1934; John H. Muirhead, *The Platonic Tradition in Anglo-Saxon Philosophy: Studies in the History of Idealism in*

England and America, London, Allen and Unwin, 1931; I. Woodbridge Riley, *American Thought from Puritanism to Pragmatism and Beyond*, New York, Peter Smith, 1941; and George Ripley and George P. Bradford, "Philosophical Thought in Boston," in Justin Winsor, ed., *The Memorial History of Boston* (Boston 1880–81), *4*, 295–330. Transcendentalism as a chapter in social history is admirably treated in Alice F. Tyler's *Freedom's Ferment: Phases of American Social History to 1860*, Minneapolis, University of Minnesota Press, 1944.

For the relations of Transcendentalism to foreign philosophies, the indispensable introduction is now Henry A. Pochmann, *German Culture in America: Philosophical and Literary Influences 1600–1900* (Madison, University of Wisconsin Press, 1957), pp. 59–255. See also Harold S. Jantz, "German Thought and Literature in New England, 1620–1820," *Journal of English and Germanic Philology, 41* (1942), 1–45; Stanley M. Vogel, *German Literary Influences on the American Transcendentalists*, New Haven, Yale University Press, 1955; René Wellek, "The Minor Transcendentalists and German Philosophy," *New England Quarterly, 15* (1942), 652–80; James Murdock, *Sketches of Modern Philosophy, Especially among the Germans*, Hartford, 1842; Walter L. Leighton, *French Philosophers and New England Transcendentalism*, Charlottesville, University of Virginia, 1908; Arthur E. Christy, *The Orient in American Transcendentalism: A Study of Emerson, Thoreau, and Alcott*, New York, Columbia University Press, 1932; and William Girard, "Du Transcendentalisme consideré essentiellment dans sa définition et ses origines françaises," *University of California Publications in Modern Philology, 4* (1916), 353–498.

The relation of Transcendentalism to Hegelian Idealism is discussed in Henry A. Pochmann's *New England Transcendentalism and St. Louis Hegelianism: Phases in the*

History of American Idealism, Philadelphia, Carl Schurz Memorial Foundation, 1948. The spread of the influence of Samuel Taylor Coleridge beyond the confines of New England Transcendentalism is treated in Noah Porter's article, "Coleridge and his American Disciples," *Bibliotheca Sacra and Theological Review*, *4* (1847), 117–71; and also by Marjorie H. Nicolson, "James Marsh and the Vermont Transcendentalists," *Philosophical Review*, *34* (1925), 28–50.

BIOGRAPHIES AND SPECIAL STUDIES OF THE TRANSCENDENTALISTS

Ralph L. Rusk's *The Life of Ralph Waldo Emerson* (New York, Scribner's, 1949) is perhaps the most useful of the Transcendentalist biographies to the present-day scholar, along with Odell Shepard's *Pedlar's Progress: The Life of Bronson Alcott*, Boston, Little, Brown, 1937; Henry S. Canby's *Thoreau*, Boston, Houghton Mifflin, 1939; and Arthur M. Schlesinger, Jr.'s, *Orestes A. Brownson: A Pilgrim's Progress*, Boston, Little, Brown, 1939. Other biographies, both nineteenth-century and recent, have been very uneven in quality. For Ripley and W. H. Channing one must rely upon the memoirs by O. B. Frothingham: *George Ripley* (Boston, 1882) and *Memoir of William Henry Channing*, Boston, 1886. The three-volume biography, *Orestes A. Brownson's Early Life, Middle Life, Latter Life* (Detroit, 1898–1900), by Henry F. Brownson, gives details not found in Schlesinger or in Theodore Maynard's useful study, *Orestes Brownson: Yankee, Radical, Catholic*, New York, Macmillan, 1943. For Parker, Henry S. Commager's *Theodore Parker* (Boston, Little, Brown, 1936) is highly readable, but must be supplemented by the nineteenth-century biographies: John Weiss, *Life and Correspondence of Theodore Parker*, 2 vols. London, 1863; O. B. Frothingham, *Theodore Parker: A Biography*, Bos-

ton, 1874; and John W. Chadwick, *Theodore Parker,
Preacher and Reformer*, Boston, 1900. The best studies of
Hedge are Orie W. Long, *Frederic Henry Hedge: A Cos-
mopolitan Scholar*, Portland, Me., Southworth-Anthoensen
Press, 1940; and George H. Williams, *Rethinking the Unitarian Relationship with Protestantism: An Examination of
the Thought of Frederic Henry Hedge (1805–1890)*, Boston, Beacon Press, 1949. See also Ronald V. Wells, *Three
Christian Transcendentalists* (cited above). For Clarke, the
volume edited by Edward E. Hale (see above) is still necessary, although a recent biography by Arthur S. Bolster, Jr.,
James Freeman Clarke: Disciple to Advancing Truth (Boston, Beacon Press, 1954), contains some new materials. For
Convers Francis see William Newell's "Memoir" (cited
above); for Margaret Fuller, Thomas W. Higginson's *Margaret Fuller Ossoli*, Boston, 1884; for Dwight, *John Sullivan
Dwight: Brook-Farmer, Editor, and Critic of Music*, by
George W. Cooke, Boston, 1898.

Several brief monographic studies of individual Transcendentalists are helpful in an appraisal of their church-
reform activities. The most important of these are "Brownson and Emerson: Nature and History," by A. Robert
Caponigri, *New England Quarterly, 18* (1945), 368–90;
and "George Ripley: Unitarian, Transcendentalist, or Infidel?" by Arthur R. Schultz and Henry A. Pochmann,
American Literature, 14 (1942), 1–19. For the relation of
Emerson to earlier religious thought: Perry Miller, "Jonathan Edwards to Emerson," *New England Quarterly, 13*
(1940), 589–617. See also René Wellek, "Emerson and
German Philosophy," *New England Quarterly, 16* (1943),
41–62; Clarence L. F. Gohdes, "Some Remarks on Emerson's Divinity School Address," *American Literature, 1*
(1929), 27–31; Francis A. Christie, "Theodore Parker and
Modern Theology," *Meadville Journal, 25* (1930), 3–17;
and Roy C. McCall, "Theodore Parker," in William N.

Brigance et al., eds., *A History and Criticism of American Public Address*, 3 vols. New York, McGraw-Hill, 1943–55.

HISTORIES AND STUDIES OF UNITARIANISM

The best full-scale study is Earl M. Wilbur's two-volume *History of Unitarianism*, Cambridge, Mass., Harvard University Press, 1945–52. But for the American movement Wilbur must be supplemented by George W. Cooke's *Unitarianism in America: A History of Its Origin and Development*, Boston, American Unitarian Association, 1902; William W. Fenn's "The Revolt against the Standing Order," in *The Religious History of New England: King's Chapel Lectures*, Cambridge, Mass., Harvard University Press, 1917; *Unitarianism: Its Origin and History* (cited above); and the standard works by Joseph H. Allen: "Historical Sketch of the Unitarian Movement Since the Reformation," in J. H. Allen and Richard Eddy, *A History of the Unitarians and Universalists in the United States*, American Church History Series, 10, New York, 1894; *Our Liberal Movement in Theology*, Boston, 1882; and *Sequel to "Our Liberal Movement*," Boston, 1897.

For the background of the Unitarian movement in America see Joseph Haroutunian, *Piety Versus Moralism: The Passing of the New England Theology*, New York, Holt, 1932; Conrad P. Wright, *The Beginnings of Unitarianism in America*, Boston, Starr King Press, 1955; Henry W. Foote, *James Freeman and King's Chapel, 1782–1787: A Chapter in the Early History of the Unitarian Movement in New England*, Boston, 1873; and H. Shelton Smith, *Changing Conceptions of Original Sin: A Study in American Theology Since 1750*, New York, Scribner's, 1955.

A bibliography of the Unitarian controversy is given in E. H. Gillett's "History and Literature of the Unitarian Controversy," *Historical Magazine*, Ser. 2, 9 (1871), 316–

24. Other accounts of that controversy, supplementing those in the denominational histories, are in George Burgess, *Pages from the Ecclesiastical History of New England during the Century between 1740 and 1840*, Boston, 1847; and George E. Ellis, *A Half-Century of the Unitarian Controversy . . .* Boston, 1857.

For descriptions of Boston Unitarianism in the period of the Transcendentalist controversy see Andrew P. Peabody, "The Unitarians," in Winsor, *Memorial History of Boston*, *3*, 467–82; Octavius B. Frothingham, *Boston Unitarianism*, *1820–1850: A Study of the Life and Work of Nathaniel Langdon Frothingham*, New York, 1890; Mark A. DeWolfe Howe, "The Boston Religion," *Atlantic Monthly*, *91* (1903), 729–38; and Clarence Faust, "The Background of the Unitarian Opposition to Transcendentalism," *Modern Philology*, *35* (1938), 297–324. Conditions in Harvard College and the Divinity School in this period are described in O. B. Frothingham, *Recollections and Impressions*, *1822–1890*, New York, 1891; Edgeley W. Todd, "Philosophical Ideas at Harvard College, 1817–1837," *New England Quarterly*, *16* (1943), 63–90; Merle E. Curti, "The Great Mr. Locke: America's Philosopher, 1783–1861," *Huntington Library Bulletin*, *11* (1937), 107–51; and George H. Williams, ed., *The Harvard Divinity School: Its Place in Harvard University and in American Culture*, Boston, Beacon Press, 1954. For later developments in Unitarian thought see John W. Chadwick, *Old and New Unitarian Belief*, Boston, 1894; and Stow Persons, *Free Religion, An American Faith*, New Haven, Yale University Press, 1947.

BIOGRAPHICAL STUDIES OF INDIVIDUAL UNITARIANS

Eliot's *Heralds of a Liberal Faith* (cited above) contains sketches of the more important nineteenth-century Unitarian clergymen. Earlier compilations are William Ware's *American Unitarian Biography*, Boston, 1850–51; and Vol. 8 of William B. Sprague's *Annals of the American Pulpit* . . . 9 vols. New York, 1857–69. See also James F. Clarke, *Memorial and Biographical Sketches*, Boston, 1878. The full-scale biographies are Eliza B. Lee, *Memoirs of Rev. Joseph Buckminster, D.D., and of His Son, Rev. Joseph Stevens Buckminster*, Boston, 1851; Daniel T. McColgan, *Joseph Tuckerman: Pioneer in American Social Work*, Washington, Catholic University of America Press, 1940; Mary E. Dewey, ed., *Autobiography and Letters of Orville Dewey, D.D.*, Boston, 1883; John Ware, *Memoir of the Life of Henry Ware, Jr.*, Boston, 1846; and William C. Gannett, *Ezra Stiles Gannett, Unitarian Minister in Boston, 1824–1871: A Memoir*, Boston, 1875.

The biographies of William Ellery Channing are W. H. Channing, *The Life of William Ellery Channing, D.D.*, Boston, 1880; John W. Chadwick, *William Ellery Channing, Minister of Religion*, Boston, Houghton Mifflin, 1903; Charles T. Brooks, *William Ellery Channing: A Centennial Memory*, Boston, 1880; David P. Edgell, *William Ellery Channing: An Intellectual Portrait*, Boston, Beacon Press, 1955; Arthur W. Brown, *Always Young for Liberty: A Biography of William Ellery Channing*, Syracuse, Syracuse University Press, 1956; and Elizabeth P. Peabody, *Reminiscences of Rev. Wm. Ellery Channing, D.D.*, Boston, 1880. Among the more specialized studies of Channing's thought, the most important is Robert L. Patterson's *The Philosophy of William Ellery Channing*, New York, Bookman Associates, 1952. See also Neal F. Doubleday, "Channing on the Nature of Man," *Journal of Religion*, 23 (1943), 245–57; Herbert W. Schneider, "The Intellectual Background of William Ellery Channing," *Church History*, 7 (1938), 13–23; and Arthur I. Ladu, "Channing and Transcendentalism," *American Literature*, 11 (1939), 129–37.

INDEX

Abbot, Francis E., 200 n.
Abbott, Lyman, 202
Abolition. *See* Antislavery
Absolute Religion (Theodore Parker's term), 106, 114, 191, 201–2
Adams, Henry, 17
Aesthetics, 29
Alcott, Bronson, 23, 28, 30, 32 n., 50, 160; *Conversations with Children on the Gospels*, 32 ff., 34 n.; conversational method, 33, 148
Alexander, J. W., 86 n.
Alexandrian period, 156
Alger, William R., 130 n.
Allen, Joseph H., 194 n., 199
American Congregationalism. *See* Congregationalism
American Unitarianism. *See* Unitarianism (American)
American Unitarian Association, 144, 195; founding, 15 f.; tracts and documents, 16; *1853* Report, 128–32; beliefs and disbeliefs, 131; *1853* resolutions, 132 and n.; Theodore Parker's reply, 132–33; modern stand, 190; sponsors Theodore Parker's writings, 199 n.

Andover Seminary, 12
Angier, Joseph, 111 n.
Anticlericalism, 161 ff.
Antislavery, 118, 128, 159, 193 f.
Anti-Trinitarianism, 6–8. *See also* God, Jesus Christ, Trinity
A priori belief, 102
Apthorp, Eliza, 183 n.
Apthorp, Robert, 183 n.
Arius, Arianism, Arian, 6 ff.
Arlington Street Church, 144 n.
Arminius, Arminian, 8
Arnold, Matthew, 72
Associationism, 169 f., 177
Atheism, 102
Atonement, 155 and n., 175
Autonomy, congregational, 6, 8–9

Baader, Franz Xaver von, 26
Baltimore, Maryland, 12
Bancroft, Aaron (father of George), 8
Bancroft, George, 8, 32 n., 47, 160; political career, 160 and n.
Banks, Isaiah, 130 n.
Baptism, 6, 150, 184
Barrett, Benjamin Fiske, 68 n.

Barrett, Samuel, 111 n., 112 n.
Bartol, Cyrus, 31, 111 n., 189; church reform, 31–32; and Theodore Parker, 121, 194 n.; reviews of Emerson's works, 192; radicalism after *1853*, 197–98
Baur, Ferdinand Christian, 55
Bellows, Henry W., 15, 132 n., 195, 201; at National Conference, 200 and n.
Benevolent Fraternity of Churches, 122, 124 n., 187
Bentley, Richard, 54
Berry Street Conference, 16, 125
Bible. *See* Scripture
Blake, Harrison Gray Otis, 68 n.
Blodgett, Levi (pseud. of Theodore Parker), 86, 100
Boston, 1, 21
Boston Association of Congregational Ministers, 16, 91; and Ralph Waldo Emerson, 70, 100; and Theodore Parker, 118 ff., 120 n., 122 f.
Boston *Courier*, 110 n.
Boston *Evening Transcript*, 110 n.
Boston intellectuals. *See* Transcendentalism (New England)
Boston *Morning Post*, 71
Boston *Observer and Religious Intelligencer*, 40 n.
Boston *Quarterly Review*, 160
Boston *Recorder*, 110 n.
Boston *Reformer*, 43, 159–60
Boston Unitarianism. *See* Unitarianism (American)
Bowen, Francis, 27, 204
Bowne, Borden, 204
Brackett, S. E., 115 n.

Brattle Street Church, 14 n.
Brazer, John, 63 and n.
Briggs, G. A., 118 n.
Briggs, George W., 130 n.
Brisbane, Albert, 171, 176 n., 177
Broad Church, 139, 195
Brook Farm, 94 and n., 175, 177, 198 n.
Brooks, Charles T., 31–32, 198 n.
Brown, John, 150
Brownson, Henry, 157 n., 158 and n.
Brownson, Orestes, 23, 28, 50, 102–3, 189; church reform, 31, 138, 152 ff., 166; social reform, 29, 41–42, 156–57, 159; *New Views of Christianity, Society, and the Church*, 32, 41 ff., 154–55; resignation from ministry, 39 n.; physical appearance, 42; biographical information, 42 ff.; ministry to working class, 43–44, 159; formation of Society for Christian Union and Progress, 43, 157; publications refuting skepticism; 43; on Thomas Carlyle, 63; on Ralph Waldo Emerson, 81–82; free pew system, 146, 184; anticlericalism, 147, 161 ff.; comparison to Theodore Parker, 153; European influences on reform ideas, 153–54; definition of atonement, 155 and n.; mystical qualities, 156; editor of Boston *Reformer*, 159–60; founder of Boston *Quarterly Review*, 160; *The Wants of the Times*, 157; "The Laboring Classes," 161 ff., 167; or-

thodox sentiments, 162; *The Convert*, 163; influence of Pierre Leroux, 164–65, 173 n.; renunciation of Transcendentalism, 164 f.; reaction to Theodore Parker's *Transient and Permanent*, 164; *The Mediatorial Life of Jesus*, 165, 168; renunciation of Unitarianism and conversion to Catholicism, 166; later career, 198 n.

Brownson's Quarterly Review, 198 n.

Buckminster, Joseph S., 14 n.

Bushnell, Horace, 46, 203

Calvinism (Genevan), 3

Calvinism (New England), 1, 2, 4, 18, 86 n.

Cambridge Platform of *1648*, 9

Cambridge Theological School. *See* Harvard Divinity School

Carlyle, Thomas, 26 f., 63, 69

Catholicism, 145, 155, 166

Chadwick, John W., 198 f.

Channing, William Ellery (uncle of William H.), 12, 14 n., 16, 32 n., 42–43, 48, 150, 205; on sources of religious truth, 18–19; contact with Transcendentalism, 31, 89 f., 149; and Orestes Brownson, 43, 160, 166, 167–68; reputation, 199

Channing, William Henry, 31, 80 n., 169, 189, 194 n., 207; collectivism, 29; church reform, 31, 138, 172–73; Brook Farm, 94 n.; associationism, 169 ff.;

summary of philosophical beliefs, 169–70; *The Present*, 170 n.; *The Spirit of the Age*, 170 n.; relations with Theodore Parker, 173 n.; Pierre Leroux's influence, 173 n.; establishment of Christian Union, 174; establishment of Religious Union of Associationists, 175; content of sermons, 176–77; decline of Associationists and later ministry, 177–78; career and reputation after *1853*, 196–97

Chauncy, Charles, 7

Cheyney, Ednah D., 183 n.

Chillingworth, William, 7

Christian Disciple, 17 n.

Christian Examiner, 17, 40 and n., 47 f., 128 n., 134 n.; miracles controversy, 56, 58, 63; reviews Emerson's Divinity School Address, 79–80; deference to Transcendentalism, 90 f.; attitudes toward Theodore Parker, 113, 115, 116 n., 121, 134–35; Frederic Hedge's articles, 139; liberalizing, 194 and n.

Christian Monitor, 17 n.

Christian Register, 17, 40 n., 43; miracles controversy, 59, 61 ff. and n.; attitudes toward Emerson, 72 ff.; defense of Andrew Norton, 89; praise for George Ripley, 94; Theodore Parker controversy, 112 and n., 134, 194; reaction to Orestes Brownson, 168

Christian Union, 174

Christian Witness, 72

Christianity, supernatural origins of, 2, 19

Church membership, 10 f.

Church ownership of property, 11

Church, Unitarian attitudes about, 6

Church vs. parish, 10

Church of the Disciples, 189; establishment and membership, 148, 150–1; statement of faith and purpose, 149; organization and rules, 149–50; pioneer symbol, 152. *See also* Clarke, James Freeman

Church of the Future, 137 ff.; basic characteristics, 142–43, 146; James Freeman Clarke's contributions, 143–44; eclectic character, 145; William Henry Channing's ideas, 170; Theodore Parker's ideas, 178–79; fates of experimental groups, 188; similarities among experimental groups, 188. *See also* Church of the Disciples, Comprehensive Church, New Church, Society for Christian Union and Progress, Twenty-Eighth Congregational Society

Clarke, James Freeman, 31, 80 n., 118, 196, 201, 207; definitions of Transcendentalism, 144–45; church reform, 31, 138, 143–44, 146–48, 151–52, 188–89; early writings and pastorate, 144; establishment of Church of the Disciples, 148 ff.; relations with Theodore Parker, 183 n.; pews and voluntary system, 184; *Manual of Unitarian Belief*, 195; *Self-Culture*, 195; *Ten Great Religions*, 195; later career and publications, 195; at National Conference, 200

Clergy: forerunners of Unitarianism in America, 7; authority in Congregational system, 9–10; rule of forfeiture, 9–10; and n.; Transcendentalist leaders, 31–32; resignations from ministry, 39 n., 198 n.; opposition to Theodore Parker, 111; young ministers converted to Transcendentalism, 128, 198–99; increasing acceptance of Transcendentalism, 192 ff.; heirs to conservative Unitarianism and moderate Transcendentalism, 205–6

Coleridge, Samuel Taylor, 26 f., 47 and n.

Collectivism, 29

Committee of Benevolent Action, 184

Communion: solidarity, 165 and n.; of saints, 177. *See also* Holy Communion

Comprehensive Church, 145. *See also* Hedge, Frederic

Concord intellectuals. *See* Transcendentalism (New England)

Confession, public, 149

Confessionalism, 98 ff.

Confucius, 78

Congregational autonomy, 6, 8–9

Congregational worship, 147, 151

Congregationalism, 2; orthodoxy, 3; parish autonomy, 8–

9; clergy's authority, 9–10; broad member participation, 147

Connecticut Puritanism. *See* Puritanism

Consociation, 9

Constant, Benjamin, 49 and n., 82 n.; historical justification of the Church, 140; influence on Orestes Brownson, 153 f., 165

Conversational method, 33, 148

Conway, Moncure, 32 n.

Corporation (parish), 10 n.

Cousin, Victor, 26, 29, 69, 82 n., 90, 102–3 f.; influence on Orestes Brownson, 153, 165 f.; eclectic philosophy, 156

Covenant, church, 8–9

Covenant, Half-Way, 10

Cranch, Christopher, 31–32, 39 n., 80 n., 198 n.

Creighton, J. E., 204

Cromwellian period, 3

Curti, Merle E., 63 n.

Daily Advertiser, 59, 110 n.

Dall, Caroline, 117 and n., 183 n.

Dana, Charles A., 176 n.

Dana, Richard Henry, 17

Darwinism, 202

Davis, George Thomas, 71 n.

Dedham, Massachusetts, 15 n.

Democratic party, 160

DeWette, Wilhelm, 55, 82 n., 83, 85, 90; *Introduction to the Old Testament*, 100, 121

Dewey, Orville, 125, 135, 198, 201

Dexter professorship, 13 f. and n.

Dial, 119, 128

Dirks, J. E., 100 n., 104 n.

Disciples of the Newness, 23

Disestablishment of Massachusetts Church, 10 n.

Divinity Hall, Cambridge, 12

Dod, A. B., 86 n.

Dorr, Theodore H., 68 n.

Driver, Thomas, 111 n.

Dunham, Z. B. C., 111 n.

Dupuis, C.-F., *Origine de tous les cultes*, 161 f. and n.

Dutch Unitarianism, 7

Dwight, John S., 31 f., 148, 171; resignation from ministry, 39 n.; later career, 198 n.; editor of *Harbinger*, 176 n.

Dwight's Journal of Music, 198 n.

East Lexington church, 38 and n.

Ecclesiastical Council, 118–19

Eclecticism, 23, 145, 150, 156

Eclectic School, 153

Editors, Unitarian, 17

Education, 159

Eichorn, Johann, 55

Elect, Calvinist doctrine of, 3, 6

Eliot, Charles (son of Samuel A.), 73 n.

Eliot, Samuel A., 73 and n., 75

Eliot professorship, 14 n., 52

Ellis, Charles M., 115 n., 183 n.

Ellis, George E., 132 n., 135

Ellis, Rufus, 134, 192–93

Emerson, Charles (brother of Ralph W.), 36

Emerson, Mary Moody (aunt of Ralph W.), 36–37

Emerson, Ralph Waldo, 28 and n., 31, 50, 207; Pantheism, 29;

Emerson, Ralph Waldo (*cont.*)
church reform, 31, 35 ff., 66–
67, 137 f.; *Nature*, 32, 34, 65;
biographical material, 34 ff.;
preaching activity, 38 and n.;
writing career, 38 f.; resignation from ministry, 39 n.;
"American Scholar" Address,
38; Divinity School Address,
64 ff., 68, 100 and n., 164;
philosophical summary, 65–66;
direct inspiration, 65–66; "obedience to self," 67, 71–72, 81;
miracles, 66; morality, 65–66
f.; controversy with Henry
Ware, Jr., 76 ff., 77 n.; relationship with Theodore Parker, 100 n., 106; interest in
historical process, 104 n.; influence on Orestes Brownson,
163; social and religious faddists, 187; gradual reaccept-
ance by Unitarians, 192–93;
The Conduct of Life, 192;
Essays, 192; "The Natural
History of the Intellect,"
193
Emerson, William (brother to
Ralph W.), 35
Empiricism. *See* Sense experience
English interpretation of Calvinism, 3
English Unitarianism, 7
Episcopal Church, 39 n., 72 and
n.
Epistemology of Transcendentalism, 102 ff.
European philosophers, 28 ff.,
140. *See also* French Eclectic
School, French writers, Ger-

man idealism, German phi-
losophy, Scottish philosophers
Evangelicalism, 203
Evangelical Missionary Society,
16
Everett, Edward, 14 n., 17
Exclusion from pulpit, 116 ff.,
125–26
Expediency, 102

Faculty of Theology, 12. *See
also* Harvard Divinity School
Fairchild, J. H., 111 n.
Fearing, Albert, 130 n.
Feast Days, Christian, 150
Federal Street Church, 15, 144 n.
Felton, Cornelius, 52, 192
Fénelon, François, 78
Fenwick, Bishop B. J., 166
Fichte, Johann, 26 f.
Fiske, John, 202
Fitzpatrick, John B., 166
Follen, Charles, 48 ff., 147–48,
153; *Religion and the Church*,
32, 49 and n., 154; biographi-
cal material, 49–50
Folsom, Nathaniel, 111
Forfeiture of parish, 9–10 and n.
Formalism, 30
Fourier, Charles, 166, 169 ff.
Fourierists, American, 170, 175
ff.
Francis, Convers, 31 and n., 50,
189; church reform, 31; *Chris-
tianity as a Purely Internal
Principle*, 32, 44; reputation,
44–45; "all-sidedness," 44–45,
52–53; career and influence
after *1853*, 197
Freedom of spirit, 67, 71–72
Free Inquirer, 42

Free inquiry, 20, 79–80; at Harvard Divinity School, 71–72, 95–96; and Andrews Norton, 95–96; in Unitarian Church, 98 ff., 120, 136, 190 n.; institutionalization of, 208

Freeman, James, 7

Free religion. *See* Free inquiry, Transcendentalism (New England)

Free Religious Association, 187 n., 200 n.

French Eclectic School, 26

French writers, 161

Friends of Liberal Religious Thought, 179

Frontier religion, 147, 203

Frothingham, Nathaniel L., 20, 31, 120, 201

Frothingham, O. B., 32 n., 128; and Ralph Waldo Emerson, 28 n.; failure of Sunday schools, 185; and Theodore Parker, 194 n.; later scientific doctrines, 198 f.; Free Religious Association, 200 n.

Fuller, Margaret, 32 n., 148, 160, 175 n.

Furness, William Henry, 50, 189; church reform, 31; *Remarks on the Four Gospels*, 32, 45, 64; naturalistic theory, 46; miracles controversy, 55 ff.; support for Andrews Norton, 89; exclusion of Theodore Parker, 126; *A Word to Unitarians*, 193 n.; influence of writings, 198

Gannett, Ezra Stiles, 15, 17 n., 94, 115, 121, 135, 201, 208; proselytizing, 17–18; and Andrews Norton, 88 f.; *Scriptural Interpreter*, 100 n.; Theodore Parker controversy, 113, 120 ff., 124 f. and n., 127; career, 122 n.

Garrison, William Lloyd, 183 n.

Gay, Ebenezer, 7

Genevan Calvinism, 3

German idealism, 25 ff., 204 f.

German philosophy, 44, 48 n., 86 and n., 88, 90; legacy to American idealism, 204–5

Gilbert, William S., 23

God: Calvinist beliefs, 3 ff.; Unitarian beliefs, 4 f., 13, 190 and n.; Theodore Parker's beliefs, 103–4, 105–6; William H. Channing's beliefs, 171–72. *See also* Anti-Trinitarianism, Confessionalism, Jesus Christ, Trinity

Godwin, Parke, 166, 176 n.

Goethe, J. W. von, 82 n.

Gordon, George Angier, 205–6 and n.

Gospel, 132. *See also* New Testament, Scriptures

Greeley, Horace, 171, 175 n.

Greenwood, F. W. P., 79 n.

Griesbach, Johann, 54

Hale, Edward Everett, 17, 151, 194 n.

Hall, E. B., 132 n.

Hancock professorship, 59 n.

Handel and Haydn Society, 180 n.

Hanover Street Church, 35

Harbinger, 176 and n., 198 n.

Harvard College and University, 59 n., 195; Unitarian influence, 11, 13 f. and n.; free inquiry issue, 71–72, 95–96; silence on Transcendentalist-Unitarian controversy, 88; and Theodore Parker, 100 n.; and Ralph Waldo Emerson, 193

Harvard Divinity School, 12 f.; Ralph Waldo Emerson's Address, 64 ff., 68, 70, 79–80; free inquiry, 71–72, 95–96; Association of Alumni, 193; and Theodore Parker, 193; and Ralph Waldo Emerson, 193; *1840–60* graduate figures, 197 n.; Transcendentalist influence, 197 and n.

Hawes Place Church, 109 f.

Hawthorne, Nathaniel, 63 n.

Haynes, John C., 183 n.

Heathenism, 109

Hecker, Isaac, 157 n., 158 and n.

Hedge, Frederic Henry, 31, 136, 205 f.; church reform, 31, 138 ff., 142–43, 145, 152; biography, 46–47; writings, 47 and n., 139; *Conservatism and Reform*, 139; *Gospel Invitations*, 139; *The Leaven of the Word*, 139; *Practical Goodness the True Religion*, 139; *Prose Writers of Germany*, 139; position in Transcendentalist movement, 139–40; and historical continuity of Church, 140; position on controversial doctrines, 140–1; defense of Unitarianism, 143; warning on speculative theology, 189; reviews of Ralph Waldo Emer-

son's works, 192; and Theodore Parker, 193 n.; editor of *Examiner*, 194 n., 195; *Reason in Religion*, 195; later career and writings, 195 and n.; at National Conference, 200

Hedge's Club, 23, 30 n. *See also* New School, Symposium, Transcendental Club

Hegel, G. W. F., 26, 55, 83, 202

Hegira, 150

Heine, Heinrich, 153 f.

Henry, Caleb Sprague, 32 n.

Hepworth, George, 194 n.

Heresy, 7, 61, 82

Higginson, Thomas Wentworth, 32 n., 128, 199, 200 n.

History: Ralph Waldo Emerson's interest, 104 n.; Frederic Hedge's interest, 140; Theodore Parker's system, 104–5

Hoar, Samuel, 132 n.

Hodge, Charles, 86 n.

Hollis professorship, 11

Hollis Street Church, 118, 183 n.

Holmes, Oliver Wendell, 82

Holy Communion: Unitarian interpretation, 6; Ralph Waldo Emerson's protest, 35 ff.; in Church of Disciples, 150; in Religious Union of Associationists, 176; Theodore Parker's views, 184

Holy Scripture, Holy Writ. *See* Scripture

Holy Spirit, Calvinist and Unitarian beliefs, 4

Hooper, Ellen, 32 n.

Hope Street Chapel, 196

Howe, Julia Ward, 183 n.

Howe, M. A. DeWolfe, 72

Howe, Samuel Gridley, 183 n.
Hudson River, Unitarian Church west of, 11 n.
Human nature, Unitarian beliefs concerning, 4 ff.
Hume, David, 83
Hurlbut, M. L., 64 and n.

Idealism, 25 ff., 204 f.
Incarnation, Theodore Parker's views, 106
Individualism of Henry Thoreau, 29
Induction, 102–3 f.
Infallibility, 106
Inspiration, Ralph Waldo Emerson's views, 65–66
Intellectuals, Boston and Concord. See Transcendentalism (New England)
Intuition, in Transcendentalism, 30, 102 ff.

Jacobi, Friedrich, 26
James, Henry, Sr., 175 n.
James, William, 204
Jesuits, 119
Jesus Christ: Calvinist and orthodox Congregational beliefs, 3; Unitarian beliefs, 4 f., 7 f., 12 f., 131, 190 and n., 201; historical anti-Trinitarian movement, 6–8; George Ripley's position, 40–41; William Henry Furness' position, 46; miracles controversy, 58; Ralph Waldo Emerson's position, 66; Theodore Parker's position, 106–7, 109, 120; Frederic Hedge's position, 140 ff.; divinity affirmed by Church of Disciples, 149; William H. Channing's views, 174, 177. See also Anti-Trinitarianism, God, Trinity
Joan of Arc, 150
Johnson, Rufus, 89
Johnson, Samuel, 32 n., 128, 198–99
Jouffroy, Theodore, 26, 82 n.
Judaism, 109
Judd, Sylvester, 32, 198 n.
Justice, implications of Transcendentalism concerning, 102

Kant, Immanuel, 90, 103; Critique of Pure Reason, 24–25; contribution to Transcendentalism, 24–25, 27
Kirkland, John T., 12, 14 n.
Kneeland, Abner, 43, 157

Labor reforms, 159
Lamennais, Abbe, 153; Paroles d'un croyant, 154 n.
Lamson, Alvan, 15 n., 122 n.
Larned, William, 115 n.
Leighton, Rufus, 183
Leroux, Pierre, 164–5 and n.; L'Humanité, 173 n.
Liberalism, viii, 2, 206; Unitarianism's contribution, 202, 205–6; Transcendentalism's contribution, 202 ff., 208
Liberals: of the eighteenth century, see Unitarianism; of the nineteenth century, see Transcendentalism
Lincoln, Calvin, 130 n.
Lion Tavern, 180 n.
Lion Theatre, 180 n.

Locke, John, 7, 19, 86 n., 204; James Walker on, 48; Andrews Norton on, 55
Longfellow, Samuel, 32 n., 128
Lothrop, Samuel K., 111, 118, 121, 135, 201, 205; controversy with Theodore Parker, 112 and n.; and the declaration of the American Unitarian Association, 129–30
Lowell, James Russell, 17, 169
Luther, Martin, 78

Mahomet, 78
Marsh, James, 32 n.
Martineau, Harriet, 157 n.; *Society in America*, 69
Martineau, James, 196; *Rationale of Religious Inquiry*, 32, 57
Massachusetts,   Unitarian churches in, 11 and n.
Massachusetts legislature, 11
Massachusetts Puritans. *See* Puritanism
Massachusetts Quarterly Review, 128
Massachusetts Supreme Court, 11, 15 n.
Materialism in the Protestant Church, 155–56
Matrimony, Theodore Parker on, 184
May, Samuel, 183 n.
Mayhew, Jonathan, 7
Mechanics Institute, 180 n.
Melodeon Theatre, 127 f., 180 and n., 187
Methodists, 147
Miles, Henry A., 130 n.
Mill, John, 54
Miller, Perry, vii

Milton, John, 7
Miracles, viii; George Ripley—William Furness controversy, 45 f., 55 ff., 57–58 ff.; conservative Unitarian position, 62 f.; Ralph Waldo Emerson's position, 66; Andrews Norton's position, 83 ff.; Theodore Parker's position, 85–86, 108, 120; Frederic Hedge's position, 141
Monthly Anthology, 17
Monthly Journal of the American Unitarian Association, 17 n., 194 n.
Monthly Miscellany, 17 n., 94, 113, 122 n., 168
Monthly Religious Magazine, 17 n., 192, 194 n.
Morison, John H., 115–16 and n., 132 n.
Morris, George Sylvester, 204
Music Hall, Boston, 128, 181

National Conference, 15; purged of radicals, 200; liberalism after *1880*, 201–2
Naturalism. *See* Transcendentalism (New England)
Naturalistic theory of miracles, 55 ff.
Nature, in Unitarianism, 19
Neoplatonism, Transcendental origins in, 28
New Bedford church, 37 f.
New Church (William H. Channing's phrase), 170
Newcomb, Charles, 32 n.
New   England,   Unitarian churches in, 11 n.

New England Calvinism. *See* Calvinism

New England Puritan, 110 n., 111

New England Transcendentalism. *See* Transcendentalism (New England)

New England Unitarianism. *See* Unitarianism (American)

New North Church, 15 n.

New School, 23. *See also* Symposium, Transcendentalism (New England)

Newspapers. *See* Periodicals and newspapers

New Testament, 5. *See also* Scripture

New Theology of the *1880's,* 202–3, 206

Newton, Isaac, 28

New York *Tribune,* 198 n.

Nicea, Council of, 6

Nightingale, Crawford, 68 n.

North American Review, 17

Norton, Andrews, ix, 13 f. and n., 17 n., 52, 60, 135; *Statement of Reasons for Not Believing the Doctrines of Trinitarians,* 13, 53; *General Repository and Review,* 13, 17 n.; *Genuineness of the Gospels,* 14, 53, 55; character, 52–53; scholarship, 53; *Discourse on the Latest Form of Infidelity,* 53, 82–83, 207; attitude toward European philosophers and theologians, 54–55; biblical scholar, 54–55; miracles, 55 ff., 83 ff.; question of "auspices," 56–57; attack on Ralph Waldo Emerson, 69–70; attack on

Ripley, 70; retort to Theophilus Parsons, 71 n.; controversy with Chandler Robbins, 73–74; *Two Articles from the "Princeton Review,"* 86 and n.; leader of conservative Unitarians, 87–89, 95–97; reaction to the *Examiner's* Transcendentalism article, 91 f.; and free inquiry, 95–96; extreme position in Transcendentalist controversy, 207–8

Novalis, 26

Noyes, George Rappall, 14 n., 63, 88–89

"Obedience to self" (Ralph Waldo Emerson), 67, 81

Old South Congregational Church, 11 n., 205

Old Testament, 14 n. *See also* Scripture

Ordaining Council, in Theodore Parker controversy, 110 ff.

Ordination, in Religious Union of Associationists, 176

Oriental religions, Transcendental origins in, 28

Original sin, 3, 131, 162

Orthodoxy: Unitarianism forced to adopt, 2, 127; meaning in American Congregational Church, 3; conversion to Unitarianism in Massachusetts, 11 and n.; objections to Theodore Parker, 111; orthodox Protestantism's contributions to church reform, 145. *See also* Calvinism; Puritanism; Unitarianism (American),

Orthodoxy (*continued*)
conservative and orthodox opinions
Osgood, Samuel, 32, 39 n., 80 n., 132 n., 189; on Theodore Parker's *Discourse*, 116–17; on Transcendental reformers, 137; career after 1853, 198 and n.
Owenites, 154, 157

Paley, William, 28
Palfrey, John G., 14 and n., 68 n., 89, 92
Panic of *1837*, 160
Pantheism, of Ralph Waldo Emerson, 29
Parish: early disputes, in Unitarian movement, 8; distinct from Church, 10; early requirements for membership, 10 and n.; political strength of members, 10 f.; choice of minister, 11; ownership of property, 11; number of Unitarian, 17
Parkerism. *See* Parker, Theodore
Parker Memorial Meetinghouse, **187**
Parker, Theodore, 28, 96–97, 135–36, 140, 160; *The Transient and Permanent in Christianity*, 40, 108–9, 110 ff., 112–13, 164; miracles controversy, 58, 85–86; pseudonym of Blodgett, 86, 100; controversy with Unitarianism, 98 ff., 107–8, 116 ff., 120 ff., 127; influence on modern Unitarianism, 128,

190 ff., 201–2; physical appearance, 99; rhetorical qualities, 99; education and early career, 99–100; philosophical and theological theories, 101 ff., 106–7 f.; theories of God and Christ, 103–4 ff., 109; historical method, 104 f. and n.; relationship with Ralph Waldo Emerson, 100 and n., 106; constructive elements in sermons and writings, 109–10; public denunciation of Church's offenses, 108–9; reform, 137 f., 178–79; *Discourse of Matters Pertaining to Religion*, 115–17, 178; criticism of Ecclesiastical Council, 119–20; edition of DeWette's *Introduction to the Old Testament*, 121; challenge to Boston Association, 123–24; and the Twenty-Eighth Congregational Society, 127 f., 180, 182, 185 f.; *Massachusetts Quarterly Review*, 128; antislavery, 128, 193 f.; controversy with the American Unitarian Association, 129–33; *Sermons of Theism, Atheism, and the Popular Theology*, 134–35; comparison to Orestes Brownson, 153; relations with William H. Channing, 173 n.; *The Idea of a Christian Church*, 178; ideas on Church structure and functions, 178–79; theories of worship, 183–84; *Experience as a Minister*, 193; later reputation, 199; extreme position in Transcendentalist controversy, 207–8

Parkman, Francis, 14–15 and n., 118

Parsons, Theophilus, 70–71 and n.

Paulist Order, 158

Paulus, Heinrich, 55

Peabody, Andrew, 90, 113–15, 137

Peabody, Elizabeth, 30 n., 32 n., 33, 160

Peace movement, 118

Peirce, Charles Sanders, 204

Periodicals and newspapers: Unitarian influence, 16–17 and n.; Andrews Norton's influence, 90–92; non-Unitarian reaction to Theodore Parker, 110 f. and n.; Theodore Parker's obituaries, 194. *See also specific titles*

Personalism, 204

Pews, 146 f., 151, 159, 184

Phalange, 171

Phalanx, 176 n.

Phillips, Jonathan, 31

Philosophers, European: contributions to Transcendentalism and Unitarianism, 28 ff., 140. *See also* French Eclectic School, French writers, German idealism, German philosophy, Scottish philosophers

Phrenology, 47

Pierce, John, 5, 111

Pierpont, John, 118 and n., 132 n., 183 n.

Platner, John W., 202

Plato, 28, 78, 202

Poland, 7

Pope, Alexander, 117 n.

Porter, Noah, 204

de Potter, L.-J.-A., *Histoire du Christianisme*, 161 f.

Pragmatism, 204

Preaching as a Christian instrument, 67

Predestination, 3

Pre-Raphaelite Brotherhood, 23

Present, 170 n.

Priestley, Joseph, 45

Princeton Theological Seminary, 86 n.

Prison reform, 118

Proprietary system, 146

Proselytizing, 17–18

Protestant Churches. *See* Calvinism, Congregationalism, Puritanism, Unitarianism

Protestant liberalism, viii, 2, 5, 202–3, 206, 208

Protestant materialism, 155–56

Purchase Street Church, 39 and n., 95 n.

Puritan churches, 8

Puritanism, 10 n.; Unitarian origins in, 3; tradition of congregational autonomy, 6, 9; worship, 6; consociation, 9; Transcendentalist origins in, 28

Putnam, George, 111 n.

Quakers, 147

Quarterly (Monthly) Journal of the American Unitarian Association, 17 n., 134 n., 194 n.

Randall, James G., 22

Reason, rationality: Unitarian appeals to, 5 f., 18–19 f.

Reason, Practical, 25

Reason, Pure, 24–25

Redemption, in Catholicism, 155
Reed, Sampson, 32 n.
Reform (church), 29, 31 f., 137 ff.; Ralph Waldo Emerson, 35 ff., 66–67, 137 f.; George Ripley, 82–83, 137, 152; James Freeman Clarke, 143–44, 146–48, 151–52, 188–89; Frederic Hedge, 142–43, 145, 152; Orestes Brownson, 152 ff., 166; William H. Channing, 172–73; Theodore Parker, 178–79; cataloguing of different nomenclature, 188. *See also* Church of the Future
Reform (social), 156–57, 185
Religious Union of Associationists: membership and articles of faith, 175–76; services of Holy Communion and ordination, 176; form of worship, 177; hints of traditionalism and orthodoxy, 177; decline, 177
Renaissance, 155
Renshaw Street Chapel, 196
Resurrection, 6, 63. *See also* Jesus Christ, Miracles
Revelation: in Unitarianism, 18–19, 98, 131; in sensationalist doctrines, 102
Revivalism, 18, 203
Richter, Johann, 26
Ripley, George, 30, 50, 60, 160, 177; collectivism, 29; church reform, 31, 82–83, 137, 152; review of James Martineau's book, 32, 57 ff.; physical appearance, 39; biography, 39 ff.; resignation from ministry, 39 ff. and n., 93; views on Jesus

Christ, 40–41; Transcendentalism in early writings, 40 f.; and Orestes Brownson, 43, 163; and Andrews Norton, 53, 70, 82–83 ff.; miracles controversy, 55 ff.; *Discourses on the Philosophy of Religion*, 82; *Specimens of Foreign Standard Literature*, 82 and n.; *"The Latest Form of Infidelity" Examined*, 84; *Farewell Discourse*, 93–94; Brook Farm, 94 and n.; Theodore Parker controversy, 112 n.; free pews, 146; *The Spirit of the Age*, 170 n.; Fourier's influence, 171; editor of *Harbinger*, 176 n.; later career, 198 n.
Ripley, Sophia, 32 n.
Robbins, Chandler, 89, 91, 111; on Ralph Waldo Emerson's Address, 72 ff.; in Theodore Parker affair, 120 f.
Robbins, Samuel, 118 n.
Royce, Josiah, 204
Russell, J. L., 118 n.

Sabbath, 67
Saint-Simon, Comte de, 165 n.; *Nouveau Christianisme*, 154; influence on Orestes Brownson, 153 f., 161
Salvation, early Unitarian beliefs, 8
Sanborn, Franklin B., 32 n., 183 n.
Sargent, John T., 111 n., 118 n., 122, 124 n., 132 n.; relations with Theodore Parker, 183 n.; Twenty-Eighth Congregational Society, 189

Schelling, Friedrich, 26; *Natur-philosophie*, 26–27

Schiller, Johann, 26, 47, 82 n.

Schlegel, August Wilhelm von, 26

Schleiermacher, Friedrich, 40, 49, 83, 90; Andrews Norton's opinion, 55; *Reden über die Religion*, 55; influence on Orestes Brownson, 153

Scottish philosophers, 19, 86 n.; Transcendentalist origins in, 28; Norton's use of, 55. *See also* Hume, David

Scriptural Interpreter, 100 and n.

Scripture: Unitarian beliefs, 2, 5, 13 f. and n.; Calvinist beliefs, 3; trinitarian and unitarian texts, 5; Ralph Waldo Emerson's views, 66; Theodore Parker's views, 106; modern Unitarian beliefs, 190 n. *See also* Miracles

Sears, Edmund H., 194 n.

Senior class at Harvard Divinity School, 68, 70, 193

Sense experience, empiricism, sensationalism: antithesis of Transcendentalism, 30, 101 ff.; in Unitarian doctrine, 19–20; effect on arts and sciences, 102

Shackford, Charles, 109, 111, 118 n.

Shelley, Percy Bysshe, 69, 81 n.

Simmons, George F., 68 n.

Simon, Richard, 54

Sin, Unitarian beliefs, 5 f. *See also* Original sin

Social principle, 146–47

Social Reform Society (Society for Christian Union and Progress), 157

Societies, religious, founded by Transcendentalists, viii. *See also* Church of the Future

Society for Christian Union and Progress, 152, 158, 189; founding, 43, 157; meetings and membership, 157–58 and n.; form of services, 159

Society for Promotion of Theological Education, 12

Socinus, Faustus (Socinian), 7, 12

Son of God. *See* Jesus Christ

South Boston Unitarian Ordination, 110 n.

Sparks, Jared, 12, 17

Spinoza, Baruch, 55, 83, 85

Spirit of the Age, 170 n., 176

Spiritualism, 105

Spirituality in Catholicism, 155 f.

Stetson, Caleb, 32, 118 n., 132 n., 198 n.

Strauss, David Friedrich, 46, 55, 83, 116; *Leben Jesu*, 55

Suffolk Street Chapel, 183 n.

Sunday school, 185

Supernatural origins of Christianity, Unitarian belief in, 2, 19

Supernaturalism. *See* Unitarianism, conservative and orthodox opinions

Swedenborg, Emanuel, 47, 63, 78, 150; Transcendentalist origins in, 28

Symposium, 23; original members, 30, 31 and n., 32 n.; first meeting, 30; duration of exist-

Symposium (*continued*)
  ence, 30 n. *See also* Hedge's
  Club, New School, Transcendental Club

Tappan, Caroline Sturgis, 32 n.
Taylor, Nathaniel, 203
Temperance, 118, 159
Temple School, 33 f.
Thayer, Charles L., 115 n.
Theism, 105
Thirteenth   Congregational
  Church, 95 n.
Thoreau, Henry David, 29, 32 n.
Ticknor, George, 17
Tolerance, toward other sects,
  203
Towne, E. C., 200 n.
Transcendental Club, vii f., 139–
  40. *See also* Hedge's Club,
  New School, Symposium
Transcendental ego (Fichte's
  term), 27
Transcendentalism   (German),
  24–26
Transcendentalism, -ists (New
  England): stereotype, vii–viii;
  choice of name for movement,
  22–23, 27 f.; definition and origin, 23 ff.; early writings, 32
  ff., 50; original group, vii f.,
  30–31 and n., 32 n.; impact on
  church reform, viii, 137 f., 145,
  187–89, 207; controversy with
  Unitarianism, ix, 1 f., 18 ff., 50,
  65 ff., 95–97 ff., 191 ff., 199 f.
  and n., 207; role of free inquiry, 20; foreign influence,
  24–26, 81; agreements and disagreements among adherents,

28 ff.; social theories, 29; clergy who resigned, 39 n., 198 n.;
  eclecticism, 50–51; support
  from Unitarian publications,
  90; epistemological theories,
  102 ff.; conversion of Orestes
  Brownson, 165; beliefs of
  William H. Channing, 170–71;
  relation to modern ecumenical
  and social movements of Protestantism, 188; influence on
  Harvard Divinity School, 197;
  legacy to American idealism,
  204; heirs of moderates, 205–
  6; contribution to humanistic
  Protestantism, 208. *See also*
  Associationism; Church of the
  Future; Clergy; Collectivism;
  Freedom of spirit; Free inquiry; Hedge's Club; Intuition; Liberalism; Miracles;
  New School; Reform, church
  and social; Scripture; Symposium; Transcendental Club
Transcendentalism, antithesis of
  sensationalism, 101 ff.
Transylvania, 7
Trinity: Unitarian rejection, 4,
  6–8, 14; Orestes Brownson,
  162; William H. Channing,
  177. *See also* Anti-Trinitarianism, God, Jesus Christ
Tübingen School, 46, 55
Tuckerman, Joseph, 14 n.
Twenty-Eighth   Congregational
  Society, 127 and n., 189; significance, 179; organization
  and activities, 180, 184 ff.; size
  of meetings, 180–1 f.; nucleus,
  183; finances, 186; decline, 187.
  See also Parker, Theodore

Unitarian, 43
Unitarian Christian, 206 n.
Unitarian Christian Fellowship, 206 **n.**
Unitarianism, -ians (American): clergy in Transcendentalist movement, vii, 31–32, 39 n.; controversy with Transcendentalism, ix, 1 f., 18 ff., 50, 65 ff., 95–97 ff., 191 ff., 199 f. and n., 207; conservative and orthodox opinions, ix f., 21, 62 f., 127, 135, 205; feud with Calvinism, 1; early liberal influence, 1 f.; early history, 2 ff., 7 ff.; negativism, 2, 12; positivism, 2–3, 13; theological beliefs, 2 ff., 6 ff., 12–13, 131; position on Jesus Christ, 4, 6–8, 12 ff., 131; congregational autonomy, 8–9; expansion of churches, 11 and n., 17 f.; educational influence, 11–12, 14 n.; documents and statements, 12–13; early leadership, 13–14, 14 n.; denominational development, 15–16; newspapers and periodicals, 16–17 and n., 90–92 (see also *Christian Examiner, Christian Register, Monthly Anthology, Monthly Miscellany, North American Review*); religious authority, 18 ff., 205–6; reason and revelation, 18–19 f., 98, 131; ambiguities of doctrine, 18–20; view of nature, 19; principles attacked by George Ripley, 40 f.; German influence, 48 n.; reaction to Ralph Waldo Emerson, 70 f., 192–93; contro-

versy with Theodore Parker, 107–8, 111, 116–17 ff., 120 f., 127, 193 ff.; *1853* Report of American Unitarian Association, 128–32; defense by Frederic Hedge and other Transcendentalists, 143; contribution to Church of the Future, 145; influence on Orestes Brownson, 156, 166 ff.; National Conference, 200 and n.; liberalization of doctrine, 201; modern concepts, 190–91, and n., 208. *See also* American Unitarian Association, Berry Street Conference, Boston Association of Congregational Ministers, Calvinism (New England), Clergy, Confessionalism, Jesus Christ, Liberalism, National Conference, Orthodoxy, Parish, Reform (church), Scripture
Unitarianism (Dutch), 7
Unitarianism (English), 7
Universalist Church, 42
Upham, Charles W., 63 and n., 87–88

Van Buren, Martin, 160 n.
Very, Jones, 32, 39 n., 198 n.
Voluntary principle, 184
Voluntary support of church, 146 f., 151, 184

Walker, James, 31, 48, 64, 79 n.; influence on younger intellectuals, 48; on Locke's philosophy, 48; affinity with Scottish philosophy, 48; mira-

Walker, James (*continued*)
  cles controversy, 58; tolerance
  of Transcendentalist view-
  point; warning to Orestes
  Brownson, 167
Walpole, New Hampshire, 43
Waltham, Massachusetts, 15 n.
Ware, Henry, Jr., 47 and n.,
  88 f.; souces of authority for
  Unitarianism, 18; relationship
  with Ralph Waldo Emerson,
  35, 76 ff., 79 n.; *The Personality of the Deity*, 77, 207; disavowal of Divine Impersonality, 77
Ware, Henry, Sr., 11, 13 f., 68 n.,
  *Letters to Trinitarians and
  Calvinists*, 13–14 and n.
Ware, William (brother to
  Henry, Jr.), 79 n.; controversy with Andrews Norton,
  89, 91 f. and n.; criticism of
  exclusion of Theodore Parker,
  126
Washington, George, 150
Wasson, David A., 32 n., 187
  and n., 198

Waterston, Robert C., 68 n., 119
  and n., 124 n.
Weiss, John (Theodore Parker's
  biographer), 32 n., 115, 185,
  194, 199; in Free Religionist
  Association, 200 n.
Wendte, Charles W., 134 n.
Western Messenger, 69, 80 and
  n.
Western Unitarian Conference,
  129 n.
Wettstein, Johann, 54
Wheeler, Charles, 32 n.
Whig Party, Whigs, 63 n., 71 n.,
  160 n., 163
Whitman, Bernard, 15 n., 43
Whitney, Frederick A., 68 n.
Willard, Sidney, 59 and n.,
  61 n.
Williams, George H., 206 n.
Wilson, William D., 68 n.
Worcester, Massachusetts, 8
Worcester, Noah, 14 n.
Workingmen's party, 42
Worship, in Unitarianism and
  Puritanism, 6
Wright, Fanny, 161

DATE DUE